THE MAURYAS

THE MAURYAS

CHANDRAGUPTA TO ASHOKA

The Backstories, The Sagas, The Legacies

DEVIKA RANGACHARI

SIMON & SCHUSTER

London · New York · Sydney · Toronto · New Delhi

First published in India by Simon & Schuster India, 2022

1 3 5 7 9 10 8 6 4 2

Simon & Schuster India
818, Indraprakash Building,
21, Barakhamba Road,
New Delhi 110001.

www.simonandschuster.co.in

Paperback ISBN: 978-81-972789-3-8
eBook ISBN: 978-93-92099-33-5

Simon & Schuster: Celebrating 100 Years of Publishing in 2024

Typeset in India by SÜRYA, New Delhi
Printed and bound in India by Replika Press Pvt. Ltd.

FSC
www.fsc.org
MIX
Paper | Supporting responsible forestry
FSC® C016779

Simon & Schuster India is committed to sourcing paper that is made from wood grown in sustainable forests and support the Forest Stewardship Council, the leading international forest certification organisation. Our books displaying the FSC logo are printed on FSC certified paper.

To Amma—my strength, my solace, my soul

CONTENTS

1

INTRODUCTION

History encompasses our past, the entirety of our lived experience and our shared inheritance. It is also a most generous discipline: everyone has access to it and can claim it as their own, and it contains within it several other fields of study that endlessly diverge and converge to reconstruct it. It can be, at once, extremely comforting and totally intimidating; unbelievably vast and highly specific. As a practitioner in this field and one who has loved it ever since she read her first work of historical fiction as a child, I feel equipped and impelled to make certain general observations about it—to lay out the ground, as it were—before I tackle the Mauryas.

Let us begin with a truism: history is selective. The history that a non-historian reads is based on the selection of facts by a historian who then, despite their best efforts, will interpose themselves between you and the fact. So if you grow up swearing belief in a particular view of history, it is because you have decided, at some point, that the historian you have read is truthful and objective, and that their facts are sacrosanct. This, as anyone who is trained in the rigours of the discipline knows, is often very far from the truth.

So how does the non-historian arrive at an objective view of the past? Put very simply, if one gathers information from various secondary sources, it is possible to garner a more or less accurate picture despite the large gaps that will inevitably exist in our knowledge given the lack of sources for some periods in history. However, it definitely does not mean that anyone and everyone can master the subject from merely ploughing through a pile of books. History is a very specialised discipline, as noted above, and you should, ideally, undergo the rigorous training and research regimen that goes with the field before you appropriate the right to make statements about it. Making sweeping assertions about the past simply because you like history and you *think* you know about it is as unfair and unjustifiable as pontificating on Physics simply because you are interested in the universe and its workings. It also does not mean, for instance, that anyone with a mastery over myth can proceed to label themselves as a historian. Myth is, emphatically, *not* history and there is nothing irreverent or injurious about reiterating this simple fact. Myths might *reflect* some aspects of the past, particularly of the times in which they were composed, but to see them as a straightforward rendition of historical fact is ridiculous and completely unwarranted.

It is also unfair to expect someone with a background in historical studies to know *everything* about the past. To say that the canvas of history is vast is akin to noting that the sky is large. History is, basically, everything that happened from the beginning of time to the present, so you cannot actually ask a specialist in medieval history, for instance, to tell you all about the Indus Valley civilisation. She will, undoubtedly, know the basics but, in all probability, not much more than that. Academics across the board are required to micro-specialise in areas of their interest and historians are no exception. Whether that is a sensible factor or not is a different discussion altogether.

Everyone is familiar with the contention that history favours the victor and suppresses facts about the vanquished and the oppressed. This is true but is, actually, the tip of the iceberg. The point is that a historical narrative cannot possibly contain the names of *each and every* person who has ever appeared on the historical stage. Consider the massive geographical breadth of this country, coupled with the thousands of regions within it with their own specific political and social trajectories. To include everyone who wielded any political and/ or social influence at all in our historical narratives would be a logistical nightmare. Textbooks would, in that case, be voluminous and near-impossible to negotiate, and general histories would be largely unreadable.

Historians who author textbooks or general narratives are, therefore, forced to make a somewhat judicious selection of some important people who left a considerable mark on history—by dint of effecting political changes, or leaving behind information on themselves in different sources, or having caught the popular imagination for a range of reasons—and omit a whole lot of others. By some tacit—and often insidious—consensus, certain names alone are mentioned repeatedly in historical delineations of the Indian past, thereby creating the impression that they were the only ones whose existence mattered.

The casualties of this approach are those who fall into the cracks of history and remain there in oblivion unless they have the fortune of being resurrected by some historian or the other to suit particular research agendas. For every individual who is 'known', there are several more—equally remarkable and noteworthy and fascinating—waiting on the sidelines for some sort of popular acknowledgement. Yet, we often lack the ability to look beyond the obvious into the enchanting shadows of the past. Ironically, though, the sources testify to their existence and provide tantalising glimpses of their personalities and contributions but they are deemed to be insignificant in the scheme of things, persons who would mar the neat outline of the ubiquitous historical narrative. Thus, they are consigned to what has been poetically referred to as 'the dustbin of history'.

Let us, for instance, talk about what history as we know it today is mostly about. It is, in fact, his-story and has very little to do with the women of the past. So the overwhelming impression conveyed—through textbooks and a majority of secondary sources—is that it was the men who went out and fought battles, founded kingdoms, made the laws, built magnificent structures and so on. There is usually a token passage on 'the status of women' in differing historical periods that, more often than not, focuses on the jewellery and clothes that they wore, which implies that all through history, women were obsessing daily about how they looked while the men did the real things. This flies in the face of the evidence that a wide range of historical sources convey about women in the past.

The truth is that women were hugely important in the political, social, economic and religious spheres in every historical period, some of them—in certain phases of the past—ruling on or behind the throne, mediating in court politics, building structures to perpetuate their names and donating to different causes—and this applies to both the royal and non-royal sections of society. Yet, most historians ignore what the sources say, in this regard, and choose to tell you a different tale altogether. The familiar spectre of the historian and their agenda between you and the source again! Thus, there is an unfortunate but concerted effort to invisibilise women and their contributions in historical narratives, leading to a male-centric—and, therefore, skewed—version of the past across age groups.

Notable exceptions to this trend are a handful of names—Razia Sultan, Rani Lakshmibai, Jahanara and Mother Teresa—and these are the ones that schoolchildren across the country obediently trot out when asked to identify some women in Indian history that they remember reading about. When, however, you ask them to name any woman before the thirteenth century, the date pertaining to Razia (the earliest woman usually mentioned), they draw a collective blank. If you extend this line of enquiry and go further back in time, some of them instinctively say 'no' when asked whether women existed during the Indus Valley civilisation, for instance, and then proceed to look sheepish when the ludicrousness of their answer dawns upon them.

Yet, such is the insidious nature of the gender bias that exists in the writing of history that leads most people to believe that women were irrelevant to the larger concerns of the past and can be dispensed with altogether. This is not to say that sources on women in history are readily available or plentiful. The further back in time you go, the more difficult it is to retrieve their presence. Yet the very fact that one can problematise the issue and be aware of the one-sided nature of most historical narratives is a promising beginning. When one is reading a purportedly 'comprehensive' history, therefore, one needs to exercise caution in one's expectations. Something or someone will, inevitably, be left out of the rendition and you need to be aware of this fact.

The selective approach to history impacts the reconstruction of the past in other ways as well, notably, when we try to put together ruling lines or dynasties: one or the other aspect will usually take precedence over others and one or more rulers will tend to be highlighted rather than all, depending on who is looking at the sources and what they are trying to say. And this brings us to the focus of this book, the Mauryan dynasty, which constitutes one of the most interesting and vibrant phases of the ancient Indian past but whose details are, by no means, completely known and whose rulers are not always accorded equal importance, their narrative being plagued, as it is, by some of the issues noted above. Sources pertaining to the Mauryas, who ruled from *c.* 324/321 BCE to *c.* 181 BCE and over almost the entire Indian subcontinent, are not necessarily plentiful but have often been used selectively so that the second Mauryan ruler, Bindusara, for instance, slips through the cracks of known history, sandwiched between his well-known father and founder of the dynasty, Chandragupta Maurya, and his even more well-known son, Ashoka, the most powerful Mauryan ruler and one of the best-known monarchs in Indian history.

Ashoka himself has spent nearly 2,000 years of floating around in half-remembered legend and tradition, in and out of public memory and more or less buried in oblivion, until a sheer accident of discovery and interpretation brought him back firmly into the light. Today, the tale of his transition from violence to non-violence is widely known as he documented this fact all over his empire, most innovatively, through inscriptions on pillars and rocks—a brilliant and pioneering method of communicating with his people. The writing and reconstruction of history, therefore, is a continuous, ongoing process. The more you know in this field, the more you realise how much you *do not* know—and therein lies the backbreaking but highly enjoyable and rewarding process of research and interpretation.

The Mauryas attempts to provide as accurate an account of the Mauryan dynasty as possible but, at the same time, involve the general reader in the evolving of a very interesting segment of our collective past whose legacy has proved to be enduring. It is meant to be enjoyed as an eminently readable tale but also as a gently informative one that attempts to draw disparate threads of this dynasty together to weave a connected narrative between its inception and the factors that enabled its rise, to those who ultimately inherited its mantle and carried it forward. The Mauryan dynasty controlled almost the entire Indian subcontinent with efficiency and administrative finesse. Small wonder, then, that it attracted so much attention in history circles and several academic treatises flowed from this. There are too many to cite, in this regard, but mention should definitely be made of R.K. Mookerji's works on Ashoka and Chandragupta, which were truly pioneering scholarly analyses, paving the way for a veritable flood of outpourings on the Mauryans.[1]

Academic works apart, there is very little available about this remarkable dynasty in a sequential, narrative form to appeal to the non-historian or non-Mauryan specialist who does not seek to engage with the dry details alone. In addition, most purportedly non-academic works on the Mauryas tend to focus solely on Ashoka, and his reign and legacy, definitely engrossing topics to capture.[2] However, to understand the breadth of his vision and the enormity of his endeavours during his reign, one needs to understand where he came from and also appreciate the fact that although pioneering, he began his reign by sitting on the shoulders of two giants, whose support he only later shrugged off when he came into his own. *The Mauryas* attempts to fill this gap.

The tale of the Mauryas actually starts with Magadha in

present-day south Bihar and the establishment of its supremacy over the other states that arose in the sixth century BCE in north India across a wide axis stretching from Gandhara in the north-west to Anga in the east and southwards across the Vindhyas to the Godavari river in the Deccan. There were many factors that ensured Magadha's success over the contemporary monarchies and oligarchies: its geographically strategic location, its natural resources, and the sheer charisma and leadership of Bimbisara and Ajatashatru, the father-and-son duo of the Haryanka dynasty who ruled it, in turn. This was also the time of what has been termed the 'heterodox' religions, mainly Buddhism and Jainism, that competed with Brahmanism, the resident heavyweight, for followers and patronage. The Haryankas were eventually replaced by the Shishunagas, a forgettable interregnum and, thereafter, by the Nandas, who further shored up Magadha's might. The Nandas are considered the first ruling line to establish an empire and some semblance of central control, building upon Magadha's resources to accumulate so much wealth and power that even Alexander the Great's soldiers balked at the thought of invading them and few among the contemporary polities dared to challenge their formidable sway. Until, of course, they were replaced by the Mauryas.

The Mauryas have several 'firsts' to their credit, beginning with the dynasty's founder, Chandragupta Maurya, who, in a sense, is the earliest emperor in Indian history whose historicity can be established on the grounds of fairly well-ascertainable chronology. This is not to say that there were no other well-known names in the narrative of the past but just that in Chandragupta's case, there is a conjunction of chronological and spatial evidence—in terms of a wide variety of sources—that enables historians to locate him in a well-defined historical context. Furthermore, the empire that he managed to establish so far outstripped earlier dynastic entities in terms of geographical extent that it occupies a hallowed space of its own. He virtually brought all of north India and most of the south under his sway, a feat that might have been attempted before but without the astounding success he (and his successors) enjoyed.

The Nanda dynasty that Chandragupta replaced, with its base at Magadha and including, within it, the Ganga valley and its neighbourhood, did not have as extensive an empire as the Mauryas nor did it have so many peoples and cultures within its ambit. There were social and cultural tensions of other kinds as well. Brahmanism, as noted earlier, was jostling with several dissident groups, prominently, Buddhism—and Jainism, to a somewhat lesser extent—not just in the philosophical realm but also in competitions for patronage. There were economic changes, too, that were often reflected in these tussles. The semi-nomadic pastoral economy of previous times and the clearing of the forests had gradually given way to a settled agrarian village economy in the area, with a preponderance of cultivators. There was, in addition, an increase in trade and communication (for which the Ganga was greatly used), and urbanism with its guilds—and the inevitable rise of certain social classes connected with these. This, in turn, necessitated a well-oiled administration with some amount of authority and control (to be able to impose taxation, among other things), which Chandragupta was able to set in motion during his time, passing the baton to Bindusara, and Ashoka was later able to cement with his policy of dhamma and its focus on social responsibility.

Sir William Jones's identification of Chandragupta as the Sandrocottus of contemporary Greek sources not only enabled the Mauryan dates to be worked out but also provided the first verifiable date in ancient Indian history, which provided the basis for subsequent datelines to be developed. Several dates and assertions mattered in this scheme of things—Alexander the Great's Indian conquests in 327/326 BCE and his death in Babylon in 323 BCE; his general, Seleucus Nikator's India campaign in 305 BCE and his subsequent clash with Chandragupta; the logical conclusion that Chandragupta must have won the Nanda throne in Magadha after Alexander's death and before the latter's generals withdrew from conquered Indian territories in 317 BCE; and the Puranic claim that Chandragupta had reigned for twenty-four years. Over years of discussions and recalculations, the general consensus is that Chandragupta Maurya ruled from around 324/321 to 297 BCE; his son, Bindusara, from 297 to 273 BCE and Bindusara's son, Ashoka, from 269/268 to 232 BCE. The Mauryan dynasty itself ended in around 181 BCE.[3]

Chandragupta's involvement with Chanakya/Kautilya, who had an axe to grind with the Nandas, who used the former as his tool to effect revenge, and who might or might not have written the *Arthashastra*, a brilliant treatise on statecraft that possibly reflected the Mauryan empire, is the subject of much speculation, as are some of the other aspects of the young king's life, and which one can attempt to make sense of by using the Brahmanical, Buddhist and Jaina literary traditions, as also Graeco-Roman accounts composed in the wake of Alexander's invasion. The same sources can also be used for Bindusara, an enigmatic character who has not received much scholarly or other attention but whose personality, such as can be discerned, was clearly strong, curious and stubborn.

The fact that he held his father's enormous empire together argues for a considerable measure of strength, control and political sagacity. His was also an enquiring and eclectic mind, reaching out to foreign ruling entities and displaying his knowledge of worlds beyond his ken in his interactions with them. Unfortunately, though, he has been completely sidelined, considered somewhat irrelevant to Mauryan analyses and, consequently, invisible to the public eye wherein he is either confused for Bimbisara of the Haryanka dynasty due to their similar-sounding names or, quite simply, ignored altogether.

Bindusara's troubled relationship with his son, Ashoka, is another aspect that comes to the fore from a perusal of the sources. The latter's desire for the throne, prompting him to kill those that stood in his way and then unleash a reign of terror at the empire's helm can be gleaned not just from the usual sources but also those specifically dedicated to him and pertaining to the Buddhist tradition. The question of whether he turned into a Buddhist in the aftermath of the bloody Kalinga war in *c.* 261 BCE and whether his political philosophy of dhamma was, in fact, the Buddha's teachings repackaged or a radical new way of thinking are some of the issues that surround this highly mercurial yet remarkable ruler who, looking for a way to unite his huge realm while making amends for the violence he had earlier unleashed, found a wonderfully pioneering way to achieve both: inscribing and disseminating his messages on stone all through his land. Consequently, Ashoka's rock and pillar edicts are great sources of information not just on him but the contemporary Mauryan context as a whole, used to understand elements of administration, religion, culture, art and architecture, to name a few.

Women have always been peripheral to narratives of the Mauryan empire; the men take centrestage. Admittedly, there isn't much information on them to begin with, but they do appear as a palpably vibrant presence through this time span ranging from Chandragupta's all-women bodyguard troop who obviously played a key role in protecting him from potential assassination bids and ensuring the dynasty's longevity; to Bindusara's intelligently ambitious queens who were anxious to promote their sons' wellbeing; to the several women connected with Ashoka, most of whom had an emphatic impact on his life and policies. Wherever possible, they have been integrated into this delineation of the Mauryan dynasty—and parallels have also been provided with similar women from the Indian past with similar trajectories, culled from my doctoral and post-doctoral research on gender in early medieval north India and Orissa, respectively,[4] to demonstrate the ubiquitous nature of the gender bias that exists in its writing.

If this narrative, however, reads more like a concatenation of stories, there is a reason: you cannot actually separate the Mauryan story from the many tales and legends that abound in religious literary traditions and other works—with regard to them as a whole and to the first three rulers, in turn. These, when seen in conjunction with archaeological evidence, help to reconstruct the dynasty's tale to a considerable extent. Remove these stories and you are left with virtually nothing! And this is, in fact, true of any part of history that belongs to an ancient context anywhere in the world. The closer you get to present times, the more profuse the sources become. The earlier it is, there is a paucity of sources, resulting in huge gaps in our knowledge. And these can usually be filled with stories, often containing nuggets of historical truth, so they should never be discounted.

Writing this book has been a confounding and liberating exercise, in turn. Straddling two ostensibly similar but radically different professions of historian and children's writer[5] has contributed to this, in no small measure. Being an academic with years of rigorous training in writing profusely-footnoted pieces on history, the temptation to weigh each sentence down with an explanatory note or citation was extremely tough to resist. The prose, consequently, felt naked and vulnerable to me. However, once I withstood the urge and, simultaneously, shook off the image of serious academics glowering at me and asking, 'But *how* do you know this or that fact? Where is the *proof*? *Where* are the cross-references?' the story and its readability—crucial elements in any well-written children's work—became paramount.

This is not to say that the historical research is inadequate or the treatment of the whole subject casual—just that the narrative is relatively uncluttered with notes that would deter from its flow or that could, quite conceivably, prompt the history-timid reader into drawing unflattering comparisons with the often-impenetrable prose of textbooks or academic works and setting the book aside forthwith. In this book, my first non-academic one for adults, the reader will find all that they need to know about the Mauryas in order to form a concrete picture of the period and the people who powered it in their minds. The narrative isn't always linear; it often veers off at a tangent to provide this or that interesting glimpse into Indian history, something that has a bearing on the issue at hand. It is hoped thereby that readers, particularly those who cordially detest history, will discover that it is, in fact, endlessly fascinating and interconnected and just so *alive* despite dealing with the dead, as it were.

Also, this book is not meant to be a comprehensive and exhaustive compendium of the Mauryan dynasty, so there is no real point in saying, 'Oh, but you didn't mention *this* particular fact about them or *that* particular fact from the *Arthashastra*!' For anyone looking to engage at depth with the subject matter of this book, there are several excellent and detailed works they can consult, a list of which is provided in the bibliography and, of course, in the endnotes that point to additional reading matter or something that will help to elucidate the point at hand. For the rest, it is hoped that they find this part of the Indian past fascinating enough to cultivate an eagerness to know more—or that they simply enjoyed themselves while reading this book. A writer (and historian) could hope for no less!

Notes

1. He also wrote on Harshavardhana of Kanauj (606-648 CE). The references are in the bibliography.
2. These are mentioned in the bibliography but two should be singled out for special mention: Nayanjot Lahiri's *Ashoka in Ancient India*, Permanent Black, 2015, which puts Ashoka under a veritable personal and professional microscope, and is an extremely well-rounded and eminently readable assessment of this remarkable ruler; and Charles Allen's *Ashoka—The Search for India's Lost Emperor*, Abacus, 2012, which details the unfolding of the Ashoka-puzzle in exciting and engaging layers.
3. Dates differ: Upinder Singh, for one, offers *c.* 324–187 BCE as the Mauryan dates. See Upinder Singh, *A History of Ancient and Early Medieval India—From the Stone Age to the Twelfth Century*, Pearson/Dorling Kindersley, 2008, pp.321, 330. For a detailed chronology of the first three Mauryan rulers, and the permutations and combinations involved in figuring out these dates, see, for instance, Allen, *Ashoka—The Search for India's Lost Emperor*, pp.296–298. See also Romila Thapar, *Asoka and the Decline of the Mauryas*, Oxford University Press, 3rd edn, 2021, pp.17–21; and Lahiri, *Ashoka in Ancient India*, pp.25, 291.
4. The references are in the bibliography.
5. Again, the pertinent references are in the bibliography.

2

MAGADHA'S RISE

Every story has a beginning and for the Mauryans, it was Magadha. This is dragging its history back somewhat but necessary to better appreciate their eventual rise and trajectory. And here, it is the sixth century BCE that marks the beginning, a crucial period in more ways than one. This itself was due to a mélange of various political, social, economic and philosophical developments. It is also seen as the onset of what is termed the early historical period in north India. Of course, there is a great deal of argument and debate about the names accorded to varied ages in Indian history and there does not seem to be any foreseeable end to it. Dates are regularly disputed; very few are set in stone, literally and figuratively. There is, however, a sort of general consensus on some of the main time blocks of the past, so we can agree that this century was an important one. Though, when a particular century (or larger timespan) is pinpointed, as in this case, it should be seen as an approximation. Changes in history occur over many centuries—a slow but continuous process.

A word about the original sources. These are always period-specific, so a particular kind of source that provides valuable evidence for a certain time span might not necessarily be useful for another. Historians usually identify and demarcate the pertinent sources for their period of study before undertaking the actual research, always keeping in mind that a new source could emerge, at any delightful point, to buttress or contest their assertions. For the sixth century BCE, both literary and archaeological sources exist. Of the textual sources, there are both secular and religious works. The latter, for purposes of convenience, can broadly be divided into those belonging to the Brahmanical, Buddhist and Jaina traditions.

The dating of these texts, though, is a huge—and hotly disputed—bottleneck. The problem usually arises when they are sometimes read as direct reflections of society and polity. An example of this is the *Ramayana* and the *Mahabharata*, the popular Sanskrit epics, that were composed over a long period of time with several interpolations. Their specific dating is a challenge, therefore, and it makes sense to use them for generalised comparisons on polity, society and culture. Again, some components of the Dharmashastra literature might or might not pertain to this specific period but can be used as general sources that reflect different aspects of the Brahmanical normative tradition.

Moreover, all three types of literary sources—the Brahmanical, Buddhist and Jaina—have some intrinsic problems. For instance, the Puranas (from around the fourth century CE), that belong to the Brahmanical corpus—collections of lore and legends that provide information on dynastic history but can be annoyingly confusing given that they sometimes contradict each other, mix up rulers of different dynasties, often describe contemporary rulers as successors and maintain a frustrating silence on rulers known from other sources. This is not always the case but it happens often enough to sound an alarm bell to the serious historian. And sometimes, they talk in an unnecessarily complicated future tense so that you are not very sure whether they are referring to things that have happened or will happen or things that have already happened but are cleverly mentioned as predictions.

Also, if you compare the dynastic history of the Buddhist and Jaina texts, and juxtapose it with the Puranic material, you find a lot of discrepancies so that it is often difficult to discern a single coherent thread. Perhaps their writers had access to different sets of details at different points of time. Or, equally, different perspectives might have created different versions. To add to the general chaotic mix, we also have several Greek and Latin accounts that provide interesting information on Alexander the Great's invasion of India (327–326 BCE)—although written long after it—and the contemporary political context of the north-west. Some of these literary luminaries were Arrian, Plutarch and Justin.

When you move to the archaeological sources, you find a focus on the Northern Black Polished Ware (NBPW), a specific type of deluxe pottery, and the culture associated with it. Historians associate early historic cultures on the basis of their particular pottery assemblages and tend to refer to past eras in what might sound like mysterious and unfathomable jargon as BRW, PGW, OCP and, in this case, NBPW. The letters refer to the colour of the pottery in each case—Black and Red Ware (associated with the Harappans), Painted Grey Ware and Ochre Coloured Pottery (associated with the post-Harappans) and the NBPW, which is technically associated with the period from the seventh to the third century BCE in its first phase.

An important piece of evidence that goes with NBPW sites is an early series of punch-marked coins, which marks the beginning of the use of money in the Indian subcontinent.

A complication arises here, though, or rather several. NBPW, totally belying its name, is not confined to north India and nor is it always black or polished. It has been found as far south as Amaravati in Andhra Pradesh, and in several shades and colours other than black.[1] This is just another indication of how complex and often baffling the process of historical reconstruction really is, definitely not something to be undertaken by the fainthearted or the untrained!

From the sixth century BCE onwards, the contours of north Indian political history become much clearer than before and prominent people mentioned in varied literary traditions can, thrillingly, be identified as actual historical figures. An important marker of this timespan was the emergence of state polities and societies along a wide axis—from Gandhara in the north-west to Anga in the east and southwards across the Vindhyas to the Godavari river in the Deccan. There were two types of rival political systems at the time—the monarchies (*rajyas*), which were mainly centred in the fertile alluvial tracts of the Gangetic valley, and the non-monarchical states (*ganas/sanghas*)—initially (and misleadingly) termed republics but, in fact, oligarchies with power exercised by a group of people—which were located around the northern edges of these kingdoms, mostly in or near the Himalayan foothills in eastern India. All three literary traditions, as well as Greek accounts, provide information on these political systems. Numismatic and epigraphic evidence also exists. The lines between them seem to have been fluid, though: the Kurus started off as a monarchy and then became a *gana*; the Videhas, too.

Thus, Buddhist and Jaina texts tell us that sixteen powerful states (*solasa-mahajanapada*) thrived in the early part of this century, apart from smaller states, chiefdoms and tribal principalities. Different texts provide slightly varying lists. For purposes of convenience, we will quote a single one, the *Anguttara Nikaya*, a Buddhist text, here. The names are in Pali, the language of the commoners, with the Sanskrit equivalents provided within brackets. Thus, the sixteen states were Kasi (Kashi), Kosala (Koshala), Anga, Magadha, Vajji (Vrijji), Malla, Chetiya (Chedi), Vamsa (Vatsa), Kuru, Panchala, Machchha (Matsya), Shurasena, Assaka (Ashmaka), Avanti, Gandhara, and Kamboja.[2]

So did these sixteen polities suddenly emerge from a vacuum? Clearly not: there are indications that the nature of political units had been changing slowly but surely over time. Later Vedic texts reflect a transition from lineage-based tribal polities to territorial states. This was not a wholescale transition, by any means, but tribes were definitely coming together to form larger political units, such as the Purus and Bharatas who merged to form the Kurus, which, according to some scholars, actually represented the first state in India. However, political transitions are usually gradual, being the culmination of several increasingly complex processes.

The emergence of a monarchical state, for instance, would undoubtedly have involved contestations, negotiations and accommodations of varied kinds, involving coercive mechanisms and control over resources in equal measure. It would also have necessitated the scripting of often-fanciful origin stories so as to legitimise the concentration of political power in the hands of a single person or family. Herein lies the basis of hereditary kingship—and an opportunity for writers of great imagination to shine. The *Aitareya Brahmana*, for instance, states that the gods were defeated by the demons because they had no king, so they elected one who led them to victory, thereby intrinsically drawing this figure closer to the divine realm.

And here we come to the knotty problem of iron. Later Vedic texts indicate a familiarity with it and its use in agriculture in the Indo-Gangetic divide and the upper Ganga valley from around 1,000 to 500 BCE. It was a significant technological advance from the copper-bronze age that preceded it but there has been much argument on the role of iron in paving the way for the emergence of the sophisticated political systems in the sixth century BCE by way of clearing thick alluvial forests and enhancing agricultural produce. D.D. Kosambi felt that the eastern movement of the Indo-Aryans was to reach the iron ores of south Bihar, thence Magadha's prominence. However, a chemical analysis of early iron artefacts at Atranjikhera point to the hills between Agra and Gwalior, and not Bihar, as the probable source of ores. Frustrating, yes, but chemistry trumps all other kinds of evidence, particularly as regards ancient India. It is dull but irrefutable.

R.S. Sharma, who claimed that iron axes helped clear the Ganga valley and expand agriculture, leading to urbanisation and the rise of religions like Buddhism in the new socio-economic milieu, was also furiously challenged. It was argued that the forests in question could have been cleared by burning, that the impact of iron technology was very gradual and not a prerequisite for urbanisation, and that the Ganga plains remained heavily forested till the sixteenth/seventeenth centuries. (It is true that largescale deforestation of the Ganga valley happened in the colonial period.)

However, while technology as a factor in historical change has to be considered along with other variables, there is general unanimity, though, that the use of iron was known almost all over the Indian subcontinent during the period *c.* 800–500 BCE—a fact that is derived not just from concrete archaeological finds but also from fortunate corroborations in literature, one of the Buddhist texts, for instance, drawing an analogy with the hissing of an iron plough that is plunged into water. Its beginnings in the Ganga valley can be traced to the second millennium BCE, its use and impact gradually widening thereon, reflected in the number and range of iron objects in the NBPW phase.[3]

The sixth century BCE in the Ganga valley was also an age of thinkers, of philosophers, of great ponderings and musings. And this is how Buddhism and Jainism, the two great 'heterodox' religions, came to be. Both had much to do with the polities and politics of the time, and the writings of both traditions are significant sources for this period despite routinely contradicting each other and often making assertions that are manifestly exaggerated.

Almost everyone is conversant with the story of the Buddha, its founder (*c.* 530–479 BCE)—of his birth as Siddhartha, son of Shuddhodana, chief of the Sakya clan of Kapilavastu; of the prophecy that proclaimed him to either become a world conqueror or renouncer; of his parents' frantic measures to ensure he fulfilled the former; of Siddhartha's sudden discovery of old age, disease, death and renunciation, in that order; and of his consequent abandonment of his wife and child, and his world of luxury, to seek the truth. The hagiographies of the Buddha—themselves an inextricable mix of history and legend—tell us that after years of penance and thought, he achieved enlightenment, delivered his first sermon in a deer park near Benares, established an order of monks and nuns called the sangha, and preached his doctrine for over four decades till his death at the age of eighty at Kusinara (modern Kasi).

Jainism, on the other hand, is older than Buddhism

and discerning a coherent historical biography from the hagiographies is as difficult in the case of Vardhamana, its exponent, as in the case of the Buddha, with the Shvetambara (white-clad) and Digambara (sky-clad/naked) traditions disagreeing on many salient aspects of his life. However, the main story is, once again, a well-known one—of Vardhamana's birth in *c.* 599 BCE at Kundagrama near Vaishali to an aristocratic family; of his renunciation of the world at a young age; of his wanderings and austerities until he attained enlightenment and became Mahavira, the twenty-fourth tirthankara of his line; of his establishment of the Jaina sangha and discipline; and of his death at the age of seventy-two at Pavapuri near modern Patna.

Reams have been written on the Buddhist and Jaina philosophies and there is no need to plunge into the details here. Suffice it to say that the Buddha and Mahavira were contemporaries, and their creeds evolved in a situation of initial urbanisation where chiefdoms were shifting to kingdoms but before the emergence of large kingdoms or empires.[4] There is some broad similarity in their teachings, too—their rejection of the Vedas' authority, their non-theistic doctrine, their emphasis on renunciation and human effort to attain salvation and their establishment of a monastic order for men and women. They are often seen as a reaction to the Brahmanical religion that endorsed social hierarchies and elaborate rituals, hence the epithet 'heterodox'—a hasty one, though, evidently based on a surface understanding of these creeds. For instance, although the Buddhist doctrine was definitely more inclusive than the Brahmanical tradition, it did not aim to abolish social differences. In fact, the Buddha saw all social relationships as chains and the cause of suffering and thus, in his view, a person needed to break away from them to attain liberation.

However, the monastic order that he created could potentially accommodate social dropouts under certain conditions; varna and jati considerations were seen as irrelevant for aspirants to the sangha. Interestingly, many brahmanas became monks and lay-followers of the Buddha despite his criticism of Brahmanical ritual and arrogation of social pre-eminence. Perhaps his teachings appealed to them in that such issues were also being discussed within their own ranks. That these converts were frowned upon by others of their ilk, though, is made clear by Buddhist texts. Incidentally, the Buddhist tradition reverses the Brahmanical order of rank and places the kshatriya higher than the brahmana. The latter term, though, is used in two senses in the Buddhist canon—as a conventional social category and as an ideal category of a wise person who led an exemplary life. The Buddha himself is addressed as 'brahmana'!

The Buddhist dhamma (featuring the four noble truths and the eightfold path) held enormous appeal for the laity due to its practical code of conduct for eliminating suffering and its accordance of importance to varied emerging social groups, such as the gahapati or householder. But what of women vis-à-vis this doctrine? Admittedly, the Buddha did accord them relevance by saying that they could aspire to the highest human goal of nibbana/nirvana but then proceeded to fetter them with dire predictions and restrictions. He did not want to establish a bhikkuni/bhikshuni sangha for women but caved in due to the pressure from his disciple, Ananda, and his aunt, Gautami, observing darkly—as per the *Vinaya Pitaka*—that his doctrine would now decline in 500 rather than 1,000 years due to their inclusion. The same noble text informs us that nuns, despite their seniority, could not revile or abuse monks and, furthermore, had to meekly accept their criticism and/or advice without returning the favour in equal coin.

Lest we intemperately accuse the Buddha of gender bias right away (and much has already been made of his abrupt abandonment of his wife, Yashodhara and son, Rahula, to traverse a higher plane), let us also consider the fact that he did give women some measure of individual agency in the religious sphere that was otherwise usually denied to them. Buddhist texts are rife with references to learned nuns and we also have the glorious, concrete example of the *Therigatha* (*Verses of Elder Nuns*), a collection of seventy-three poems composed by seventy-two nuns, who had advanced quite a bit on the spiritual road.

And let us also remember that women donors, as a collective identity, are more visible in the Buddhist cause than in any other throughout early Indian history. Yet just to confound, here is an interesting anecdote from the *Anguttara Nikaya*. While at the house of Anathapindika, a prominent gahapati of Shravasti, the Buddha's ears were assailed by persistent noise, the source of which, the former unhappily informed him, was his daughter-in-law, Sujata, the child of wealthy parents and a law unto herself, incapable of restraint from any quarter. The Buddha proceeded to give the errant Sujata a lecture on the seven kinds of wives that existed. Hell awaited the first three kinds whose crimes ranged from being wilful and indolent to neglectful and loud, while heaven was the reward for the other four types who basically looked after their husbands in every which way.

Sujata suddenly had an inexplicable character transformation and opted for one of the latter categories—that of the slavelike wife/dasisama who is calm, patient and obedient, and remains meek while her husband beats her up. Presumably, quiet reigned in Anathapindika's household thereon but the point is that recalcitrant wives *did* exist in all their intractability, resisting patriarchal strictures and generally being heard. That Sujata subsequently chose the most servile form of wifehood might equally reflect the (male) writer's wishful thinking and his keen desire to reinforce the norm in a situation where it was continually being challenged.

The Jaina doctrine, while being somewhat similar to the Buddhist, focuses largely on ahimsa or non-violence/non-injury towards other living beings, which, especially in the case of its monks and nuns, was observed to an extraordinary degree. For instance, they were forbidden from bathing or walking in the rain so as not to harm water bodies, from digging the earth so as not to kill earth bodies, from fanning themselves so as not to harm air bodies, from lighting or extinguishing flames so as not to harm fire bodies, and from walking on greenery or touching living plants so as not to harm vegetable bodies. Certainly not a discipline for the absentminded!

However, Jainism was able to strike a practical balance between the worlds of monasticism and the householder. People of all varnas and social categories could enter the Jaina sangha. Yet once again, there was an odd relationship that it sported with Brahmanism. There is a highly dramatic story in the *Uttaradhyayana Sutra* of a Jaina monk in search of food who stumbles upon some brahmanas intent on a sacrifice. They refuse him food and, weirdly, attack him with sticks and canes until a demigod/yaksha intervenes whereupon they capitulate and seek the monk's pardon, who, in turn, graciously proceeds to upbraid them on the futility of sacrifices and the wisdom of the Jaina way. To further complicate the issue, all the chief disciples of Mahavira were brahmanas belonging to the Magadha area who apparently entered the sangha with several of *their* disciples. In fact, the Jaina texts say, the brahmana varna was instituted by the first Jaina tirthankara's son and, furthermore, only a Jaina monk was worthy of being called a brahmana.

Turning from these excessively convoluted claims to the issue of women, the Jaina tradition, too, had a problematic relationship with them. They were seen as a generally avoidable danger, whose friendship and company ought to be shunned by monks, but were, equally, seen as deserving of a monastic order. In fact, at the time of Mahavira's death, there were apparently 14,000 monks, 36,000 nuns, 1,59,000 laymen and 3,18,000 laywomen. The figures speak for themselves. Curiously enough, though, the issue of clothing became a key element in the vigorous Jaina debate on gender and salvation. The Digambara order (mentioned earlier) for whom nudity was a prerequisite (clothes being seen as possessions), claimed that a woman who clearly could not roam around naked could, therefore, not attain salvation and had to be reborn as a man to attain this goal. The Shvetambaras disagree: clothes were optional and both men and women could attain salvation. And yet, here is a reality check—nuns, irrespective of their seniority, had to offer respectful salutations to the monks at all times. Moreover, they were supposed to confess their errors to the monks and be rebuked by them but it was never a vice versa situation. And the Digambara order, in particular, seems to have nurtured a morbid fear of menstruating women and the generally unspeakable things that went on with their anatomy. Some of the explanations proferred thereof would put the most imaginative writer of fiction to shame.

Time for another curious and convoluted tale, at this juncture, that involves women and food. This one exemplifies the Shvetambara belief that women could attain salvation or jinahood and focuses on Malli, their nineteenth tirthankara, who was, in fact, a woman—although she became one only because of cheating in a previous birth, if we may be allowed to preempt the story a bit. Accordingly, Malli's soul was born, in a previous life, in a king named Mahabala. At some point, Mahabala, along with his seven friends, renounced the world in order to become Jaina monks. As part of their new regimen, they undertook to observe the same number of fasts but Mahabala was soon champing at the bit and devising innovative ways of skipping meals, thus ending with a greater number of fasts than originally agreed upon.

Other than this, though, his conduct was exemplary and so, he was deemed worthy of becoming a jina. However, his meal-skipping deed to rack up his fast-tally cast a long shadow for which, after spending some time in heaven, his soul had to be resigned to the fact that it was reborn in a woman's body, that of a princess named Malli. His seven friends, on the other hand, were reborn as kshatriya warriors of neighbouring kingdoms. Inevitably—and ironically, given their previous mutual relationship—they all desired Malli and fought with each other for her hand. This had the unfortunate result of making Malli renounce the world in disgust whereupon she promptly attained enlightenment and became the nineteenth tirthankara, thereby constituting the single exception to the rule that a jina should be male.

Incidentally, the Digambaras scoff at this fanciful tale. For them, the nineteenth tirthankara was a man named Mallinatha who was very firmly a prince, not a princess, and who became enlightened after becoming a Digambara monk. However, Malli did not ever become the object of popular worship, although a ninth century image of her has been found that sports long hair and breasts. Not surprisingly, the number of Digambara nuns did decline over time. The Buddhist bhikkuni sangha was similarly affected, performing a disappearing act of sorts among the Theravada communities of Sri Lanka and southeast Asia. In fact, both Buddhism and Jainism disappeared in slow stages from the central scheme of things but that happened over a long span of time and in a different period altogether.

The point of this somewhat tangential discussion on religion is to reiterate the fact that the sixth century BCE was an age of increasing levels of complexity. Urbanism, new socio-economic groupings and new philosophies were among the changes that marked the age—and as the development of Buddhism and Jainism and their rivalry with a well-entrenched Brahmanism played out in the background of the tussle between the new political systems that emerged in this period, it becomes important to consider them before we tackle the main story.[5]

Notes

1. See, for instance, Nayanjot Lahiri, *Ashoka in Ancient India*, Permanent Black, 2015, pp.46, 326 (endnote 8).
2. For details of these states and their locations, see Singh, *A History of Ancient and Early Medieval India*, pp.260–269. See also pp.280–287 for an excellent account of the archaeological and literary profiles of these early historical cities.
3. Romila Thapar, for one, points out that the extensive use of iron in the Megalithic sites of the peninsula largely predates urban centres and the coming of the Mauryas. Iron production was recorded but it was not the sole agent in the creation of cities. Urbanisation would have required other factors besides. See Romila Thapar, *Asoka and the Decline of the Mauryas*, Oxford University Press, 3rd edn, 2021, p.324. See also Singh, *A History of Ancient and Early Medieval India*, pp.240–242, 253–255 for details on early iron age cultures in the subcontinent and the impact of iron technology on the history of ancient India.

4. See ibid., pp.312–313.
5. This is, in fact, seen as the age of the second urbanisation in the north (the first was the Harappan), although its foundation was laid in preceding centuries, around 800 BCE. The dates for the south are different, though. Urbanism was based on steady agrarian supplies, leading to burgeoning settlements, crafts, trade and money, and political leadership to oversee it all. See ibid., 278–279. Singh also points to the irony in the increasing range of material goods alongside emerging doctrines that advocated their renunciation (p.288).

3

THE CONVOLUTED HISTORIES OF BIMBISARA AND AJATASHATRU

Amongst the sixteen entities of the sixth century BCE at the beginning of the early historical period in north India, there was a tussle for power; some main contenders emerged and were, basically, the ones that had to be taken seriously. These were the kingdoms of Kashi (the region of Benares), Kosala (on Kashi's east), Avanti (the region of Malwa) and Magadha (modern-day southern Bihar), and the republic of the Vrijjis (parts of Bihar and Nepal). Their mutual relations spanned wars and alliances, and skyrocketed or plummeted depending on the political exigencies of the moment.

Let us cite the case of the Sakyas of Kapilavastu, a sangha, and the rajya of the Kosalans, narrated by Buddhist tradition. Prasenajit, the ruler of Kosala, admired the Buddha and thought he would marry into the Sakya clan to which the latter belonged. The lineage-proud Sakyas dragged their feet over this, loath to hand over one of their princesses to Prasenajit but too afraid of his power to refuse. So they cleverly presented a slave girl, Vasabhakkhattiya, daughter of a Sakya chief and a slave woman, to Prasenajit as the ideal candidate. Marital bliss followed, along with two children, Vidudabha, a boy, and Vajira, a girl. Inexplicably, everyone remained in this happy delusional haze for ages until Vidudabha decided to visit his maternal grandfather and got to know his mother's antecedents. Prasenajit's knee-jerk reaction on learning the awful news was to shoot the messenger, so to speak, and disown his son. He also disowned his hapless wife.

The Buddha entered the scene, at this point, and convinced the highly-excitable (and, clearly, highly-impressionable) Prasenajit that the father's social status was all that really mattered. So the latter called back the banished duo. When the darkly-brooding Vidudabha became king, however, he massacred the Sakyas in belated revenge. Now whether or not this tale is true is a matter for conjecture. It should be noted, though, that the massacre is sculpturally depicted in many stupa sites and is recalled in later Buddhist tradition, so there could very well be an element of truth in it. There are several other enchanting stories of the weird clashes between the rajyas, and between them and the gana-sanghas, all embellished with fascinating (and probably embroidered) detail in the texts.

Incidentally, some nationalist histories tended to compare the ganas of the sixth/fifth century BCE with the republics of Greece and Rome, and draw parallels between them and modern democratic systems. However, the former were not democracies in the strict sense of the term. Instead, they were ruled by an aristocracy, comprising the heads of the leading Kshatriya families, and headed by the chief of the aristocratic council. The best-known example, in this regard, is that of the Lichchhavis of Vaishali who apparently had 7,707 rajas (kings) to govern the realm, and a similar number of subordinate kings, military heads and treasurers. Given that their tendency to argue among themselves is also documented by Buddhist texts, one can only imagine the terrible chaos and sheer noise that must, inevitably, have ensued in the process. Admittedly, the numbers provided by the texts are exaggerations but they definitely indicate that the Lichchhavis had a large assembly and that their heads called themselves raja.

That Brahmanical texts are comparatively stingy on details regarding the ganas is not surprising. Kingship was the pivot of the Brahmanical social and political system, and kinglessness was a state to be avoided at all costs. There were other fundamental differences between the two rival political entities. For instance, some of the more powerful monarchies developed a standing army that was recruited and maintained by the state, and which was to be in perpetual readiness to fight battles if the need arose. On the other hand, ganas, such as the Lichchhavis, had strong armies that turned to other professions when not engaged in warfare.[1]

Additionally, the egalitarian concept of governing through debate and discussion exposed the ganas to a considerable degree of internal dissension, a strength-turned-weakness that was fully exploited by the aggressive and more cohesive monarchies. There is an interesting account in a Buddhist text, the *Lalitavistara*, that encapsulates this point. While the Buddha contemplates his next birth, the appropriateness of his future family is discussed by the other divine beings who summarily dismiss the Lichchhavis of Vaishali as a probable option. One of the reasons proferred is that everyone in this place thinks of himself as a king. The Buddha could obviously not be born into a family of such swollen egos and general disorder!

Fast-forwarding a little, we can see how this glorious political experiment of the ganas met its end. In the fourth century CE, Chandragupta I, the first prominent ruler of the Gupta dynasty, married a Lichchhavi princess, Kumaradevi, and this was duly memorialised on gold coins issued for the occasion. Obviously, therefore, the Lichchhavis were still a force to reckon with all those centuries later if the mighty Guptas were seeking an alliance with them. The product of this marriage, Samudragupta, is even known as *Lichchhavi-dauhitra* (grandson of the Lichchhavis) in inscriptions. Ironically, though, Samudragupta's hugely successful military campaigns probably finished the ganas or consigned them to a subordinate role. So while the monarchies were quietly and persistently expanding their ambitions and aspiring to universal rule, the ganas, whose history covers around a thousand years, could not match this fervour with their typical system of governance and military organisation, and succumbed to several military defeats at the hands of the former. And the monarchies—or, particularly, one—reigned supreme.

So now we come to Magadha, the kingdom that ended the nearly hundred-year-old rivalry between the sixteen states by triumphing over them all and becoming the centre of political activity in northern India—a position that it maintained for several centuries. This state would roughly correspond to the Patna and Gaya districts of Bihar today. On the north, west and east, it was bound by the Ganga, Son and Champa rivers, respectively, and it had the Vindhyan range to its south. The Puranas, as well as the Buddhist and Jaina texts, provide information on Magadha's rise to power but, of course, they contradict each other and offer differing dynastic sequences, among other things. The story is one of blood and gore, though, in all three traditions, involving a ruthless quelling of internal and external rivals.

Magadha's meteoric rise to political glory began with Bimbisara. He is said to have belonged to the Haryanka dynasty, although a Buddhist text, the *Mahavamsa*, notes that he was made king by his father at the tender age of fifteen, which probably indicates that he was not the founder of the dynasty. Some other texts indicate that he was, initially, a senapati (commander-in-chief) of another political line, the Vajjis. His origins are shrouded in fog, therefore, but all sources agree that he was Magadha's first important king. It is difficult to assign precise dates to him but a more or less acceptable time bracket, involving complex calculations of varied regnal years with reference to the date of the Buddha's death, is 545–493 BCE.[2]

All through history, when rulers sought to enhance their power, they made clever marriage alliances. The idea behind this was that if you married the daughter of your enemy, the latter had no choice but to become your friend. If this was done several times over, your resources and allies could be multiplied. Then you could cast your net wider, and find more people to conquer and more marriage alliances to fix. So while these bonds might not always have been personally enjoyable for the two persons involved, it made perfect political sense—and Bimbisara was not immune to its charms. The *Mahavagga*, a Buddhist text, talks of his five hundred wives—a highly unlikely number! What we do know is that he married Mahakosala, the sister of Prasenajit, the king of Kosala, which brought him a village in Kashi as dowry. Bimbisara also married a princess of Videha; Khema, the daughter of the Madra ruler of central Punjab; and a Lichchhavi princess from Vaishali. These politically strategic alliances gave him the means to expand his kingdom and elevate its status.

Accordingly, after strengthening his northern and western boundaries, he waged war on the kingdom of Anga to the south-east and annexed it. This was a smart decision because

Anga controlled the trade and the routes to the ports in the Ganga delta. These ports, in turn, had commercial links with ports on the coast of Burma and the east coast of India, leading to an economic windfall for Magadha. Prince Kunika, Bimbisara's son, was appointed governor at Champa, the capital of Anga. Yet, it wasn't as if Bimbisara's relations with all the contemporary states were antagonistic. There is an account of him sending his personal physician, Jivaka, to King Pradyota of Avanti (in the Malwa region of central India) when the latter was ill, which implies that the two were on reasonably friendly terms with each other.

More than anything, it helped that Bimbisara's capital at Girivraja (identified with Rajagriha)—a beautiful city in itself—was surrounded by five hills that formed a natural defence barrier, an effective deterrent to those aggrieved by Magadha's aggression and who might have wanted to give it a taste of its own medicine. The kingdom itself was very large with thousands of prosperous villages, if one goes by the *Mahavagga*. Buddhist texts refer to these villages being governed by assemblies under village headmen. They also mention high-ranking officials who probably had executive, military and judicial functions in the overall administration.

In addition, the king's standing army was maintained through state revenues and was composed of carefully-recruited Magadhan loyalists rather than mercenaries, definitely a huge factor in their high rate of military successes. Bimbisara, therefore, was clearly a visionary of sorts, and a highly-intelligent and pragmatic ruler besides. He is also supposed to have handpicked his ministers and to have never ignored their advice. Some of his close friends and followers are mentioned in the sources—a flower-gatherer named Sumana who provided the king with a daily heap of jasmine flowers;

a minister called Koliya; a treasurer, Kumbhaghoshaka; and the physician, Jivaka, mentioned earlier—a very eclectic mix of companions, indeed.

And where did Bimbisara's religious loyalties lie? Both Buddhist and Jaina texts squabble over him but their sparring in prose does not leave us any the wiser. A Jaina text, the *Uttaradhyayana Sutra*, claims that Bimbisara was an ardent follower of Mahavira whom he apparently visited along with his wives, kinspeople and staff. Buddhist texts, on the other hand, note that he was devoted to the Buddha and that they met, for the first time, a few years after the latter's enlightenment. The Buddha is also supposed to have visited Rajagriha with his disciples whereupon Bimbisara went into some kind of hospitality overdrive, hosting lavish meals for the retinue and showering them with gifts, while also, presumably, listening to their teachings. The physician, Jivaka—who seems to have been dispatched all over the place during his service—was sent to attend to the Buddha and his monks, at one point.

Interestingly, some of the rules that the Buddha laid down with regard to monks eating fruit and the observance of the monsoon retreat (vassavasa) were apparently in response to issues and queries raised by Bimbisara. The king is also supposed to have lessened the ferry charges for all ascetics after an incident when the Buddha did not have the money to pay the ferryman who took him across the Ganga. All these are riveting stories with or without any historical basis but they do, collectively, reiterate one important fact: Bimbisara was a formidable political figure who wielded a great deal of influence. Why else would both religious traditions scramble to claim him as their own?

History has repeatedly shown (and been repeatedly

ignored, in this regard!) that the more powerful and influential you are, the more likely you are to have enemies. And these enemies can be closer home than you realise—the classic viper in the bosom syndrome. In Bimbisara's case, it was his son, Ajatashatru, who turned his last days into a sort of Shakespearean tragedy. Ajatashatru's tale has all the ingredients of a racy modern thriller—rivalry, murder, suspense, treachery and gory revenge—and is a classic case of how truth is often stranger than fiction. Although the tale might have been expanded and embroidered in varied ways over time, the main facts are startling. Ajatashatru's is also a cautionary tale of what happens if power goes to one's head.

We have already come across this saturnine personality under his other name of Kunika, who was made governor of Champa on his father's conquest of Anga. Having had a tantalising taste of power during this stint, therefore, he began to chafe at the prospect of waiting in the wings until he could ascend the Magadhan throne in the fullness of time. And so, he decided to script his father's death. Here, again, there are several intriguing discrepancies between the versions of the Buddhists and the Jainas. According to the Buddhist tradition, Ajatashatru was egged on in his evil endeavour by the Buddha's wicked cousin, Devadatta. (The former is supposed to have made a clean breast of his crime to the Buddha, at some point, when belatedly seized by remorse.)

Meanwhile, the Jaina tale is of a hair-raising and rather ludicrous set of events. According to it, Ajatashatru imprisoned his father so that he could become the king. After his initial shock and disbelief, Bimbisara apparently resigned himself to his fate, preparing for a life in fettered captivity. At this point, a twist in the tale emerged. One of Bimbisara's wives, Chellana, displayed so much devotion to her husband in prison that Ajatashatru was filled with regret at his deed. Accordingly, he raced towards his father with an iron club in his hand with the intention of breaking his chains and releasing him. The sight of his son rushing towards him with a weapon made Bimbisara blanch. Fearing the worst, he promptly consumed some conveniently handy poison to end his life. Which version contains the truth is anybody's guess but both of them highlight an important fact: Ajatashatru was definitely involved in his father's death, which happened around 493 BCE.

And so, this is how Ajatashatru became the king of Magadha. Although the kingdom continued to prosper under him, this did not mean that his horrific deed was forgotten. On the contrary, it was to cast a very long shadow and one of the initial repercussions was Ajatashatru's dramatic embroilment with Prasenajit, the king of Kosala, whose sister, Mahakosala, had—as mentioned earlier—married Bimbisara. Prasenajit was appalled at Bimbisara's murder and his trauma was aggravated by the fact that Mahakosala died of grief soon after. A pastmaster at kneejerk reactions, he decided to take back the village in Kashi that had been given as part of his sister's dowry. This resulted in a war between Kosala and Magadha that spooled out in an utterly tragi-comic manner. Both rulers were locked for a very long time in a sort of back-and forth combat with no clear victor.

At one point in this long-winded tussle, Prasenajit was defeated and had to race back to his capital for safety. At another, Ajatashatru was captured but his life spared. Peace was eventually restored through a treaty, according to which the disputed village in Kashi was returned to Ajatashatru, who also received a princess of Kosala, Vajira, in marriage. Soon afterwards, Prasenajit was deposed in a palace coup and set out towards Rajagriha to seek his enemy-turned-friend's help. However, he died outside the city gates before help could get to him. And that was the end of this very strange bond.

Ajatashatru, on the other hand, shrugged off this minor roadblock and set out to expand Magadha in every possible manner. There is no better way to demonstrate his political prescience and cunning than his conflict with and eventual victory over the Lichchhavis of Vaishali. The latter had become an extremely powerful confederacy at this time but Ajatashatru had it in his sights and was determined to break its back using any means possible. The fact that he was related to the Lichchhavis was, of course, no deterrent to him whatsoever as he set about finding excuses to quarrel with them and, eventually, wage war. It should be noted here that the identity of Ajatashatru's mother is unclear with both the Kosalan and Lichchhavi queens often cited as probable options. He was related to both of them, though, by virtue of their being Bimbisara's wives.

The reasons for the conflict between Ajatashatru and the Lichchhavis, as revealed by the sources, were varied but that he actively fostered it is undeniable. However, the Buddhist texts tell us that it was the Lichchhavis who actually commenced the hostilities because they broke their promise to share the contents of a jewel mine equally with Ajatashatru. The mine in question had been discovered at the foot of a hill at a port on the Ganga. The Jaina texts, on the other hand, insist that the entire problem started when Ajatashatru's stepbrothers, princes Halla and Vehalla, refused to hand over to him a remarkable elephant called Seyanaga who regularly sprinkled water on the women of the court with his trunk, and a valuable necklace of eighteen pearl strings that their father, Bimbisara, had given them. Apparently, the princes ran off with these two coveted items to their maternal grandfather in Vaishali and this precipitated the entire fight. (It must have been an onerous task—racing down the roads to Vaishali with a lumbering, water-sprinkling elephant in tow—but the princes were clearly a spirited duo and managed to reach safety unscathed.)

The main point of conflict, though—if we are to discard the other enchanting but eminently silly reasons—was something else altogether. Control over the river trade, as also a clash between two entirely different political systems—one a kingdom and one an oligarchy—was at the heart of the issue. Buttress this with Ajatashatru's single-minded desire to establish Magadhan supremacy and you have all the central causes of this clash. Yet Ajatashatru now came up against a reality check. The Lichchhavis, as noted earlier, were militarily powerful and actively supported by various other rulers, principally Kosala, which was—for obvious reasons—no longer Magadha's ally. It was clear, therefore, that he could not defeat them in straightforward combat. Other, more insidious means were the need of the hour. These might take time but he could be a patient man if he wanted.

And so, Ajatashatru embarked upon one of the most prolonged and ruthless campaigns of treachery that early India had ever witnessed. His diabolic plan was to destroy the Lichchhavis from within so that they would eventually turn upon themselves, and he could then sweep in and vanquish them. Accordingly, he sent his minister, Vassakara, to Vaishali on a mission of subterfuge to gradually create dissension within the Lichchhavi confederacy. Even the meaning of his name was appropriate: 'rainmaker'! The undercover assignment took from around 484 to 468 BCE but, to Ajatashatru, these sixteen years were time well-spent. When he finally attacked

Vaishali, the once firmly-united Lichchhavis were so busy fighting among themselves about how they should respond that it was child's play to defeat them.

In the interim, Ajatashatru ordered fortifications to be constructed at Pataligrama on the Ganga to aid his campaign. This later became the famous city of Pataliputra. Later, when in the midst of battle, Ajatashatru employed two new weapons to deadly effect, according to the Jaina texts. One was a catapult that could throw massive pieces of stone; the other was a chariot that had an attached mace and cutting edges, as well as a concealed place for the charioteer to sit in and drive through the enemy ranks, while mowing them down. Both these wrought havoc in the ranks of the Lichchhavis. Magadha's victory was a foregone conclusion and while the Lichchhavis sat around licking their wounds, Ajatashatru went on to defeat Chanda Pradyota of Avanti as well. So, all in all, although he might have obtained the throne through dubious means, Ajatashatru proved to be an even mightier king than his father.

Even if Ajatashatru barely troubled to hide his Machiavellian side from the world at large, he was, ironically but very clearly, a diplomat. The Buddha was an important figure at the time and it made sense for him to make a public display of his reverence, as his father did before him. This was, in all probability, the reason behind Ajatashatru's dramatic show of regret before the Buddha for Bimbisara's murder, documented in Buddhist texts. His visit to the Buddha was considered a pivotal event in the Buddhist tradition and this is memorialised in a second century BCE relief panel on one of the railing pillars of the western gateway that once stood at the Buddhist site of Bharhut near Rewa in central India.

The panel is made up of four scenes showing a royal

procession with the king and his queens riding on elephants towards the Buddha, and, subsequently, offering their worship to him or, rather, to the footprint-bearing throne that symbolises the Buddha.[3] A Prakrit inscription to the side reads *Ajatasatu Bhagavato vandate* (Ajatashatru worships the Lord [Buddha]), confirming his identity. Incidentally, this panel also provides evidence of his many wives—poor, hapless creatures tied in holy matrimony to that fearsome and definitely unpleasant character. Ajatashatru's purported link with Buddhism seems to have continued even after the Buddha's death when he apparently went to Kusinara to claim a portion of the latter's relics. He is also supposed to have built many relic stupas around Rajagriha, and repaired monasteries in and around the city. Additionally, he is credited with hosting the first Buddhist council of eminent monks in Rajagriha soon after the Buddha's death.[4]

The Jainas, however, stood their ground in this game of appropriate-the-ruler. They stoutly present Ajatashatru as an ardent follower of Mahavira, waxing eloquent about his frequent visits to the latter, as well as their conversations at Vaishali and Champa. The king is also supposed to have strictly adhered to Mahavira's teachings. The contradictions between the traditions continue well into the aftermath of Ajatashatru's demise in *c.* 461 BCE. The Buddhist texts describe the four kings who succeeded him as patricides or those who had killed their fathers, perhaps indicating that Ajatashatru had set a certain unsavoury pattern into motion. His immediate successor was either Udayibhada or Udayin, depending on whether you favour the Buddhist or the Jaina narrative. To spice up the proceedings, the Puranas insert a ruler named Darshaka before him.

Udayin was *not* a patricide, the Jaina texts say. Instead,

he was a devoted son who served as his father's viceroy at Champa before becoming the king and founding the city of Pataliputra. It seems that Udayin's piety was, literally, the death of him. Described as a devout Jaina with a penchant for frequent fasting, he was apparently killed by an assassin hired by the king of Avanti while listening to a religious discourse. The Puranas note that Udayin was succeeded by Nandivardhana and Mahanandin. The Buddhist texts, however, list Anuruddha, Munda and Nagadarshaka as Udayibhada's successors. If your head is reeling with all these names, consider the plight of the historian who has to sift through a veritable mountain of red herrings to get at the single, elusive fact—not just now but at every single juncture of the past.

As a fascinating postscript to Ajatashatru's murky deeds, it seems as if the Lichchhavis had their final revenge many years later when Shishunaga, who was, according to one text, the son of a Lichchhavi ruler of Vaishali and had his second capital there, replaced the Haryankas on the throne of Magadha. The people of Magadha seem to have driven out the ruling Haryanka family and elected him, an *amatya* (high-ranking official), as king. The whys and wherefores of this are a trifle unclear. What we do know is that he successfully vented his ire on the Pradyota dynasty of Avanti—as all Magadhan rulers did!—and probably annexed Vatsa and Kosala as well. Kalashoka was Shishunaga's son and successor, who oversaw the shifting of the capital to Pataliputra and the second Buddhist council at Vaishali.

And that was pretty much it. The Shishunaga dynasty's tenure was short but definitely not sweet. It came to a gory end when the king and his sons were murdered by the ones who started the Nanda dynasty. This, in turn, means that the Mauryan tale is about to start. However, in order to better appreciate its nuances—and the sheer impossibility of the task that Chandragupta and Kautilya took on—we need to discuss the Nandas and their rule over Magadha in a little more detail.

The founder of the Nanda dynasty, according to the Puranas, was someone called Mahapadma, who was the son of a king of the Shishunaga dynasty and a shudra woman—and this, due to their strict avowal of Brahmanical prescriptive strictures, results in their branding him and his successors as *adharmika* or those who do not follow the norms of dharma. The Buddhist tradition, with considerably more delicacy, describe the Nanda kings as 'of unknown lineage'. They insist, however, that the founder of the dynasty was one Ugrasena, a frontier man who fell into the clutches of a gang of robbers, became their leader and eventually led them to several military successes. The Jaina tradition, not to be outdone, adds its bit to the confusing mix by noting that the first Nanda king was the son of a barber and a courtesan. The Greek writer, Curtius, though, decides to clarify this point and claims that the first Nanda king was a barber who became the lover of one of the previous queens and killed her husband, the Shishunaga king, at her prompting.

The three traditions agree that there were nine Nanda kings in all but just as we are breathing sighs of relief at this fortuitous unanimity, they begin to confound each other—and us—all over again. So while the Puranas describe the first Nanda king as the father and his eight successors as his sons, the Buddhist texts insist that all of them were brothers. The former is stingy on information, only naming Mahapadma, who attained sole sovereignty, and one of his sons, Sukalpa. However, the Buddhist tradition, via the *Mahabodhivamsha*, painstakingly provides a full list: Ugrasena,

Panduka, Pandugati, Bhutapala, Rashtrapala, Govishanaka, Dashasiddhaka, Kaivarta and Dhana. Of these, only the first and the last need concern us here.

That Mahapadma Nanda was a successful military ruler is possibly indicated by the Hathigumpha inscription of Kharavela (a very interesting ruler, in turn, but a story for another time and tome), which mentions a king named Nanda building a canal and either conquering a place in Kalinga or taking away a Jaina shrine or image from there. It should be noted here that whenever there is evidence of rulers of the past building structures in territories other than their own, historians always sit up in excitement because this is the time-honoured method of demonstrating superiority or influence over contemporary rulers, which might not always be documented in other original sources. By extension, a place named Nau Nand Dehra or Nanded on the Godavari has been viewed as indicating Nanda rule over the Deccan. However, this is slight evidence, at best, and we can't really postulate the extension of Nanda rule into the Vindhyas. Incidentally, if you are wondering why a Jaina image was the bone of contention, Jaina texts strongly insist that the Nandas had several ministers with Jaina leanings.

We also know that the Nanda kings strengthened the foundations of their predecessors on the Magadhan throne, the Haryankas and the Shishunagas, and managed to create what is seen as the first great empire of north India. Magadha's ideal geographical position—the perimeter of five hills around the old capital, Rajagriha, and the new capital, Pataliputra's location at the junction of the Ganga and Son; the Ganga and its tributaries, the Son, Gandak and Gogra, connecting Magadha with important trade routes; the access to fertile soil, and timber and elephants in the adjoining forests; and the proximity to the Chotanagpur plateau with its minerals and raw materials—had, as noted earlier, given it an unassailable lead over all contemporary powers. Add to this the willingness of its resourceful rulers—of which Magadha clearly had no dearth!—to experiment with strategic military campaigns and marriage alliances alike and you have a win-win situation. Before you eagerly look for more details, though, a word of caution: we have barely any details of the administrative, economic or military structure of early Magadha and so we are left clutching at vague, incidental references, filling in the gaps as best as we can with supposition and surmise—as is the case with huge chronological swathes of ancient history.

We may now skip almost the entire Nanda list to arrive at Dhana Nanda, the villain of Kautilya's story and the one against whom his ire was mainly directed. Indigenous sources refer to his enviable wealth, his greed, his exploitation of his subjects and his (unsurprising) lack of popularity thereby. He was also rumoured to have a huge and formidable army, the very thought of which would deter potential invaders. In addition, Dhana Nanda had the historical fortune—or misfortune, as matters turned out!—to be ruling Magadha at the time of the invasion of Alexander the Great.

And now it becomes necessary to take a few steps back and understand how this cataclysmic event came to be, why it forms a crucial background to our story and the manner in which it ties in with Dhana Nanda's tale. A digression, therefore, but an entirely justifiable one! Alexander of Macedon, his short but remarkable life immortalised in story and song, and on screen, was one of those maverick military geniuses who appear all too infrequently on the canvas of history and who act swiftly and efficiently to achieve their grandiose goals before they disappear just as swiftly, leaving the entire world gasping in their wake.

So, in a nutshell, at the time of Alexander's invasion (327–326 BCE), the Persians had nominal sway over their twentieth and once most prosperous satrapy or province, the Indus valley. This province itself had been acquired in the sixth century BCE when the Persian empire extended upto the north-western borders of the Indian subcontinent and the Achaemenid king, Cyrus (558–529 BCE) destroyed Kapisha that lay to the south-east of the Hindukush range. It quickly became the jewel in the Persian crown, as it were, for according to the Greek historian, Herodotus, the tribute from this province—360 talents of gold dust (and that is an enchanting description, indeed!)—amounted to more than that from all the other provinces put together.

However, as the Persian empire waned after the death of Xerxes (486–465 BCE), its hold over 'India' declined, although 'Indians' continue to be mentioned as its subjects, now under Artaxerxes II (405–359 BCE). Later, the army of Darius III (336–330 BCE) apparently included 'Indian' troops. Apart from the military and political consequences of being hitched to the Persian wagon, India also imbibed the Kharoshti script, derived from Aramaic, the official script of the Persian empire, which Ashoka makes clever use of at a later stage—but we are getting ahead of ourselves now, so back to the story.

There are detailed and oft-exaggerated accounts of Alexander's India campaign through Greek accounts. According to them, Alexander managed to defeat the Persian army led by Darius, leaving this erstwhile glorious empire in shambles, and then turned his attention to its eastern provinces, establishing outposts in Afghanistan before heading further. The Greeks make much of this because Alexander had to confront a number of warring principalities in the north-west, not the least of which was Astes, the Assekenoi stronghold, whose defence was, interestingly, headed by the late king's mother. Nothing and no one could stand for long, though, in the Macedonian conqueror's way. Thus, his army easily crossed the Indus in 326 BCE whereupon Ambhi, the ruler of Taxila, extended his support, thereby betraying his cousin, Porus or Puru/Paurava, who ruled the region between the Jhelum and Chenab. The former clearly didn't know that his reputation would be blackened thereon through poems and narrative hand-wringing of varied kinds.

The subsequent encounter between Porus and Alexander has passed easily into legend—the former's defeat and the latter's appreciation of his bravery, resulting in the reinstatement of Porus as ruler (more on this later). Ambhi apparently skulked in the shadows for ever more because of his dastardly deed while Alexander's halo only grew brighter due to his genuine appreciation of bravery and honesty, as exemplified by the leonine Porus. His magnanimity notwithstanding, Alexander was able to move further and conquer the region between the Chenab and Ravi.

Yet here is where this golden general's plan began to go downhill. His soldiers, initially caught up in his world-conquering enthusiasm, now began to realise that this grandiose endeavour necessarily involved discomfort and drudgery, along with the pain of homesickness—a horribly toxic brew. And so, they sulked and clamoured to go home, bewildering poor Alexander who was all set to move beyond the Beas. In a pragmatic attempt to salvage the situation, Alexander did the next best thing, under the circumstances—he began his homeward journey, entrusting the territories he had conquered to satraps or governors and Madeconian garrisons. His way back involved confrontations with ganas, such as those of the Mallas and Kshudrakas, but he managed to shake them off without much effort and finally reached the Indus delta from where he took the land route home towards Babylon. Alexander died, suddenly and inexplicably, two years later. Had he lived, it is well within the realms of possibility that he would have conquered the world! We have to settle for reams of fiction and silver screen versions of his tale instead.

And this, therefore, is when the Mauryan tale actually starts.

Notes

1. Ancient Vaishali is identified with Basarh in the Muzaffarnagar district of Bihar. This is where the 'coronation tank' of the Lichchhavis was discovered, pertaining to the second century BCE.
2. For the chronology of the early dynasties of Magadha and the calculations involved, see Upinder Singh, *A History of Ancient and Early Medieval India—From the Stone Age to the Twelfth Century*, Pearson/Dorling Kindersley, 2008, p.270.
3. Ajatashatru sits on the royal elephant with the others accompanying the leader controlled by, significantly, female mahouts. Prasenajit of Kosala is also depicted in this scene. For a description, see Nayanjot Lahiri, *Ashoka in Ancient India*, Permanent Black, 2015, p.90.
4. Incidentally, the Pali canon refers to Bimbisara and Prasenajit gifting land to brahmanas, so it is not as if the former, for instance, only favoured the Buddha to the exclusion of other creeds.

4

KAUTILYA AND THE KNOTTY PROBLEM OF THE *ARTHASHASTRA*

The Mauryan saga begins with Chandragupta Maurya, the founder of the dynasty and the one who inaugurated its greatness. His story, though, is such a curious mélange of tales, legends, claims and counter-claims that it is often impossible to separate the grain from the chaff, as it were. One can begin by examining the available sources for the Mauryan period in general and tackle the ones that pertain specifically to him later. It is near-common consensus to ascribe the first place, in this regard, to the *Arthashastra* of Kautilya, a detailed treatise on statecraft and politics, although the term *artha* itself refers to material well-being. The text, therefore, in its own words, is the branch of learning that deals with the acquisition and protection of the earth, which is the source of people's livelihood.

Most historians believe that the *Arthashastra* was written in the fourth century BCE by Kautilya, a person of multiple addresses given that he was also known as Chanakya or Vishnugupta—his *gotra* name, a patronym and personal name, respectively—who became Chandragupta Maurya's chief or prime minister after helping him overthrow the Nandas.[1] The text itself states that 'this work, easy to learn and understand, precise in doctrine, sense and word, and free from wordiness, has been composed by Kautilya'.[2] A subsequent verse notes that 'this *shastra* has been composed by him, who in resentment quickly regenerated the *shastra* and the earth that was under the control of the Nanda kings'.

One form of speculation is that Kautilya wrote this text after having been insulted by Dhana Nanda, the last Nanda king and before joining forces with his protégé, Chandragupta. Conversely, he could, equally, have written it when he had placed the latter firmly on the Magadhan throne and turned his musings on statecraft into concrete notes. With the discovery of interpolations and other historical calculations in the *Arthashastra*, it (or rather, its core) is now seen as having been partly composed in the Mauryan period with some additions and revisions spilling over into the early centuries CE. All of its statements cannot, therefore, be read as direct reflections of Chandragupta's time for this is fraught with reconstructive dangers. It can be used as a source for certain aspects of the period, though. And similarities between terms used in the *Arthashastra* and the Ashokan edicts certainly suggests that the Mauryan rulers were acquainted with it.[3]

We also have the *Indica* of Megasthenes, the Greek ambassador of Seleucus Nikator, one of Alexander's inheritors, to Chandragupta's court, which is a memoir of his travels and experiences in India, and has survived largely through quotations in later works. It merits a chapter all to itself owing to its delightful inconsistencies and exaggerations, so we will get to those later. We also have a few other texts that are immensely useful in reconstructing the early part of Mauryan history: the verse-drama, *Mudrarakshasa*, written by Vishakhadatta, a fifth century CE playwright, which tells the story of Chandragupta Mauryas's ouster of the Nanda king with the help of Kautilya in which Chandragupta is the prime mover of the plot; and the twelfth century Jaina text, *Parisishtaparvan* by Hemachandra (containing the histories of the earliest Jaina teachers), which tells pretty much the same story but with a different take on Kautilya's origins and his part in the whole affair. And then you have the Puranas of the Brahmanical corpus with their (often garbled and confused) king lists. For every phase of Mauryan history, the Buddhist, Jaina and Brahmanical literary traditions have to be taken in conjunction.

And then, of course, we have the weightiest category of all—the epigraphs left behind by the third Mauryan emperor, Ashoka, who spoke directly to the people all over his vast realm through these permanent missives on rocks and pillars. The whys and wherefores of Ashoka's endeavour will be examined in detail, subsequently, so this tantalising curtain-raiser should suffice for the moment. There are certain literary sources that pertain specifically to Ashoka, and others that provide information on the Mauryan period as a whole. Among them are the *Ashokavadana*, a text devoted to Ashoka and his life (which is a part of a larger text, the *Divyavadana*, a Sanskrit anthology of tales of Buddhist saints; it may have originally existed as an independent text and was written after his time in the second century BCE by the monks of the Mathura region), and the Sri Lankan chronicles, the *Dipavamsa* and the *Mahavamsa*, the oldest historical records of Sri Lanka, dated to around the fourth and fifth centuries CE, respectively. More details of these will be revealed as we go along (as will the names of other texts that are on other subjects but prove surprisingly helpful with Mauryan details).[4]

Archaeological remains also exist for the Mauryan period: the NBPW, associated with what is termed the second urbanisation (or the so-called Ganges civilisation), is its counterpart but, in fact—and as noted earlier, it was in use even before. It is generally a bit difficult to pinpoint archaeological data that can provide concrete dates for the Mauryans. We can, of course, produce Ashoka's epistolary work in stone as providing additional evidence, as also some sculptural and architectural elements thereof. Remains from Kumrahar and Bulandibagh are connected to Pataliputra, the Mauryan capital, and others pertain to important sites, such as Taxila, Mathura and Bhita.

Numismatic evidence exists, too: the Mauryan period is synonymous with punch-marked coins, usually of silver, with interesting symbols on them that have, unfortunately, been assigned the deeply prosaic names of 'crescent-on-arches, tree-in-railing and peacock-on/-in-arches',[5] conveying little or nothing about their meaning and symbolism. Scholars with imagination have suggested that the tree-in-railing carving represents the Buddha's enlightenment and the arches on the others represent stupas. However, in the realm of academia, such conjectures are seen as little more than wild surmises, so all we can safely say without being frowned upon is that these definitely had some political significance as they were issued by the state.

The *Arthashastra* also refers to varied alloyed silver coins (*panas*) and copper coins (*mashakas*). These seem to have circulated all through the Mauryan period and until the Bactrian Greeks, particularly in northwest India, the Ganga basin and the upper Deccan. For coin and number enthusiasts, here are a few more details (which you could skip if you do not belong to this ilk!): half, quarter and one-eighth *panas* were in circulation; there were sixteen *mashakas* to a *pana* and four *kakanis* to a *mashaka*; there were one *mashaka*, half a *mashaka*, one *kakani* and half-*kakani* copper coins; the smallest coin was, therefore, one hundred and twenty-eighth the value of the highest; and the highest cash salary was forty-eight thousand *panas* a year (incidentally, the chief queen was among those in this exalted bracket), the lowest being sixty.[6]

Before we get to the one who inaugurated the Mauryan tale, Chandragupta, we have to explore the story of his purported mentor, Kautilya, the author of the *Arthashastra* and a fascinating character in himself, renowned for his unbelievably shrewd and devious mind that bordered on brilliance—and for his general paranoia. Let us begin at the beginning. Kautilya is popularly seen as the person who engineered Chandragupta's ascension of the Magadhan throne by successfully scheming against and overthrowing the Nandas whom he had sworn to supplant on account of their mistreatment of him. All sources of Indian tradition—the Brahmanical, Buddhist and Jaina—are in broad agreement on this.

Like most pivotal characters of the Indian past, Kautilya has engendered all sorts of speculation on his origins. To obfuscate matters further, legends place him all over the map. One holds that he was an impoverished brahmana from Kerala who somehow found himself in Dhana Nanda's court in Pataliputra.[7] Another tale claims that he was a north Indian brahmana, born and educated in Taxila/Takshashila, who came to Pataliputra to show his philosophical prowess through debate. Apparently Pataliputra, at the time, was *the* place to be as regards learning and in whose rarefied intellectual atmosphere you could meet the proponents of varied systems of thought and all manner of creative stalwarts.

A somewhat strange image of Kautilya emerges from the

Buddhist sources that balance his intellectual highs against his physical lows. Thus, he was, apparently, a highly learned man who could spout the three Vedas, devise strategies on demand, and knew everything there was to know about intrigue and policy but, on the other hand, was ugly, with an unflattering complexion and deformed limbs. Jaina tradition chips in at this point and agrees with the Buddhist texts that he was fairly hideous to behold—and this on account of an added disadvantage.[8] If we are to believe them, then, Kautilya's parents noticed that he was born with a full set of teeth and were awfully dismayed as this was the mark of a future king.

Therefore, they had his teeth removed, which had the net result of making him uglier. This was because one or both of them did not want him to become a king—an inexplicable parenting compulsion, this, and one wonders whether it was attributable to their extreme modesty or extreme reserve. Perhaps they habitually shrank from the limelight and wanted their son to emulate them in this. According to some Buddhist versions, Kautilya's mother feared he would neglect her if he became a king, hence the dental dictate. Time was to turn their desire on its head, though, for their very average looking, presumably toothless, son proved to have an excellent set of fangs that could bite hard when needed, as it were, and went on to become one of the greatest kingmakers in Indian history. Looks, clearly, aren't everything!

So what was Kautilya's problem with the Nanda king, Dhana Nanda, which impelled him to rebel and, further, replace the latter on the throne with his own protégé? Dhana Nanda's name epitomised the state of the Nanda empire at the time of his clash with Kautilya: it was rich, prosperous and likely to continue in this vein for as long as it was considered impregnable, which it virtually was. The only problem was that Dhana Nanda's fondness for his wealth had turned him into a money-extractor and an inveterate miser (the fact of his riches, incidentally, being known all over the realm, even meriting a description in the Tamil work *Ahananuru*). This is not a combination that would endear any ruler to his subjects and there were already rumblings among the disgruntled populace. There are several, clearly exaggerated tales of Dhana Nanda's wealth. Its worth was purportedly around eighty crores and was buried in a secret spot in the Ganga riverbed—a decidedly odd choice for a hidden stash![9]

Dhana Nanda's purported origins did nothing to mitigate matters. His father, reportedly a barber (as noted earlier), had the dubious distinction of coming to power after murdering the previous king at, apparently, the reigning queen's behest. This murky state of affairs would have been ideal fodder for gossip and so, the tale remained fresh and in circulation through the years, and thereby firmly in the public memory. This is, incidentally, another reason behind newly-established dynasties all through history scrambling to invent impeccable genealogical origins for themselves, particularly if they came from obscure ones. A pure-blood family tree was the best safeguard against rebellion. And this was exactly what Dhana Nanda did not possess! The ground was already being prepared for an alternative but he just did not know it.

The revenge motif is a fairly ubiquitous one in stories of the ancient world—and Kautilya's tale was no different. There are differing versions of the exact skirmish between him and Dhana Nanda but a general agreement on the broad details. Most concur that Kautilya, having entered Pataliputra, decided to sit down and partake of a feast that had been laid out at court, although whether this was after his participation in a debate or at another place altogether is a point of conjecture. Dhana Nanda seems to have made a grand entry, at this juncture, and the first thing his eye fell on was Kautilya eating away. Unfortunately, Kautilya, unschooled in the intricacies of status and hierarchy at court, had chosen to sit at a seat reserved for royalty and this infuriated the arrogant king. Rushing forward, he confronted Kautilya, demanding that he stop his meal forthwith and remove his offending presence from the chamber. Inwardly boiling with rage but outwardly stoic, Kautilya continued to eat, prompting Dhana Nanda to hurl further invectives at him.

Most ascetic male figures in the ancient literary tradition seem to have had hair-trigger tempers, causing all sorts of problems and complications thereby—and Kautilya was no exception. Two inflated egos and two strong wills locked horns, causing complete chaos in the dining chamber. It ended with Kautilya's furious declaration that he would not tie his topknot until he had destroyed the Nanda dynasty by its roots. (This, incidentally, is a much-favoured scene in screen versions of this story; the scope for drama is immense!) He stormed out of court, consumed by rage, and wandered up and down the land in search of a way to achieve his goal. Dhana Nanda, meanwhile, dismissed the whole laughable matter from his mind, little knowing that he had cut his nose to spite his face, so to speak.

Another (Buddhist) version has Kautilya actually working for Dhana Nanda to administer his hoarded wealth. However, it seems the king's obvious distaste for the ascetic's purported ugliness prompted him to dismiss Kautilya (one wonders why he appointed him, in the first place, if he couldn't bear to look at him!), which, thereupon, had the latter vowing revenge and, moreover, escaping from the royal clutches as a naked Ajivika ascetic (we will come to the Ajivikas later). His meanderings, thereafter, brought him to Chandragupta.[10] Incidentally, the *Mudrarakshasa* concurs that Kautilya was dramatically expelled from the place of honour assigned to him at the Nanda court, which had him invoking revenge on the entire Nanda clan.

Kautilya's dilemma was solved, in due course, when he met Chandragupta but we will reserve that story for later and come to the *Arthashastra*. The text itself came to light in a very interesting way. In 1905, R. Shamashastry, a librarian at the Mysore Government Oriental Library, received a Sanskrit manuscript from a pundit, which, though written in a crisp style that was not easily comprehensible, noted that this *Arthashastra*, composed by Kautilya, represented the collation of treatises aimed at the acquisition and protection of the earth. Shamashastry's cognisance of the text being an ancient but authoritative work on statecraft led to his translating it in installments for a scholarly journal, *The Indian Antiquary*. The complete text was published in 1909, followed by an English translation in 1915, leading to great excitement in scholarly circles and the subsequent unearthing of several manuscripts and commentaries of the original text. Thereafter, Kautilya's *Arthashastra* was translated into various Indian and foreign languages and a critical edition, using the many manuscripts and commentaries, was published by R.P. Kangle in 1960–65.[11] The text was now firmly part of the public domain, sparking off heated debates on its date, authorship, content and contemporary relevance.

If one were to condense the arguments into a single essence, it would be this: did the *Arthashastra* belong to the Mauryan period at all? As noted earlier, some historians view it as an integral part of this timespan, written by Kautilya/

Chanakya who masterminded Chandragupta's bid for power, while others believe the text to be a compilation of observations by different authors at different points of time, and of a much later vintage. This seemingly intractable issue has been approached by historians with methodical and detective-like zeal ever since the text's discovery and perusal. In order to arrive at the truth, let us break the problem into smaller, palatable portions.

What, to begin with, is this text all about? It is, in fact, the first Indian text to define a state. The word *artha*, usually seen in its most basic sense as money or wealth, occurs in Sanskrit literature, normative and otherwise, as one of the worthy goals of human existence. The *Arthashastra*, on the other hand, explains *artha*, or material well-being, as the sustenance or livelihood of men, stemming from the earth inhabited by people. Or in another less-convoluted way, it is the branch of learning that deals with the means of the acquisition and protection of the earth, which is the source of people's livelihoods; thus, the science of statecraft. This work of—it must be stated—pioneering brilliance consists of fifteen books or *adhikaranas* of which the first five deal with internal administration, the next eight with inter-state relations and the last two with miscellaneous issues.

The text definitely works as a ready reckoner for anyone wanting to assume and maintain supreme power, demanding a higher-than-average level of comprehension and intelligence to understand the intricate ins and outs of the devious strategising recommended. To quote a simple example, your neighbour's enemy is actually your friend whom you can use to outwit the former. By extension, that neighbour-turned-friend's friend is actually your enemy because he might join hands with the former to oust you. Thus, the sequence facing a king—or rather, aspiring conqueror—is the enemy, the (conqueror's) ally, the enemy's ally, the ally's ally, the enemy's ally's ally and so on, depending on the proximity of territories.[12]

Likewise, behind the conqueror lie the enemy in the rear, the ally in the rear, the rear enemy's ally, the rear ally's ally and so on. All this might very well make your head swim but as the *Arthashastra* clearly implies, acquiring power and holding on to it is no joke, and definitely not a course of action to be undertaken by the feeble-minded or faint-hearted. It requires brains, courage, shrewdness and farsightedness, along with a general dislike and suspicion of people and an ability to be impossibly devious—all of these exemplary virtues being exhibited by the esteemed author himself, if popular stories pertaining to the Mauryan times are to be believed.

The traditional view of Kautilya having written the *Arthashastra* that directly pertained to the Mauryas has often been questioned, as noted above. The verses that mention Kautilya as its author (cited above) have been seen as later insertions into the original text and it is argued that his name in the colophons could, equally, be interpreted as 'as taught or held by Kautilya'. Additional evidence has also been cited: Patanjali's *Mahabhashya*, a book on grammar which mentions the Mauryas and Chandragupta's assembly, makes no reference to Kautilya. Nor does, Megasthenes in his *Indica*. However, as the *Mahabhashya* is, essentially, an illustration of grammatical rules and mentions historical personalities only incidentally, and the *Indica* survives only in bits and pieces paraphrased by later writers, their omission of Kautilya's name as clinching proof is a dubious argument, at best. This is, very clearly, the work of someone who has bloodied his hands in political wrangling.

A word about the *Indica* here—as Megasthenes was at

Chandragupta Maurya's court, it is presumed that whatever he wrote is an accurate, eyewitness account of the time. Unfortunately, Megasthenes seemed to have a propensity for jumping to wild conclusions. Perhaps he was in a tearing hurry to note his views or, equally, might have harboured preconceived notions about the people he had been sent to live with. Accordingly, he declares, among other things, that they did not know writing—an observation that, quite conceivably, would have outraged the Mauryan writer par excellence, Ashoka, for one! Therefore, the assertions of this worthy Greek should be taken with a pinch of salt. By extension, his not mentioning Kautilya means very little in the scheme of things.

To demonstrate the extent to which scholars will go to prove their contentions, let us consider the illustrative case of Thomas Trautmann who actually made a statistical analysis of the *Arthashastra*, wherein he focused on the differences in the words that occurred often in the various books that comprised the text. His conclusion was that three or four authors had contributed to its composition, which finally happened by *c.* 250 CE and so, while Kautilya could very well have written a part of the *Arthashastra*, he can't be seen as the author of the entire work. Therefore, Trautmann asserts, the *Arthashastra* should not be seen as a historical source for the Mauryans. As with every other historical hypothesis, though, this claim was roundly criticised and the text reinstated as sound evidence of this period.[13]

Let us also remember that the Mauryan realm was a huge entity and, while the *Arthashastra* might appear to refer to a smallish state in its discussion of inter-state relations, it completely stresses imperial ideals and ambitions, and of the perspective of a *vijigishu*—the aspiring conqueror—who wants to subdue the entire subcontinent, which, incidentally, is exactly what the Mauryans did, barring a few regional entities that remained outside their grasp. The framework provided of an elaborate administrative structure also indicates that the author had a large, well-established political structure in mind, one that he might very well have seen or, even, helped to evolve.

Yet, the text maintains an infuriating silence on the Mauryas and their empire, as also key words like Chandragupta or Pataliputra, the capital. One way of resolving this mystery is to look at the motive behind the text: this is a work on the theory of statecraft, which envisages an ideal and not an actual state. Kautilya could very well have been a powerful seer but for him to display such an intricate knowledge of politics, state mechanisms and the socio-economic realm presupposes his existence in this very system—a mighty state marked by sophisticated methods of governance. And he simply used it as a model for his theoretical state.

More statements have been used to reinforce this argument. Stylistic considerations place the *Arthashastra* as older than Vatsyayana's *Kamasutra* and the *Manusmriti*, both texts pertaining to the early centuries CE, so that slots it neatly into the Mauryan period or very nearly thereabouts. Certain other references, such as to the Ajivika sect, the sangha politics and the widespread establishment of agricultural settlements, are, once again, seen as quintessentially Mauryan features and connections, as does the intricate administrative structure gleaned from the text that quite clearly does not pertain to any other known dynasty. Therefore, some part of this work was definitely composed in the Mauryan period by a person named Kautilya. It could have been a living work, so to speak, that he expanded based on the evolving situation he was part of.

Of such contentious arguments are historical debates woven, then pulled into inextricable knots and finally unravelled to reveal a single shining truth—or truths. Spare a thought here for the beleaguered historian, sifting through texts and other evidence, and proposing a tentative theory only to be howled at by his ilk on grounds of dating and content and logic. And so, the poor soul, eyes fixed on the holy grail of historical fact, repeats the cycle ad nauseum until proven right. Even so, there are always some naysayers lurking in the shadows.

Now picture, if you will, a brooding genius, his mind crammed with conspiracy theories and solutions thereof, raking you with his suspicious eye as you walk by, ready to despatch his spies on your tail and quite certain you are up to no good. You cringe as you soldier on but nothing and no one is safe from his hawk-eyed gaze. And woe betide you if the evidence is damning. This is what it must have felt like for anyone at the court of Chandragupta, Kautilya's precious ward and sovereign, whom he was determined to protect at all costs and in extraordinary ways. We will examine some of Kautilya's weirder security stipulations as we go on.

The text, though, is, undoubtedly, a work of sheer brilliance. It is as if Kautilya sat down and thought about *each and every* aspect of governance, administration and daily life that exists in a modern state (and the detailing *is* modern, in every sense of the word, even though the context is the ancient world), and then formulated rules and prescriptions covering every single miniscule detail with (fairly draconian) punishments recommended for dereliction of duty and every conceivable lapse thereof, so that if you pick it up today and read it, you will find it difficult to identify any aspect of living in a socio-political context that he has not already considered and included. The scope and breadth of vision is staggering—and the text also displays a very shrewd understanding of human propensities and frailties. It is a magnificent treatise, stemming from a magnificent mind—and despite the quibbles over authorship, should be regarded as such. In the process of penning his thoughts, though, Kautilya might very well have rendered earlier works on politics and statecraft redundant.

Notes

1. Works belonging to a later date, such as Kamandaka's *Nitisara*, Dandin's *Dashakumaracharita*, Vishakhadatta's *Mudrarakshasa* and Banabhatta's *Kadambari*, support this contention. See L.N. Rangarajan, ed. and trans.*Kautilya—The Arthashastra*, Penguin, 1992, pp.1–78 for a general and very useful introduction to the text.
2. See ibid., p.79. See also Upinder Singh, *A History of Ancient and Early Medieval India—From the Stone Age to the 12th Century*, Pearson/Dorling Kindersley, 2008, p.322. She cites verses 1.1.19 and 15.1.73 of the *Arthashastra*, respectively.
3. See, for instance, Romila Thapar, *Asoka and the Decline of the Mauryas*, Oxford University Press, 3rd edn, 2021, p.12.
4. The *Vamsatthapakasini*, for one, which is a tenth century commentary on the *Mahavamsa*, but lurks here in the endnotes because readers might find it difficult to pronounce!
5. Singh, *A History of Ancient and Early Medieval India*, p.329. See also, Thapar, *Asoka and the Decline of the Mauryas*, pp.366–375 for details of the Mauryan coins and symbols.
6. The others were the minister, the priest and the army commander. See Rangarajan, *Kautilya—The Arthashastra*, p.87.
7. Ibid., p.4.
8. Ibid.
9. It has been suggested that the rumours of the Nandas's wealth were because they were the first dynasty to have issued coins on a large scale. See Thapar, *Asoka and the Decline of the Mauryas*, p.368.
10. See R.K. Mookerji, *Chandragupta Maurya and His Times*, Motilal Banarsidass, 1966, rpt.1988, pp.20–21 for more details.

11. R.P. Kangle, *The Kautilya Arthasastra (Part 1)*, University of Bombay, 1960; *The Kautilya Arthasastra (Part II)*, Motilal Banarsidass, 1972 (rpt 2000); *The Kautilya Arthasastra (Part III), English Translation with Critical and Explanatory Notes*, Motilal Banarsidass, 1965 (rpt 2000).
12. Rangarajan, *Kautilya—The Arthashastra*, p.521, 6.2.18.
13. For details of Trautmann's analysis and the objections raised, see Singh, *A History of Ancient and Early Medieval India*, p.323.

5

THE GREEKS (AND ROMANS) WHO WROTE

Kautilya and Ashoka were not the only writers of the Mauryan period who wielded their pen, so to speak, in a prolific manner. The works of Megasthenes, the Greek ambassador to Chandragupta's court (mentioned earlier), and later Graeco-Roman writers who appraised and abstracted his text, deserve closer scrutiny not just because of their content but also, more enchantingly, on account of the sarcasm and annoyance that routinely pervade the latter. This is one of the first instances in the world of historical evidence of a dual commentary—of Megasthenes noting down what he saw and heard, and of his ilk later analysing his comments. In the process, much of ancient Greek attitudes towards history writing, as also the Indian subcontinent, are revealed in tantalising layers.

So why was Megasthenes sent to Chandragupta Maurya's court in the first place? And why did this Greek feel impelled to write his *Indica*? Let us take those questions in sequence. To understand who Megasthenes was, we have to move backwards to the invasion of the north-west of India by Alexander of Macedon (327–326 BCE, alluded to earlier; his dates were *c.* 356–323 BCE), that most intriguing and exciting character who might very well have taken over the entire world if destiny had allotted him more years to live. As it was, he died ridiculously young, at the age of thirty-three, but managed to make himself gloriously famous even so. There is, in fact, an interesting story of a meeting between Chandragupta and Alexander but more on that later.

In the power struggle that ensued for Alexander's empire, Seleucus Nikator, who inherited the eastern provinces of Alexander's empire, and proclaimed himself the king of Mesopotamia and Persia in 305 BCE, decided to reclaim Alexander's territories beyond the Indus, which had gone back into Indian hands. In doing so, he seems to have clashed with Chandragupta Maurya (Androkottus or Sandrocottus, 'king of the Indians', in Greek accounts; as also Sandrokoptos, the most accurate version). This run-in probably happened in around 301 (305?) BCE and the treaty that followed indicates that Seleucus had clearly bitten off more than he could chew, reinforced by the Greek historians being unusually coy on its details, with Pliny alone admitting to the loss of Greek territory.

So Chandragupta, in return for five hundred (of his nine thousand) elephants, secured the territories of Arachosia (the Kandahar region of south-east Afghanistan), Gedrosia (south Baluchistan) and Parapomisadai (the area between Afghanistan and the Indian subcontinent). If these names seem wildly unfamiliar, it is because they are the Greek equivalents of the actual ones—and as we are talking about Greeks, it is only appropriate to use their terms. Also, Chandragupta might or might not have made a marriage alliance as part of this treaty. The world of popular media would like to think so whereby much is made of his Greek wife in serials and stories but there is no conclusive proof of her identity.[1] Equally, the treaty could also be interpreted as having paved the way for inter-marriage between the Greeks and the Indians, and Chandragupta could very well have decided to be the first beneficiary, in this regard, marrying the daughter of Seleucus by his Persian wife, Susa.[2] And it is also possible that a Mauryan princess was given to the Seleucid house.

Megasthenes now slips into the historical limelight as he happened to be the representative of Seleucus Nikator at the court of Sibyrtios, the governor of Arachosia, one of the territories that Chandragupta obtained. Much in the fashion of present-day diplomats being peremptorily uprooted and transplanted by their masters, Seleucus included Megasthenes in his treaty with Chandragupta. (Interestingly, Seleucus's son and successor, Antiochus, whose sister would have been a queen or princess at the Mauryan court depending on whom she married, also sent his envoy to the Mauryan court—Deimachus, when his turn came.) And so, Megasthenes left Arachosia and arrived in Pataliputra, presumably aching to record his new adventures in a new land.

And thus, the *Indica* was born, documenting all that this important Greek saw and experienced during his sojourn at the Mauryan court. Ironically and inexplicably, though, this ancient travel memoir speedily vanished in its entirety—and there is a whole detective story there, waiting in the wings. For our purposes, suffice it to say that the *Indica* lives on in a highly fragile and tenuous manner—in fragments preserved in later Greek and Latin works, particularly in the works of Diodorus, Strabo, Arrian and Pliny.

This should have been enough to treat it as a valuable source for the Mauryas, yet one is always told to treat this work with extreme caution, a veritable hot potato in the fingers of an evidence-hunter. So what exactly did Megasthenes say?

What did he deem worthy of inclusion in his work? He seems to have started with the usual, run-of-the-mill recordings of India, its shape and size (as discernible to his largely untrained eye), its rivers, soil, climate, flora and fauna, its administration and society. And some of its stories, of course. These, along with a few wildly-implausible tales that he seems to have dreamt up rather than seen, make his work a page-turner—or would have if it had existed in its full form!

We could consider many illustrative examples but, perhaps, a few would suffice. Here is an enchanting one: Megasthenes's description of men living on a mountain called Nulo who had particularly arresting feet in that not only did they turn backwards but each foot had no less than eight toes. Trying to allocate a factual match for this would confound any scholar! Consider, too, the accounts of men living on other mountains who were, essentially, hunters and fowlers, but who had heads like dogs and conversed through barking. And then, there were the gold-digging ants who apparently occupied the mountains in the north-west.

If you are feeling a trifle dizzy on reading this, think of historians from the ancient times to the present grappling with the text and wondering whether Megasthenes merely had a keen sense of the absurd or was so enamoured of the sights and sounds around him that his fevered imagination conjured up fantastical images visible only to him. The alternative is too awful to contemplate—people with rotating feet and/or canine heads, barking at each other as they went about their work, carefully avoiding the ants and their gold-rush frenzy, all the while. A sojourn in the hills would take on impossibly sinister meanings, in that case! You can understand, therefore, why historians are somewhat wary of using the *Indica* as an impeccable source for Chandragupta Maurya and his times.

Nevertheless, let us turn to those who got the *Indica* hot off the press, so to speak—the ancient Greek and Roman scholars who cited it in their own works, although they differed in the extent to which they used it to buttress their own. Diodorus Sicilus, for instance, a historian from Agyrium in Sicily (as his name implies!) wrote in a prolific manner in the second half of the first century BCE. Of his forty books, only a few have survived but these describe Alexander's India campaign, as well as the country in general, based on the *Indica* and other sources. Here is where Diodorus differs somewhat from his Megasthenes-quoting peers: he refrains from making any nasty, snide remarks about the Greek but he definitely leaves out some of the latter's weird observations and stories about India and its people.

Meanwhile, Strabo, a geographer and historian from Pontus in West Asia, wrote seventeen books at around the same time as Diodorus, of which the fifteenth deals with India and Persia. This man was, among other things, a pastmaster at criticism and sarcasm. Poor Megasthenes wouldn't have stood a chance against him had there been an actual confrontation between the two! Behold his scathing indictment: 'Generally speaking, the men who have hitherto written on the affairs of India were a set of liars—Deimachus holds the first place in the list, Megasthenes comes next, while Onesicritus and Nearchus, with others of the same class, manage to stammer out a few words (of truth)...No faith whatever can be placed in Deimachus and Megasthenes. They coined the fables concerning men with ears large enough to sleep in, men without any mouths, without noses, with only one eye, with spider legs, and with fingers bent backward...Both of these men were sent as ambassadors to Palimbothra—Megasthenes to Sandrocottus (Chandragupta), Deimachus to Amitrochades

(Bindusara), his son—and such are the notes of their residence abroad, which, I know not why, they thought fit to leave.' The ancient equivalent of a modern literary review that completely pans the book! Strabo also notes that both these Greek writers accused each other of lying and observes: '... they all frequently contradict one another. But if they differ thus about what was seen, what must we think of what they report from hearsay?'

Let us also consider the views of Arrian (*c.* 96–180 CE), a curious mix of statesman, soldier, philosopher and historian, from Nikomedia in Bithynia. Not only did he write the *Anabasis* on Alexander's Asian campaigns but also unabashedly borrowed the title of *Indica* for the continuation of his work. Of this, the first part describes India, using the accounts of Megasthenes and Eratosthenes as sources, the latter being a formidable Greek polymath and chief librarian at the library of Alexandria in the third century BCE. Arrian trusts Megasthenes slightly more than his fellow-writers, although still critical of him, and manages to couch his criticism in refined terms. Consider the following statement: '...Megasthenes, so far as it appears, did not travel over much of India, though no doubt he saw more of it than those who came with Alexander... for, as he tells us, he resided at the court of Sandrocottus, the greatest king in India, and also at the court of Porus, who was still greater than he.'

Arrian goes on to note that despite this, '...we have no real knowledge of the country: since this is the sort of account which Megasthenes gives us of an Indian river: Its name is the Silas; it flows from a fountain called after the river, through the dominions of the Silaens, who again are called after the river and the fountain; the water of the river manifests this singular property—that there is nothing which it cannot buoy up, nor anything which can swim or float in it, but everything sinks down to the bottom, so that there is nothing in the world so thin and unsubstantial as this water…' Convoluted, indeed—and one can imagine Arrian shaking his head in dignified grief at Megasthenes' wild surmises.

Gaius Plinius Secundus (*c.* 23–79 CE) or Pliny the Elder, the much-quoted Roman scholar, is another prolific writer who frowns upon Megasthenes and his ramblings. His tome, *Naturalis Historia*, consisting, in turn, of thirty-seven books on diverse subjects, such as geography, ethnography and zoology, uses the *Indica* as a source, although—as he himself asserts—it is a clearly dubious one. Here is his succinct observation: 'India was opened up to our knowledge…by other Greek writers, who, having resided with Indian kings—as for instance Megasthenes and Dionysius—made known the strength of the peoples of the country. It is not, however, worthwhile to study their accounts with care, so conflicting are they, and incredible.'[3]

Then they all go slightly berserk while describing the Mauryan king's public appearances, culled from the *Indica*, clearly.[4] Strabo holds forth on royal processions that featured elephants adorned with gold and silver, attendants bearing vessels of gold (some with goblets of six feet in breadth, if you please!), a profusion of precious stones cleverly woven into sundry garments, and wild beasts and birds (apparently leopards ambled along with buffaloes), so that the impression conveyed is one of extreme colour and exotic sounds and general magnificence. Or sample Curtius's description of Chandragupta Maurya's public face wherein he sat in a golden-and-pearl palanquin, robed in purple and gold, while his attendants bore silver censors and perfumed incense all down the roads that he chose for his promenade, as it were.

Bodyguards brought up his rear, some of whom carried branches of trees on which birds perched, 'trained to interrupt business with their cries'.

And let us not forget the unbearable excitement caused when the king ceremonially washed his hair on his birthday during which he apparently liked to receive presents of birds and beasts; the wilder, the better. So deer and rhinos and panthers huddled, so to speak, by his feet, along with cranes and geese and wild pigeons. How much hair was washed, in the process, and what sort of order was required to keep the live gifts away from the king and his ablutions is a matter for conjecture. Also, what Kautilya thought of this strange mix of flora and fauna and humans and tresses and general chaos is not clear. So is this an entirely fanciful rendition of events? That, too, isn't clear.

There is a lot more besides but this is, more or less, the salient narrative. So there you have it—study the *Indica* at your peril. But is this work really so useless? The answer is a resounding no. These ancient writers who quoted Megasthenes were targeting an educated Greek audience who sought to learn about new lands, and their aim was not only to educate but also to entertain. So the parts that were culled from the *Indica* were those that would amuse and interest their readers the most. Consequently, the parts that were left out, owing to their presumably dry nature, might have been of immense value to historians. There is, therefore, a sameness to their works—despite being separated by time, interest and style—in that they talk about aspects that were common to India and Greece, as well as those that were markedly different. The parts that lay between these two discourses were clearly and unceremoniously dropped from the narrative—and these were, in retrospect, the truly valuable bits.

So, much is made by them of indications that India, too, was once inhabited by primitive tribes, and that arts and other cultural attributes were invented on a gradual basis. Similarities were spotted in the philosophical realm as well—in the views of the Brahmanas and the Greek ideas of the world and soul. Here was an ideal country where there was no slavery and no theft, no lending or borrowing of money on interest, no knowledge of writing and no drinking of wine except for sacrificial purposes—all of which, of course, flies in the face of hard evidence. Grandiose parallels were drawn with Egypt and Europe: the Ganga and the Indus were akin to the Nile and the Danube. And then, the unbelievable and wondrous inversions of nature and beast: the one-horned horses with deerlike heads; the huge snakes that could swallow stags and oxen whole; the Silas (earlier cited) in which nothing could float; the sheer captivating breadth and diversity of flora and fauna in this exciting new land.

These works had an agenda of their own, and what Megasthenes saw and heard at the Mauryan court was not, by any means, their exclusive priority. Arrian, for one, confesses that his main preoccupation was with the manner in which Alexander brought his army from India to Persia and not necessarily the manners and customs of the Indians, who should be treated '…as a mere episode'. It is not even clear whether these writers had direct access to the *Indica* or whether they had to rely on yet another secondary account of the text. It is grossly unfair, therefore, to blame Megathenes for the later whimsical paraphrasing of his work even though that is, ironically, the only way in which it lives on.

What, then, can we glean about Chandragupta and the Mauryan court from the much-maligned Megasthenes? For a start, he got several things right about the ancient city of

Pataliputra (the Greek Palimbothra), the capital of Magadha and the first Mauryan rulers, and archaeological evidence—that is usually seen as a clincher in such arguments. Megasthenes describes the city as surrounded by a wooden wall with towers and openings for shooting arrows, beyond which was a moat.[5] The exact location of Pataliputra has been hotly-debated but ancient ruins that can be connected to the Mauryas in this city have been identified at several places in modern Patna; particularly at Kumrahar, where there are remains of a pillared hall with ten rows of eight pillars each; and Bulandibagh to its north-west where remains of a wooden palisade of two parallel walls have been found. These might, quite conceivably, be the remnants of the wooden fortifications of Pataliputra as described by Megasthenes.

The environs of the palace itself have been discussed by Arrian and Claudius Aelianus (second-third century CE), a Roman scholar whose work on zoology went by an engaging title, *On the Peculiarities of Animals*. Arrian cites Megasthenes as claiming that the inhabited portion of Pataliputra stretched on either side to an extreme length of eighty stadia (over nine miles), its breadth was fifteen stadia (one and a quarter miles) and a ditch of thirty cubits in depth surrounded it. The wall had five hundred and seventy towers and sixty-four gates. Megasthenes either painstakingly counted and measured away or relied on official data, in this regard. Either way, it was a clearly massive and impressive city, and an immaculately guarded one besides. A very discouraging sight to potential invaders—and obviously designed for this very purpose!

Aelian, on the other hand, contents himself with describing the wonders within. He manages to paint an exceedingly charming picture of exotic birds traipsing around the palace grounds, and waxes eloquent on parrots and their virtues before moving on to the enormous, tame fish in the palace ponds, who were presumably unruffled by the Mauryan princes' attempts to sail boats in their waters, and the magnificent plants and trees that apparently never shed their leaves, being untouched by age. While this might be an accurate rendition of the *Indica*'s notes, one wonders whether Kautilya, for one, would have allowed untrammelled nature to exist thus. He would have cast a jaundiced eye at the dancing peacocks and probably had their feathers examined for hidden weapons, and hauled the princes up by the scruff of their necks if they so much as dared set a toe in the water!

Furthermore, Megasthenes, as noted by Strabo, also reveals some interesting aspects about the king's routine—and these tie in neatly with Kautilya's strictures, which we will come to later. That the king was always surrounded by women bodyguards is an exciting nugget of information that assumes pivotal importance given that the throne was initially fragile but managed to root itself firmly in Mauryan hands after its slightly shaky start—and these women must have contributed to this in no small measure. When the king hunted, for instance, in a fenced enclosure, 'shooting arrows from a platform in his chariot, two or three armed women stand beside him, and also in the unfenced hunting-grounds from an elephant; and the women ride partly in chariots, partly on horses, and partly on elephants, and they are equipped with all kinds of weapons, as they are when they go on military expeditions with men'. So the king's care was 'committed to women': thus Strabo quoted from the *Indica*.[6] But consider this tantalising comment, too: 'And a woman who kills a king when he is drunk receives as her reward the privilege of consorting with his successor; and their children succeed to the throne.' Clearly, therefore, women in the Mauryan court were both saviours and destroyers. They protected the king but he was also vulnerable to attacks by them.

However, another example of Megasthenes's wild imaginings is his observation on the Indian people, whom he rather arbitrarily divides into seven tiers. If we combine the remnants of his remarks from Diodorus and Strabo, we can extricate these groups as philosophers, farmers, herdsmen and hunters, artisans and traders, soldiers, overseers and the king's counsellors. Nine, in fact, but we mustn't quibble because the categories that he lumps together are actually partners of a kind. The more critical fact here is that this motley collection of professional groups and administrative officers does not correspond to either the varnas or the jatis. The only logical assumption, therefore, is that they must have sprung out of the Greek writer's head, although, as Upinder Singh points out, his comment might have been modelled on the redoubtable Herodotus's classification of Egyptian society into seven similar classes.[7]

Megasthenes goes on to claim that no one in India could marry outside their *genos* (a Greek word that refers to one's clan or relationships of descent) and nor could they follow another's occupation. To give him his due, though, he was interpreting what he saw through his Greek-specific lens—something he can hardly be faulted for!—and, as Romila Thapar notes, *did* manage to spot two of the crucial aspects of the caste system—hereditary occupation and endogamy, the latter being the custom of marrying only within a community/clan or tribe. Philosophers were greatly respected, it seems, and Strabo divides them into the *brachmanes* (brahmanas) and *garmanes* (shramanas or Buddhist monks), so this ties in with what we already know.

Yet if we attempt to draw parallels between the *Indica*

and the *Arthashastra* as regards the society, we immediately run into trouble. For instance, Megasthenes makes the blanket statement that Indian society did not have any slaves. Kautilya, on the other hand, talks at length about *dasas* or slaves: he enumerates their categories (temporary and permanent depending on their work, situations of enslavement and whether they were employed by private citizens or the state), their treatment and related penalties (those who sell a pregnant slave without maternity arrangements and/or causing her to miscarry are to be punished) and rules for their manumission (on paying money or if a *dasi* bore her master a son; the child would be considered the father's legitimate heir). Much later, Ashoka's Rock Edict 9 urges courteous behaviour towards *dasas* and other menial staff as part of dhamma or spiritual philosophy. Furthermore, where Kautilya indicates growing strictures for untouchables, such as *chandalas* and *shvapakas* (the latter refers to dog-breeders) having to live at the very edges of settlements, Megasthenes remains completely silent.

So what exactly was Megasthenes doing, veering between the factual (the description of Pataliputra, for one) and the fanciful (most of his other observations!)? As noted earlier, he was, perhaps, so overwhelmed by his surroundings that he did not stop to think through his observations or even consult a local cultural interpreter in his rush to write them down. Equally, perhaps, he was eager to show off his knowledge of a new and thoroughly (to him) exotic place to his family and compatriots, banking on their total ignorance of it. No one he knew was going to contradict or challenge him; on the contrary, admiration would envelop him wherever he went on account of his writing. Even in the Mauryan court, his erudition would be remarked upon in envious tones. Therefore, he wrote and wrote, blissfully keeping all filters at bay. His enthusiasm for the task is praiseworthy; not, though, his discernment.

And of such conflicting material are the sources of the ancient world made!

Notes

1. Once again, the Greeks and Romans are silent on the details, implying that it was an unequal marriage settlement whereby Seleucus gave his daughter to Sandrokoptus, or to his son and heir. See, for instance, Charles Allen, *Ashoka—The Search for India's Lost Emperor*, Abacus, 2012, pp.60–61. Incidentally, Seleucus outlived all his rival successors to become the last of the Macedonian generals who had fought alongside Alexander. At seventy-seven years of age, he set out in 281 BCE to take possession of Macedonia and Thrace for his son, Antiochus, only to be murdered by a son of his late friend-turned-enemy, Ptolemy of Egypt. See p.62.
2. See, for instance, ibid., p.368.
3. All these quotes are from Upinder Singh, *A History of Ancient and Early Medieval India—From the Stone Age to the 12th Century*, Pearson/ Dorling Kindersley, 2008, pp.325–325.
4. See, for instance, R.K. Mookerji, *Chandragupta Maurya and His Times*, Motilal Banarsidass, 1966, rpt.1988, p.62.
5. The dimensions given by him indicate that this was a long and narrow city. See Nayanjot Lahiri, *Ashoka in Ancient India*, Permanent Black, 2015, p.53. Incidentally, the ditch in front of the city walls was meant both for defence and for the city's sewage.
6. Mookerji, *Chandragupta Maurya and His Times*, p.343.
7. Ibid., p.339.

6

KAUTILYA'S CAREFULLY DRAWN-UP WORLD

Let us revisit the *Arthashastra* before we engage with Mauryan politics because this tome provides a great introduction—or background, as it were—to ruling and living at the time. However, we will merely contend ourselves with some of the more interesting and thought-provoking themes that run through it. Hopefully, this will enthuse many more readers to tackle the text in its entirety without their hearts quailing at the thought. Kautilya may be stern but he can also be delightfully acerbic and candid—and this is where the text comes alive. What follows, therefore, is a sort of dipping into his magnum opus and, by no means, a comprehensive analysis of its content.

The *Arthashastra* essentially deals with the state as a concept and is concerned with the security and foreign policy imperatives of such an entity, small though it may be, in a context where it jostles with numerous other small states. The focus, therefore, is to strengthen it internally and externally, so that it can occupy a pre-eminent position. The state that Kautilya envisages, by extension, is extremely well-organised and structured and, consequently, awe-inspiring. At the centre of this magnificent polity was the king (the *vijigishu*; in his words, the king who wants to win or the would-be conqueror). Kingship was a fiercely contested and sought-after possession at the time but if you were to consider Kautilya's view of the king's world and his duties within it, your heart would go out to the poor soul who must live in a highly-dangerous scenario of perpetual murder attempts while barely getting any time to breathe.

Consider Kautilya's structuring of a typical day in a king's life. The *Arthashastra* recommends that the royal day be divided into eight parts each, thereby constituting a block of sixteen units of time.[1] Each unit, in turn, consisted of one and a half hours devoted to particular work/activities. So here we go with the eight parts of the king's day beginning right after sunrise: receive reports on defence and accounts; examine urban and rural affairs; bathe, eat and study; receive revenue and assign tasks to the heads of department; consult the council of ministers and receive secret information from spies; relax or hold further consultations; review troops, elephants, horses and chariots; and discuss military policy with the commander-in-chief of the army.

And here is how the king should spend the eight parts of the night: interview secret agents; bathe, eat and study; retire to bed with a background music of instruments; club two units together and continue to sleep; wake to the sound of musical instruments and mull over the day's work, as well as the science of statecraft; consult counsellors and despatch secret agents; receive the priests' blessings, and see the physician, chief cook and astrologer. At dawn, the king was to circumambulate a cow and its calf, as also a bull, and then move to the assembly hall to execute the first eight parts of the day. And so on and on.

Yes, you would definitely feel for a mortal who had to

follow such a cheerless routine, however exalted his status. With a paltry four and a half hours of sleep and without the liberty to ponder over, say, the day's meal at dawn, requiring, instead, to consider the dark realities of statecraft, one can imagine any king's reaction to this ghastly regimen. The stern Kautilya must also have anticipated some amount of reluctance, or even mutiny, on the part of the king, and so he hastily adds a disclaimer: if the latter does not want to follow this routine, he is free to divide the day and night into different parts according to his abilities, and figure out what he wants to do.

The prescription is, of course, for an *ideal* king—for whether he liked it or not, Kautilya had to factor in human frailty, however immune to it he himself was! The subjects mirror the king, he cautions, though. If he is energetic, so will they be. If he is lazy, well, then, his subjects will emulate him and eventually eat up all his wealth. And there is a far worse consequence of royal indolence: the awful spectre of the enemy who has his eye on the throne and will oust the careless incumbent at the slightest opportunity.

This brings us to Kautilya's somewhat over-the-top precautions to ensure the king's safety in a world that is otherwise filled with political malevolence and backstabbing. He is never safe, and neither he nor those around him can relax their vigil for a moment lest some potential assassin creeps up and does his treacherous work. What further complicates matters is that the greatest threat is posed by those closest to the king—vipers lurking in his bosom again. To drive home his point, Kautilya painstakingly cites examples of some unfortunate royal personages who were killed by their sons, wives or brothers.

However, while a prince can, at any point, seize the

country's resources for himself and his friends, he can be kept in check through ministers and the like. So any threat that he poses can be countered but the same is not true of women close to the king: the 'king's favourite cannot be controlled because she is (stubbornly) childish and (usually) associates with harmful persons'.[2] Queens and princes could either act in collusion against the king, according to the *Arthashastra*[3], or separately, queens having apparently killed their royal husbands 'by putting poison in their food, with a poisoned ornament or jewel, or by a concealed weapon'. Much fodder for writers of historical crime fiction here!

Kautilya's ideal king, though, should immediately adopt pre-emptive measures to thwart any such dastardly scheme in the making. And so, to begin with (and as confirmed by Megasthenes via Strabo), he shouldn't sleep during the day—and even at night, he must change his bed and sleeping quarters at frequent intervals. Thus would a lurking assassin be completely confounded. This also immediately conjures up visions of a sleep-deprived king, staggering around the palace and trying hard to keep abreast of important matters while constantly peering into the shadows.

There is more. Kautilya gives elaborate instructions on how the palace (which had its own inner fortifications of ramparts, a moat and gates, and segregated sleeping quarters) should be provided with manifold secret emergency exits.[4] His architectural design bristles with mazes, subterranean passages, hidden staircases, hollow pillars and collapsible floors. (One wonders how the palace inmates navigated these veritable death-traps. Anyone who wasn't an expert map-reader was clearly doomed!) Everything entering or leaving the palace complex was to be closely examined. Spies in varied guises were to infiltrate all parts of the kingdom to smoke out traitors and plots in the making. Whatever the king consumed by way of food and drink was to be tested before it made its way to his mouth, the food itself being prepared in a kitchen that was constructed in a secret place. No raiding the shelves for food at night by hungry royal children. They, presumably, didn't know the kitchen's location, in the first place!

Apart from his personal guard of women archers, the king was to surround himself at all times with people he could trust, although all ministers, even the closest and most important ones, were to be given regular loyalty tests. Intricate arrangements to guard the king against poison, fire and snakes were also to be put in place. Kautilya does go a little over-the-top when it comes to the recruitment of secret agents. The requirements are very precise and exacting, and it definitely was not a job that anyone could just saunter up and sign up for. After emerging from what seems to have been a highly-specialised training course, the agents were assigned manifold tasks, as detailed in a section on covert operations—to protect the king, ferret out plots and sniff out traitors, create chaos in enemy camps and/or infiltrate their forces, identify those amenable to bribes and test the loyalty of ministers and others close to the king.

Among their more interesting tasks was helping the king to demonstrate his divine connections, so to speak, for specific purposes—and, therefore, demanding a certain histrionic ability on their part. Governance is always smooth when a ruler sports a divine aura but more so if he can be shown to have the private ear of the gods. Kautilya's helpful recommendations, in this regard, point to a highly-refined sense of the dramatic, among other things: for instance, agents were to conceal themselves in tunnels or inside images in temples so that the king, while worshipping, could carry on a conversation with the deity; they could even rise out of water, pretending to be *nagas* (snakes) or the god of water (Varuna), so that the king could have a casual chat with them. This was to be accompanied by various chemical experiments to create illusions (fire on water and the like) before the presumably gobsmacked public, so that the king rose sky-high in their estimation.

Being an agent wasn't just a male prerogative, though. Kautilya recommends that 'poor but intrepid widows' could, equally, be recruited in the service of the state, after which they could disguise themselves as wandering nuns, for instance, and move around freely with their antennae out for insidious plots.[5] He further notes that women agents who were comfortable with water could be used to demonstrate the king's ability to talk to mermaids and snake-maidens (*naga-kanyas*).[6] So picture, if you will, the king stepping into a sacred space and conversing with the idol/s enshrined therein, while beautiful apparitions floating on the water awaited their turn for a discussion—and, in the meantime, fire and smoke issued from sundry mouths in the background. The public would have watched, wide-eyed, and then retreated to discuss—in hushed, awestruck tones—the divine being that was their ruler. A highly-effective ploy in discouraging dissension—rebelling against a semi-god (or a demigod!) was just asking for trouble, after all!

The bottomline, to Kautilya, is that the king is always vulnerable and cannot really trust anyone around him in an atmosphere where everyone is eyeing the throne and will resort to all sorts of devious, savage ways to nab it. 'No enemy shall know his secrets,' he vows. On the other hand, the king should be privy to 'all his enemy's weaknesses. Like a tortoise, he shall draw in any limb of his that is exposed'[7]—

an endeavour, which, if constantly practised, must have been utterly exhausting! Chandragupta's eventual abdication of the Mauryan throne begins to make more sense, in this context. If he had had to adopt some, if not all, of Kautilya's measures while on the throne, a religious life would have seemed like a wonderful, relaxing alternative to him!

So does this ideal polity that Kautilya envisages correlate to an actual geographical space in the *Arthashastra*? He declares, rather grandly, that 'of the whole world, the northern part of the country' from the Himalayas to the seas 'is marked out as the natural sphere of imperialism' (*chakravarti-kshetram*). R.K. Mookerji speculates that he had in mind the empire already established by Chandragupta in northern India by extinguishing the remnants of Greek rule in the Punjab, quelling the Nandas of Magadha and drawing Saurashtra in western India into his imperial ambit.[8] It is a rich land, avers Kautilya, with immense potential in economic and human resources, and bristling, therefore, with possibilities for an able person at the helm to capitalise upon. But the central point of whether he was looking backwards (to an existing political realm) or forwards (to an ideal political realm) remains unclear.

Did the Mauryan king do anything apart from batting off death threats, then? Well, for a start, he was the pivot of the political system that Kautilya visualised, the power at the centre of the monarchy. And although the *Arthashastra* discusses in depth the acquisition, maintenance and strengthening of political power, it also stresses the moral duties and responsibilities of the king. These include protecting his subjects in every which way (including from a diverse range of wrongdoers like deceitful artisans, thieves, murderers and their ilk), and ensuring their welfare and prosperity. Thus, his happiness is inextricably wound up with that of his people, and it is incumbent on him to protect the social order and do things that are beneficial to himself and everyone else.

If this is strongly reminiscent of a benevolent father hovering around his children and anxious about their welfare but knowing, all the same, what is best for them, you are completely justified in thinking so. In fact, the idea of a paternalistic rule that is raised by Kautilya in his text is brought to triumphant fruition by Ashoka in subsequent times with his own unique twist to it—but more on that later. Suffice it to say that a blend of the *Arthashastra* and Ashoka's inscriptions gives us plentiful information on the Mauryan political system and its machinations. We will come to this in due course. These strictures aren't exactly binding but, as Kautilya warns, a king 'who flouts the teachings of the Dharmashastras and the Arthashastra, ruins the kingdom by his own injustice'.[9] Ignore them at your peril, then, Mauryan king!

Kautilya's brisk, commonsensical directives for society show him at his best. Consider this singularly pithy saying: 'Wealth will slip away from that childish man who constantly consults the stars. The only (guiding) star of wealth is itself: what can the stars of the sky do?'[10] One imagines the realm's astrologers howling in dismay. This, too—his cynical appraisal of corruption in the ranks: 'Just as it is impossible to know when a fish moving in water is drinking it, so it is impossible to find out when government servants in charge of undertakings misappropriate money.'[11] (This, incidentally, was also a concern for Rudradaman of the Junagadh inscription of *c.* CE 150 in Saurashtra—who mentions Chandragupta and whom we will come to soon—who scouts around very carefully before entrusting the repair of the Sudarshana lake reservoir to an incorruptible official.)

And yet, it wasn't as if Kautilya was above resorting to underhand ways if his purpose was served—the ends justifying the means, as it were. Consider his singular methods of collecting revenue to make it appear as if the king wasn't involved in the least:[12] for one, a secret agent could pose as a trader, coin examiner or goldsmith, and collect, in the process, money on deposit and as loans. This could, in turn, be 'stolen' by other agents for the treasury's benefit. For another, the property of anyone accused of a crime could be confiscated by using one of several drastic methods, ranging from the milder woman-as-blackmailer ploy, to the brutal usage of someone on death row to falsely convict him, to the impossibly convoluted use of an agent to pose as an ascetic and trap him into performing occult rituals and then accuse him of sorcery.[13]

As noted earlier, the punishments for errors and aberrations are stringent and unsparing: physical maiming and/or hefty fines are all par for the course. Everything is aimed towards the rolling of the state's wheels without a single piece of grit coming in the way. Therefore, if a state functioned with the *Arthashastra* as a guide, it would be a sort of utopia with no crime, no dissent, and no interference in governance and conquest and eventual glory. Was this, in fact, the case with the Mauryans? Its greatest rulers—who also happen to be the first three in sequence—might or might not have followed these strictures but all were highly individualistic in their approach to ruling and managed to cover themselves in glory in varied ways, nevertheless. To use a modern analogy, if you will, it matters little if you swotted away at a guide book or just used your brains to ace a test!

Before we wrap up this quick survey of Kautilya's excellent work, here is another noteworthy aspect: the text's recognition of prostitutes as an autonomous body of women dealing with the state on their own without any male intermediary as regards the payment of taxes. The income from their establishments needed to be scrupulously accounted for with details on payments and expenses, and the profits made. One can imagine the less mathematically-inclined among them wrestling with accounts and figures and intricate calculations! The revenue, already stipulated by the text and likely to rise in times of financial stringency,[14] was to be handed over to the Chief Controller of Entertainers[15]—a post that must have been much sought after in that it sounds marginally less taxing (and no pun is intended here!) than, say, that of the Chief Superintendent of Warehouses. It would have also meant a certain measure of cultural and artistic hobnobbing that would have relieved the otherwise deathly grim picture of work that emerges from the text, involving, as it did, the supervision of other entertainers, too, such as actors, dancers, singers and musicians.[16]

Although brothels and similar places of entertainment were strictly state-controlled,[17] space was accorded to individual prostitutes as well provided they dutifully paid their taxes. Incidentally, the Chief Controller of Entertainers (although Kautilya refers to him by the more prosaic Head of the Department of Courtesans/Prostitutes) was apparently responsible for the training of courtesans and protecting the interests of prostitutes but no special qualifications are stipulated for this job. Clearly, this ability came naturally to men, which is a wonderful thing, indeed, if you consider it! But Kautilya hedges his strictures with welcome safeguards: raping a prostitute was a crime, inviting censure and punishment.[18] In fact, he has a whole chapter on sexual offences where he shows little patience with rapists and their ilk—or with anyone flouting varna and other rules to indulge their passions, for that matter. And, of course, anyone caught having sexual relations with the queen was to be boiled alive on the spot.[19]

Incidentally, the Mauryan king, in Kautilya's world, had three grades of women dancing attendance on him: the lowest was to hold the royal umbrella and pitcher, the next one carried the fan and the highest grade served him while seated on the throne. Moreover, Kautilya envisaged a constant influx and outflux of these women keeping in mind the vagaries of age. Thus, the elderly women staff were continually transferred to the royal kitchens or storehouse and the recruitment process went on, and so, everyone was constantly and gainfully employed. Of course, if some woman wanted to opt out of this cycle, she could pay 'a ransom' of twenty-four thousand *panas*—an interesting choice of word, that![20]

And now that we have sketched the world that the Mauryan king would (or did) inhabit, let us finally turn to Chandragupta, the one who started it all.

Notes

1. See, for this, Upinder Singh, *A History of Ancient and Early Medieval India—From the Stone Age to the 12th Century*, Pearson/ Dorling Kindersley, 2008, p.342.
2. L.N. Rangarajan, ed. and trans. *Kautilya—The Arthashastra*, Penguin, 1992, p.110, 8.4.24–26.
3. Ibid., p.130, 1.20.15–17.
4. See, for instance, Nayanjot Lahiri, *Ashoka in Ancient India*, Permanent Black, 2015, pp.60–62.
5. Rangarajan, *Kautilya—The Arthashastra*, p.470, 1.12.4, 5.
6. Ibid., p.496, 13.1.3–6.
7. Ibid., p.151, 1.15.60.
8. See, for instance, R.K. Mookerji, *Chandragupta Maurya and His Times*, Motilal Banarsidass, 1966, rpt.1988, pp.73–74.
9. Rangarajan, *Kautilya—The Arthashastra*, p.118, 8.2.12.

10. Ibid., p.222, 9.4.26.
11. Ibid., p.251, 2.9.33.
12. Ibid., p.243, 5.2.46–51.
13. Ibid., pp.243–244, 5.2.52–68.
14. Ibid., p.317.
15. Ibid., pp.231–232, 2.27.6–8, 10, 24–27.
16. Ibid., p.317, 2.27.25.
17. Exhaustive details for their functioning are provided: see ibid., pp.320–324.
18. Ibid., p.446, 4.13.38, 39.
19. Ibid., p.447, 4.13.33.
20. See, for instance, Mookerji, *Chandragupta Maurya and His Times*, pp.59–60.

7

CHANDRAGUPTA MAURYA

PART I

So how did Chandragupta Maurya, the first hero of the Mauryan saga, happen to cross paths with the formidable Kautilya? And who *was* he, to begin with? Let us answer the second question first. The three religious traditions cheerfully contradict each other with regard to Chandragupta's mysterious origins, as with most other things, and the historian is left to make of their divergent assertions what they will. Accordingly, in Buddhist texts, such as the *Digha Nikaya* and the *Divyavadana*, the Mauryas are described as hailing from a Kshatriya clan named the Moriyas who ruled at Pipphalivana. On the other hand, the *Parishishtaparvan* claims that Chandragupta (and here you might need to hold your breath!) was the son of a daughter of a chief of a village of peacock tamers or *mayura-poshakas* (the peacock is *mayura* in Sanskrit; *mora* in Pali).

The *Mudrarakshasa* of Vishakhadatta, which describes Chandragupta's ascent to power and has been variously ascribed to periods from the late fourth century to the eighth century CE, talks of the hero's low social origin. Then we have an infuriatingly tantalising reference by Kshemendra and

Somadeva, early medieval writers of Kashmir, to Chandragupta being the 'son of the genuine Nanda' (*purva-nanda-suta*). Are we to understand, then, that Chandragupta was actually of royal Nanda blood who revolted against his own people and claimed the throne? A distinctly unhelpful statement is added by Dhundiraja, a commentator on the *Vishnu Purana*: Chandragupta was the eldest son of Maurya, son of the Nanda king Sarvarthasiddhi, by Mura, who was the daughter of a hunter.

Lest you begin to tear your hair out by the handful, let us hasten to add that this is the typical situation that prevails during any reconstruction of identities pertaining to the ancient period—loads of assertions and counter-assertions, some of them seeming to have been made for the sheer fun of it alone, and the historian making their slow and painful way through the pile of genuine facts and red herrings to arrive at the holy grail of historical truth! One may add here, as a telling aside, that such frenzied speculation is never the lot of women in the past, even truly remarkable ones who left a trail of evidence behind. No one really cares who they are and where they came from because history is—and has always been—about the men.

What we know about Chandragupta is that he ruled from 324/321 to 297 BCE, first establishing himself in Punjab and then moving eastwards until he gained control over Magadha. The only epigraphic evidence that we can definitely connect to him is the Junagarh inscription of Rudradaman, which attributes the beginning of the construction of a water reservoir known as the Sudarshana lake to Vaishya Pushyagupta, the provincial governor of Chandragupta Maurya. It was eventually completed by Tuhshaspa, the governor of the area during Chandragupta's grandson, Ashoka's reign.

The reservoir was used as a dam all through the Mauryan period and beyond, the waters of the lake being used for irrigation, and stimulating the agricultural growth and prosperity of the area. Rudradaman was a ruler of a line called the Kardamakas, a branch of the Shaka-Kshatrapas, from *c.*130 to 150 CE. On the self-same reservoir capitulating to a storm during his reign, he brushed aside the naysayers—and there were many!—and decided to repair and restore the lake. Once he had done so, he proceeded to record his deed on a rock for posterity—and this is how we establish a connection between him, the lake and Chandragupta. Of such fortuitous discoveries is history constructed—or rather, reconstructed!

And so, this excellent record, dated to CE 150, is inscribed near the top of the Girnar/Junagadh rock (the inscription is interchangeably named after both places) in the Brahmi script. Consisting of twenty lines of writing, it holds the distinction of being the earliest long inscription in Sanskrit in the Indian subcontinent. Parts of the text have been ravaged over time and cannot be read without difficulty. At one point, in the mid-1800s, a well-meaning, pious but blundering Jaina used gunpowder to widen the pilgrim trail that led up Girnar's sacred mountain.[1] The explosion blew off a corner of the Girnar rock at a critical part, obliterating some vital names that were a part of the Mauryan emperor, Ashoka's edicts on the same rock and deeply frustrating historians thereby.

However, Rudradaman's record remained intact, one that seems to have been composed with great care and elegance. The rock itself was clearly a much sought-after proclamatory material in early times because, as noted above, it also contains a set of edicts of Ashoka and an inscription of the Gupta king, Skandagupta. While the former contains Ashoka's views on dhamma/dharma (and we will come to this at a later stage), the latter talks of the Sudarshana lake being repaired yet again after a storm and the breach taking two years (from CE 456–57) for Skandagupta's governor of Saurashtra, Parnadatta, to rectify through his son, Chakrapalita, who was in charge of that particular city.

A troublesome water body, indeed, but one that could evidently be tamed repeatedly! Rudradaman himself, clearly a budding water resource engineer, appears to have been a very interesting character but that is a story for another time. Suffice it to say that the fact that he decided to record his reservoir-wrestles for posterity on the Junagadh rock speaks volumes about him and his priorities in a milieu where the only thing that rulers usually recorded about themselves were their military successes.

On the question of how Chandragupta met Kautilya, which is where his story actually takes off, stories abound, each jostling the other to claim historical veracity, and all equally gripping and fascinating. Let us consider the two main ones, though (and this might occasion some quibbling, there being differing views on their relative importance!), and in chronological sequence. The first of these apparently occurred when Kautilya was roaming around the Magadhan realm (or on the run from the Nandas, depending on the story you pick!), still smarting from Dhana Nanda's cavalier treatment of him and mulling over his plans for revenge. At the time, Chandragupta was young, no more than eleven or twelve years of age but already, so this particular story goes, sporting the demeanour of a king and, at the point when Kautilya first saw him, holding a mock court with his friends. Chandragupta was the king, and the others had divided up the roles of robbers and officers between them.

It seems that Kautilya watched, unobserved and rapt,

as the young Chandragupta, seated regally on a tree stump, swiftly dispensed justice after first carefully scrutinising the incriminating evidence and satisfying himself as to the guilty party. The thieving arms were to be chopped off—an order that was carried out with much boisterous enthusiasm and realistic screaming—and everyone was thoroughly enjoying themselves when Kautilya, probably wincing at the noise, decided to step forward and make himself seen. The other boys scattered in confusion when this unsmiling stranger walked into their midst but Chandragupta remained poised and grave, as befitted a king. Kautilya fashioned a test on the spot (a recurrent motif, again, in most ancient tales; nothing is immediately straightforward but once a qualifying test has been passed, all falls into place!), introducing himself as a poor brahmana in need of largesse.

Chandragupta, barely pausing for thought, decided to gift his supplicant a cow (in another version, a herd of cows) to cover his needs and, in the process, passed the test with flying colours. The solemn bestowal of a stick-as-cow followed, after which Chandragupta was thoroughly interrogated by Kautilya. The boy was, it seems, the son of a hunter (cowherd, in some versions), and Kautilya couldn't help but marvel at his regal dignity and confidence that belied his humble origins. Also, he couldn't help feeling thrilled: he had found his tool for revenge and his future king, in one lucky stroke. Accordingly, he would take the boy along and groom him for his role.

And so, after dispensing with the preliminaries—persuading the boy's parents to let him go with a thousand *panas* to spur them on and informing Chandragupta that his life was about to radically change—Kautilya set forth on his mission with renewed vigour. One wonders how Chandragupta would have reacted to this electrifying news. He was probably thrilled at the thought of future adventures but also, quite conceivably, nervous at the prospect of accompanying this stern-faced stranger on his unnamed journey. But here, a note is injected into the tale that shows this to be Chandragupta's destiny. His father apparently informed Kautilya that Chandragupta was not his real son—he had been discovered abandoned near a cowshed as a mewling infant and there was speculation that he was of noble birth. So in following Kautilya, he was merely fulfilling the role he was born to assume, which was definitely not that of a hunter (or cowherd!).

The spate of theories regarding Chandragupta's birth explains the vagueness in these tales. The peacock motif clings stubbornly to him in most of them; the 'peacock on arches' symbol later becomes emblematic of the Mauryan coins. Apart from the origin-guesses mentioned earlier, he has also been connected to the Sakya clan of the Buddha, a descendant settled in eastern Magadha, famous for its peacocks. Or perhaps his family came from the mountain region of Meru on the northwest, which might explain why two of Ashoka's Major Rock Edicts, Mansera and Shahbazgarhi, are located as gateways to the region.[2] His link, however with the peacock totem is undeniable, hence the name of the dynasty he started.

One of the more convoluted Buddhist versions has the pregnant queen of the conquered hill-town of Moriya-nagara fleeing on the heels of her husband's murder, along with her older brothers, to Pataliputra. When Chandragupta was born, she placed the child in a vase and left him at a cattle-pen. Despite the odd choice of baby receptacle and locale, the infant survived, watched over by a herdsman and huntsman, in sequence, the latter being the foster father whom Kautilya later bought him from.[3] And, incidentally, this same tradition insists that Chandragupta later married the daughter of his oldest maternal uncle, who had accompanied his mother to Pataliputra, and made her his queen. Anyway, the more ambiguous the origins, the more explanatory tales and variations there are—and this is true of any notable personage of the past who rises, all of a sudden, as if from nowhere, as it were.

As for Kautilya, at this moment, he was now firmly back on track and revenge seemed within grasping range. These are the bare essentials of the story but there are other tangential storylines and complications that have been tagged on to the original tale to give it more colour and excitement. One of these is the inclusion of a prince named Parvata/Pabbato, one of Dhana Nanda's sons, who feared for his life at court and who, having abetted Kautilya's escape from the palace after his unfortunate skirmish with the king, decided to accompany him on his travels in the hope of getting the throne someday with his new friend's help.

As it happens, despite faithfully tagging on with Kautilya and later, vying with Chandragupta for his favour, Parvata meets a sorry end. Chandragupta is forced to murder him in pursuance of some ghastly loyalty test that the Machiavellian Kautilya had thought up; also, an early indication of the latter's absolute ruthlessness in pursuance of his goal/s. Although mentioned in the *Mahavamsa*, the story veers just a little too much in the direction of purple melodrama to actually ring true but it is an interesting one, nevertheless. It was clearly fashioned to reinforce not just Chandragupta's ability to take unpalatable decisions for a cause (and thereby his complete suitability to rule) but also the intense bond between mentor and disciple.

Yet, here is the second of the two noteworthy tales—and it is much more convoluted than the previous one. It takes, as its premise, that the Nandas were cousins of the Mauryas and virtual rulers of Magadha. According to this story, the Nandas, who wanted to eliminate their cousins, invited the latter for a hunt and a celebratory dinner. The day's proceedings went well until it was dinner time when the Mauryas were told that there was no sitting space in the palace's main hall and food would be served to them in the cellar. This should have raised even an infant's suspicions but the Mauryas were clearly good-natured and gullible, and meekly followed their gracious hosts down to the cellar where—and this is frankly weird—they failed to notice the Nandas pretending to serve them but actually slinking out of the cellar in turns! It was only when the door banged shut that they realised their predicament, and then proceeded to starve and die, one after the other. Chandragupta, the hero of our story, remained alive, though, and was eventually hauled out of the cellar and thrust into a jail, vowing to take revenge on his family's murderers.

At this point, a neighbouring king who wanted to attack Magadha, devised a ruse by which to ensure that the feared Mauryas were, in fact, dead. Accordingly, he sent a caged lion to Pataliputra with its tamer who challenged the people to set the animal free without breaking open the cage. Predictably, Chandragupta was the only one who took up the gauntlet and by a complicated series of moves, which involved parading an elephant before the lion, realised that the latter was, in fact, made of wax and manipulated by its tamer's magnetic staff. So he set fire to the offending contraption for which he was rewarded by the Nanda king with the post of the state guesthouse's manager in the wild hope that he would enrage some brahmana who would thereby curse and destroy him.

The king's decidedly odd logic was turned on its head

by Kautilya who now entered the scene in a dramatic way. Chandragupta saw him uprooting all the grass in his path because the blades had had the temerity to poke his feet and promptly invited the irascible brahmana to a meal. This dinner invitation led to an exchange of confidences on both sides but before more secrets could be spilled, the Nandas entered the guesthouse and became immediately and terribly annoyed that a shabbily-dressed brahmana was being fussed over and cossetted. In the ensuing tumult, the Nanda king pulled Kautilya to his feet whereby his knotted hair came undone and swung loose—and the latter swore to destroy the perpetrator of this awful deed.

The story now becomes so impossibly complex that it is nigh-impossible to follow its twists and turns. Once he deemed Chandragupta capable of effecting his revenge, Kautilya recruited an army, a motley crew sourced from all over, including Greek mercenaries. And then, he, basically—and very cleverly—turned friend against friend and enemy against enemy and everyone against everyone else until the path was clear for Chandragupta to kill the offending Nanda king on the battlefield and claim Pataliputra as its new ruler, while Kautilya grimly but triumphantly knotted his hair once more. A bizarre but wonderful story indeed and a classic example of the sort of frustrating source material that a historian routinely confronts!

But let us flesh out this story with some basic details. Master and disciple began their grand campaign of unseating Dhana Nanda on the Magadhan throne by attacking some central cities only to meet with unanticipated resistance and failure. The story seems to have spread like wildfire among the populace: one presumes this was on account of the plan's temerity and the fact that bad news is always savoured. One needs to backtrack a bit, at this juncture, though. Prior to their impetuous assault on the Nanda heartlands, the duo had been hard at work. Chandragupta wasn't merely a puppet being dragged around by the masterful Kautilya and passively doing his bidding. Kautilya made sure that he was put through his paces in every sense of the word, most probably at Taxila, which was the last word in learning at the time, hosting students of haughty and humble backgrounds, and offering a grounding in everything that you conceivably needed to succeed in life.[4]

Accordingly, Chandragupta had to master every single science and art that Kautilya saw fit for him to study, the aim being to make him physically and intellectually formidable. In addition, he was subjected to regular spot tests by Kautilya to ensure that his training was impeccable and had soaked into every pore of his being, so that it was literally coming out of his ears. This argues a high level of intelligence and receptivity in Chandragupta; Kautilya would have ruthlessly discarded him if it were otherwise and hunted for a replacement revenge-tool without a single qualm.

While this was happening, Alexander of Macedon decided to make his Indian foray (alluded to earlier), and Kautilya was quick to appraise the situation and capitalise on it—although the attempt very quickly went pie-faced, as it turned out. Much has been said and written on the encounter between Alexander and the dastardly Ambhi, who ruled the land between the Indus and Jhelum rivers, and who cravenly capitulated to the former without offering a single moment's resistance. Alexander promptly heaped gifts on him and a much-relieved and gratified Ambhi offered arms and hospitality in return—and, furthermore, offered to help the conqueror subdue his longstanding enemy, Porus/Puru, who ruled the land between the Jhelum and the Chenab.

Things went downhill very quickly for Ambhi at the resultant battle of Hydaspes/Jhelum, fought in 326 BCE (which witnessed Alexander's dramatic fording of the monsoon-swollen waters of the Jhelum virtually under Puru's nose and leading to his consummate victory). He almost lost his life at Puru's hands and, moreover, had to suffer the ignominy of seeing his old rival being treated with grace and dignity by Alexander. Incidentally, the brief but crisp conversation between Puru and Alexander moved swiftly into the ranks of legend, and has been immortalised in poetry and prose through the ages (Michael Madhusudan Dutt's wonderfully poignant poem, 'King Porus—A Legend of Old', comes to mind, for one). It seems Puru was asked by his vanquisher how he would like to be treated. Puru's magnificent retort was that he should be treated as a king; if their roles had been reversed, he would have behaved thus. It was Puru's turn to have gifts heaped upon him by a deeply impressed Alexander, who, additionally, returned his kingdom to him. (Incidentally, this battle more or less sapped the spirit of Alexander's army that clamoured to return home. This effectively put paid to his plans of ranging further afield, to Magadha and even beyond—but this occurred a little later.)

Sniffing out opportunities was Kautilya's forte and here was a heaven-sent one. Chandragupta was immediately despatched to Taxila, where Alexander was at the time, to win him over as an ally.[5] If all went well, this brilliant military genius would be another feather in Kautilya's cap; he would hasten the conquest of Magadha and the dethroning of Dhana Nanda. As it happened, though, the rumoured meeting did not go well, as usually happens when arrogance meets arrogance head-on. Chandragupta, presumably sporting a swollen head on account of being Magadha's uncrowned king-elect, said or did something in Alexander's presence that annoyed him terribly.

This was purportedly nothing more than addressing Alexander as his equal but the latter, flush with his victories and surrounded by fawning flatterers like Ambhi, did not take kindly to it. The net result was that a chastened Chandragupta had to literally flee from Alexander's presence. Meanwhile, Ambhi, sore since the landmark battle in body and spirit, tried to gain brownie points with the mighty conqueror in a highly clumsy fashion: he apparently threatened all sorts of dire consequences if Kautilya didn't send Chandragupta back to apologise to Alexander and had his ear chewed off for his pains.

Some good came out of this awful imbroglio, though, in the form of a heavenly sign—or something that Kautilya *chose* to interpret as such. While racing away from Taxila, Chandragupta, overcome by the noon heat, at a point, decided to sleep. One wonders at his equanimity in this life-threatening situation but perhaps taking power naps while in dire straits was part and parcel of Kautilya's training! He woke abruptly, a short while later, to face the simple but terrifying fact that a tiger stood over him, licking off his sweat with its raspy tongue. It then looked long and deep into his eyes before sauntering off, leaving a petrified Chandragupta to make sense of what had happened. He would later swear to Kautilya that the tiger had seemed to *bow* to him. And Kautilya, who knew that his pupil was not subject to flights of fancy and never lied, suspended his habitual disbelief in superstition and grew equally excited. This was some sort of powerful omen; it was almost as if Chandragupta had been touched by a divine hand and anointed the king. It was time for them to strike!

Incidentally, the divine portent in question changes somewhat depending on the version you read. Here, for instance, is what the Roman writer, Justinus, has to say about our hero and the sign: 'This man was of mean origin, but was stimulated to aspire to regal power by supernatural encouragement; for, having offended Alexander by his boldness of speech, and orders being given to kill him, he saved himself by swiftness of foot; and while he was lying asleep, after his fatigue, a lion of great size having come up to him, licked off with his tongue the sweat that was running from him, and after gently waking him, left him.'[6] Sidestepping Kautilya and being less than complimentary to Chandragupta was probably Justinus's reaction to their ostensibly audacious plan: of trying to rope the mighty Alexander into their kingmaking scheme and assuming he would be happy to help. The thing is that he *might* have helped and changed his—and our—history altogether but we will never really know what exactly transpired in that chamber in Taxila!

And so, we get back to where we were where the conniving duo, floating along in the euphoria occasioned by signs, launched their grand assault on the Nandas. The whole enterprise was a humbling endeavour—their calculations were way off, their reading of the public mood incorrect and their assessment of the Nanda resistance woefully inadequate. All the major towns and cities stood firm and despite their army growing from a ragtag crowd to a respectable size over the years—even featuring the fierce Arashtraka tribes ('stateless' people often identified with the Kambojas northwest of Kashmir)—they were not able to make a dent anywhere they went. Attacking Pataliputra right away was not an option: Dhana Nanda's massive army was stationed there and rumours about its invincibility were strong enough to have even dissuaded Alexander's soldiers from indulging their master's whim and venturing in that direction.

Tales of the duo, at this juncture in their campaign, range from the prosaic to the wildly lurid. An example of the latter is when they were fleeing the Magadhan forces, at some point, and found themselves by a lake with a pursuing (Nanda) horseman hot on their heels. Kautilya did a quick wardrobe change, donning a mendicant's robes and rubbing dust all over his face, and ordered Chandragupta to jump into the lake and hide. When the soldier on horseback came up, Kautilya told him that a man had just jumped into the water. While the excited soldier began to throw off his armour to follow suit, Kautilya chopped off his unfortunate head. Chandragupta emerged from the lake, immensely gratified at his master's quick thinking—and presumably grateful that holding his breath underwater for prolonged periods of time had been part of his training schedule!

This is just one among the several hair-raising tales of Kautilya's alleged brutality, and his obstinate pursual of the job at hand whereby nothing and no one was allowed to interfere. Yet, he was considerably chastened. The Nanda empire was seemingly impregnable and unvanquishable, and the thought of Dhana Nanda having the last laugh must have been impossibly galling to him. Kautilya was also keenly aware that he and Chandragupta were becoming a laughing stock among the people. The latter were a bit of an enigma, in any case. On the one hand, they squirmed under the savage Nanda hand but on the other, they closed ranks with him when it mattered.

Thus, casting about in his mind for workable solutions, Kautilya stumbled upon the incident that triggered a major rethinking of strategy on his part (mentioned in both Buddhist and Jaina traditions)—the one where he witnessed a woman rebuking her son for eating a hot dish from the centre rather than the sides and burning his tongue thereby. She likened the unfortunate boy to Chandragupta and his foolish scheme of seizing an empire from where it was strongest rather than from the sides.

Something clicked in Kautilya's mind during this irritable woman's rant and he changed his plan immediately (and it *is* gratifying to note than a woman is given credit, in this regard). From now on, they would attack the Nanda empire obliquely, from its frontiers and outlying areas, and work their way steadily and stealthily to its heart—just as you would approach a dish of steaming porridge (or *roti*/ bread, as some versions go). This necessitated an entirely new set of allies and Kautilya set his giant brain to selecting them. The use of the word 'selecting' is appropriate here—once Kautilya had identified them, they would inevitably and inexorably be drawn into his grand web through intrigue whether they wanted to or not. Parvataka, the ruler of a mountain fastness, was the first major recruit to their cause.

He is a bit frustrating to identify, though—some versions claim that he was Dhana Nanda's son, Parvata, who, however, had already been killed by Chandragupta, if you remember, so this is untenable. Jaina accounts describe him as the king of Himavatakuta or the mountain country, which some see as modern-day Himachal Pradesh or Kashmir. Another wild surmise is that he was, in fact, Porus/Puru, clearly masquerading under a different name. However, as Parvataka is shown as a *mleccha* or outcast in the *Mudrarakshasa* and Porus belonged to a Kshatriya race, this theory holds no water, too—and this is compounded by the fact that Greek sources insist on Porus having eventually died at Alexander's hands. So unless there were a lot of resurrected souls wandering around and joining the anti-Nanda cause, we must presume that Parvataka was a different person altogether! The *Mudrarakshasa* lists Chandragupta's other allies—the Greeks, Scythians, Kambojans of Gandhara and the Nepalese or Kashmiris—all from the northwest or beyond.

Another story pops up, at this juncture, which compels us to sit back and marvel at Kautilya's sheer ingenuity. It is situated at a time when the duo had begun to experience some success—belatedly but, nevertheless, sweeter for the delay. They had stuck so far to their altered plan of focusing on cities on the Nanda empire's frontiers—and had picked them off, one by one, in a steady, relentless fashion. Their numbers had swelled considerably by now for there is nothing like a successful track record, however small, to attract supporters and win over vacillators. Occupying units held sway in the conquered units and Pataliputra was drawing tantalisingly closer.

At this exhilarating point, though, a particularly intractable city (frustratingly unnamed) stood in their way. The Jaina texts note that the duo's siege of this city had yielded no result and if this state of affairs continued, their resources would be stretched and, eventually, snap. Besides, the spies (and Kautilya already had a huge force of them, cleverly hidden in plain sight in key places and keeping him clued in, at all times) reported discontented rumblings and general homesickness among the soldiers—a malady that Kautilya simply could not afford to have on his hands. Chandragupta, always privy to his master's moods and findings, also chafed at the bit.

It was time for action and Kautilya rose to the occasion by unleashing his theatrical abilities for the second time around (although there might have been several more that we are unaware of). Donning his favourite mendicant robes again, he prepared to infiltrate the stubborn city before Chandragupta's startled eyes and was annoyingly cagey when questioned except for murmuring something about the temple of the Seven Mothers (*sapta-matrika*) within its walls and instructing his baffled disciple to temporarily withdraw his troops on the morrow. When the guards on the city's bafflements saw Kautilya approaching the gates, they were dumbfounded. How clueless could this ascetic be that he didn't know the city was under siege and that they couldn't open the gates! But Kautilya was nothing if not thorough and managed to put on an act so convincing that the soldiers could not bear to disappoint this mild man, desperate to worship at the temple of the Seven Mothers within.

After much discussion and shaking of heads, here was their compromise solution: they let down a rope ladder, up which the mendicant—suddenly transformed into an athletic soul—swarmed with alacrity. Once in, Kautilya made his way to the temple, made a great show of devotion and then began to suss the mood of the people thronging around the shrine. Within minutes, he had heard enough: they were sick of the siege and were willing to do anything to see it lifted. Life and business had come to a standstill, and they could not care less about the politics behind it. It was time for Kautilya to move among the crowd, gently insinuating that the siege couldn't *possibly* end as long as the Seven Mothers protected the city. And as the enemy could happily camp outside for another six months, all was well, wasn't it? Well, no, it clearly wasn't, or so their faces said, and Kautilya spoke a little bit more about the Mothers' protection and the resultant impregnability of the city, and so on and so forth. At some point, he tactfully removed himself to the anonymity of a night shelter.

The following morning, the temple was in the eye of a storm. Someone had removed the Seven Mothers from the shrine and there was no knowing who had done it or why. It was rumoured, though, that a wise sage had predicted that this was the only way to lift the siege—and someone had decided to act upon it. More people were spilling out onto the battlements, pointing in wonder at the enemy's retreating army and in no time at all, a clarion call was sounded: the siege had ended. Kautilya backed away from the jubilant crowd and slipped out of the now-open gates.

Of course, in a matter of moments, Chandragupta's forces swooped in—and the rest, as they say, is history.

Notes

1. See Charles Allen, *Ashoka—The Search for India's Lost Emperor*, Abacus, 2012, pp.177–178.
2. See ibid., p.364.
3. For details, see R.K. Mookerji, *Chandragupta Maurya and His Times*, Motilal Banarsidass, 1966, rpt.1988, pp.229–233.
4. See, for instance, ibid., pp.16–17.
5. There is an altogether different view, too—that Chandragupta offered to help Bessos, the satrap of Bactria, and then switched sides to join Alexander. As Sisikottus/Sashigupta/the Moon-Protected, he helped the latter to subjugate his own mountain people (in Charles Allen's view, the Ashvakan horse-people of the lunar/Chandravanshi dynasty who were mercenary cavalrymen under Alexander) and then brought Porus over to his side. See Allen, *Ashoka—The Search for India's Lost Emperor*, pp.364-366.
6. Deepa Agarwal, *Chanakya—The Master of Statecraft*, Puffin/Penguin, p.79.

8

CHANDRAGUPTA MAURYA

PART II

And so to the mother of all battles—Dhana Nanda's colossal army against Chandragupta's comparatively small one—but the former's back had been broken with tales of the latter's astonishing success, and the entire thing was a bit like the parable of the elephant and the ant whereby the former succumbed and quite quickly at that. We have highly exaggerated figures of this clash (one hundred crore soldiers, ten thousand elephants, one lakh horses and five thousand charioteers are supposed to have died, according to the *Milindapanho*, a Buddhist text)[1] but there are no real corroborative accounts to verify the facts. Chandragupta's army varies from adequate to massive depending on who is telling the tale but the size can be inferred by a process of intelligent deduction.[2] So here goes: the Greek account of Dhana Nanda's army estimates it as two lakh infantry, twenty thousand cavalry, three thousand elephants and eight thousand four-horsed chariots, so Chandragupta's army would have had to be roughly comparable in number or, perhaps, even larger in order to triumph.

And here we have Arrian's astute mathematical

observations: each chariot in Chandragupta's army carried two soldiers and the driver; and each elephant carried three archers, besides the mahout; therefore, the total number of soldiers in his army would have been six lakh infantry, thirty thousand cavalry, thirty-six thousand men on elephants and twenty-four thousand men in chariots, with the staggering total of six lakh ninety thousand—and this excludes camp followers and attendants at large. Or we could discard the complicated calculations and just trust Pliny who says that Chandragupta had six lakh infantry, thirty thousand cavalry and nine thousand elephants, and probably eight thousand chariots like the Nandas. The non-mathematically inclined need not concern themselves with these figures but to those who love numbers and their tales, these statistics are infinitely fascinating!

Also, this obsession with elephants vis-à-vis battles was completely warranted on account of their sheer size and volatile nature, which routinely resulted in the (perhaps unfortunate) trampling of the enemy—and this, incidentally, is a feature that remains constant in warfare all the way down to the Mughals. But pertinent to our purpose is the fact that Magadha was the undisputed leader in elephant procurement, training and deployment. Kautilya himself talks of the east (*prachya*) as the region with the best elephants, while the *Mahabharata* echoes his sentiments, claiming that the Prachyas/easterners were brilliant at elephant-fighting.[3]

Megasthenes was an elephant-noter, too: he says that the largest elephants in the land were of the Praisian, or of the land of the Prasii/eastern people—in other words, Magadha. In fact, the elephants that Chandragupta later gave Seleucus Nikator despite being 'past their sell-by date' apparently helped the latter in his struggles against the other

Greek generals, resulting in him being one of the prime winners.[4] The presumption, therefore, is that Chandragupta had considerably more elephants than Dhana Nanda and they probably swung the battle his way.

And of course, Chandragupta must have acquitted himself honourably in this defining battle of his life. This had a little to do with his training, and obviously a lot to do with his courage and grit and determination and ambition—for too often, what is lost in accounts of Chandragupta are these very qualities. The accent is usually on Kautilya who, being the overpowering figure that he is, dominates the entire narrative in most instances, reducing Chandragupta to a silent, passive figure who tags along with him, falls in with his plans and mutely becomes the next Magadhan king, seemingly without a single original thought in his head. Yet, let us remember that his was no easy task: to take a leap of faith and trust a virtual stranger with your destiny requires a sort of mental toughness and resilience that is not immediately evident in most people—and, moreover, he was extremely young when he put his life in the hands of the redoubtable Kautilya.

Lots changed after the battle—the Nandas vacating the throne and Kautilya finally tying up his hair, for a start. A dispirited Dhana Nanda apparently offered his apologies to Kautilya and asked that his wife and daughters be spared, which set the wily mentor's brain on another track altogether. Accordingly, when the dust had settled and Dhana Nanda had left Pataliputra (incidentally, it is a bit odd that Kautilya spared his life; logically, he should not have left any rebellious elements around to foster problems at a later stage but we do not know anything for certain, so we just have to assume that he was in a particularly charitable mood then), Kautilya proposed that Chandragupta marry Durdhara, the exiled king's youngest daughter (in one version, Chandragupta's maternal cousin), who, when the prospect was mentioned, was, it seems, none too loath to marry the young man—and Chandragupta, too, wasn't averse to the idea, so all was well.

Again, odd that love would blossom in the heart of one whose father had just been shoved off his throne but perhaps pragmatic considerations were uppermost in Durdhara's mind—and perhaps Chandragupta was irresistible. Also, it made supreme political sense, at this point—the Nanda rule would meld seamlessly into the Mauryas, making one happy family, as a result. Uniting two ruling lines by the replacer marrying into the displaced was a ploy that was used time and time again through the ages. Let us move away from India for a change and consider world history. Think of the unison of the warring families of the Yorks/Plantagenets and Lancasters in medieval England, for instance, with the marriage of Henry of Lancaster with Elizabeth of York, thereby starting the Tudor dynasty, in which their son, Henry VIIIth, had a starring role, at a subsequent point, with his wife-killing penchant (this fact is expressly mentioned for those who have little idea of English history but who would have read about this impossibly eccentric king *somewhere* or the other, so it puts the whole thing into context!).[5] Anyway the point is that Kautilya was employing this diplomatic device much before this time—and it was eminently successful except that Durdhara eventually died in a dramatic way (mentioned later) due to the former's machinations.

But we are getting ahead of ourselves here, so back to the marriage and Kautilya's satisfaction at pulling off this diplomatic masterstroke. If we go by the stories, the atmosphere was marred a bit by the news of Dhana Nanda having been set upon by robbers while on his way out of the city and killed. This was unfortunate but not entirely regrettable—it meant one less thorn in the flesh for the duo to worry about for their attention was completely occupied by a potential mess: it was not only that random Nanda adherents were hatching plots to murder Chandragupta—or so it seemed to the ever-suspicious Kautilya—but also that the question of who should actually sit on the vacant throne had not quite been settled. When Parvataka and other powers had been roped in as allies, this delicate issue had been skirted and so, everyone thought they would be king after the Nandas, particularly the mountain ruler who fancied himself as the main contender. Accordingly, his clamours grew shriller and more insistent till the point when Kautilya regretfully informed his protégé that they couldn't risk an open rupture with Parvataka and would have to make arrangements for his crowning.

Needless to say, Chandragupta was deeply chagrined. The Magadhan throne was always supposed to have been his—and he had endured much in his pursuit of it. So to be told at the very last minute that plans had changed must have stirred up all sorts of violent emotions in his breast. Luckily, his training was immaculate and stood him in good stead now. Where a normal man would have raged, he remained deadpan and impassive. Besides, his years with Kautilya had taught him to expect the unexpected and read through the latter's doublespeak—and there *was* something very suspicious in his master's sudden and meek capitulation to Parvataka, so he wisely decided to hold his counsel. Also, Kautilya had a lot on his plate, at the moment. Prominent among the Nanda flagbearers was his erstwhile prime minister, Rakshasa, who indicated through every single expression and word that he heartily disliked the change of guard, and was going to cause trouble.

Accordingly, Chandragupta withdrew to focus on his domestic change of scene while Kautilya immersed himself in the findings of his massive spy network (grown from a small and dedicated band to an ungainly behemoth), emerging now and then to pacify the restive Parvataka. Meanwhile, the citizens of Pataliputra and the larger Magadhan realm wondered what on earth was going on. What *was* going on was something nasty and convoluted, something that Kautilya, however, was able to pounce on and thereby divert events from taking a tragic turn to a more cheerful outcome (at least, for him!) altogether. It seems that Rakshasa, brooding over the state of affairs and sorely missing his former employer, had devised the perfect solution. Astutely divining that it was Chandragupta among the many claimants to the throne whose cause was the strongest, he decided to focus on getting rid of him. Once Chandragupta disappeared from the scene, all would be well.

And the perfect ploy presented itself in the form of a much-feared and much-deployed figure: the *vishkanya* or snake-maiden—basically, a girl who had been fed small amounts of poison from childhood so that, in time, her very touch was fatal. As you can imagine, such people were in great demand for use against enemies, although, in all probability, not in possession of a great personal life—there would have been an obvious paucity of friends, for one! Making a lot of money was, perhaps, the only benefit of this profession. That—and presumably the ability to stroll through reptile-infested areas with an air of cool nonchalance! Predictably, these girls—who seem to have been around in Nanda times and even earlier—had made their way irrevocably into lore and legend where the very mention of them would make everyone's hair stand on end.

And it was one such girl whom Rakshasa decided to employ against Chandragupta. He had not reckoned with Kautilya, though, who had spent a lifetime anticipating *precisely* such attacks from people around him. To cut a long and rather complicated story short, Kautilya sniffed out the plot, intercepted the *vishkanya* in question while on her way to Chandragupta's chambers and promptly despatched her to Parvataka's instead where, to the court's shock and horror (and one person's jubilation), he was found dead the following morning. This was another brilliant move; two enemies had been defanged in one stroke—Parvataka, to contemplate his life in his afterlife and Rakshasa, to contemplate his elderly but very dangerous opponent who was clearly miles ahead of him. All fight momentarily oozed out of the latter; other minor contenders to the throne hurriedly opted for the discretion-over-valour policy and rehearsed their speeches of loyalty to Chandragupta. And with his perfect resolution of this potentially sordid mess, Kautilya began to soar even higher in Chandragupta's estimation.

Everything fell into place very quickly after that. Chandragupta became the new ruler of Magadha and Kautilya, his hair firmly knotted and his thrill of sweet revenge firmly suppressed, began to devote his extraordinary mind to getting the kingdom together and, basically, keeping everything in place. If we go by the *Mudrarakshasa*, though, it was not exactly easy. The populace was bewildered and annoyed at having to keep up with these constant changes at the helm, and Parvataka's son, Malayaketu, suddenly became fractious and demanded that the throne go to him as his father's heir. Fortunately, the ambiguously-worded treaty that the duo had concluded with Parvataka while initially roping him in had *not* mentioned an heir (Kautilya thinking several steps ahead, as usual!) and this was now waved in Malayaketu's face. However, Rakshasa, the inveterate brooder, chose this moment to join Malayaketu's ranks and revive his 'anyone-but-Chandragupta' campaign.

However, fortune favours the brave—or the wily, depending on how you choose to interpret the word—and Kautilya (who was both!) threw his all into forcing these two main irritants off the scene. What happened, thereafter, is full of intricate detail and would make your head swim but suffice it to say that Kautilya managed to get hold of Rakshasa's signet ring (hence, *mudrarakshasa*, the title of the play) from his unsuspecting wife and used it on a forged letter to convince Malayaketu that the minister had ordered his father, Parvataka's death. This had a predictable end: Rakshasa could not argue his way out of this and the two allies had an acrimonious parting of ways. Subsequently, Kautilya, in recognition of Rakshasa's stubborn determination and dogged loyalties (however misplaced!), co-opted him onto Chandragupta's side, intending to use his special skills for the latter's benefit, at some future date.

While all these political permutations and combinations were going on, the people were running riot in every sense of the term. It is a simple equation (and always has been through the ages)—when there is no tangible leader, small-time thugs *will* emerge and create chaos. And the populace of the erstwhile-Nanda-now-Maurya realm, to begin with, was as variegated a mix as one could find, comprising foreigners at the north-western end, jostling with people in different stages of social evolution in the heartland and elsewhere—tribes, nomads, townsfolk, rural folk, religious sects, linguistic cultures and so on and so forth. No easy matter to rule this unwieldy entity whose denizens were, in any case, irritable and bewildered with the political changes and general chaos!

And so it was, at that point, and the victorious duo hastened to mend matters on a war footing. Anyone recruited in Chandragupta's cause had to be incorruptible and principled and intelligent—and, presumably, there were loads of such people around because the ranks filled up quite quickly with Kautilya keeping an eagle eye over them all. His spy network was already doing yeoman service in keeping plots and pretenders at bay, freeing him to scout around for a suitable person to employ as Pataliputra's mayor (*nagar-adhyaksha*)—a key position deserving of a worthy incumbent.

Kautilya's methods and motives were always rather odd and this case, too, was no exception. The story goes that while he was walking around the city (no doubt keeping an eye on everyone and everything), he came upon a weaver who was, inexplicably, setting fire to large portions of his own house. This demanded a closer scrutiny and Kautilya interrogated the man. It turned out that this was the weaver's radical solution to ridding his house of a bug infestation—and Kautilya immediately knew that he had found his man, the logic being that if he could burn his *own* house to stamp out bugs, then he could, equally, go to drastic lengths to stamp out lawlessness. This was a bit of a shot in the dark but the weaver took over his new responsibility with fervour and ferocity, justifying Kautilya's foray into human psychology. Of course, there is a parallel Buddhist story that talks of Chandragupta summoning a former acquaintance, Maunitapasvi/Maniyatappo, to restore order in the city, which he promptly succeeding in doing.

And that, as they say, was that. The rest of the Magadhan realm followed Pataliputra's example and settled down to a normal life, presumably gossiping about their young and charming king, and enjoying their release from Dhana Nanda's exactions. Chandragupta, in turn, settled down to the onerous duties of rulership with, of course, Kautilya breathing down his neck but in a different way. As noted elsewhere, we presume that he followed Kautilya's rigorous regimen, which demanded a lot of discipline and self-restraint, and became an immensely successfully ruler—both within, where he managed to keep excellent control over his administration and subjects; and externally, where he balanced equations vis-a-vis other powers with the finesse of a fencing pro.

At the very least, this is what seems *likely*. Most of the stories surrounding the Mauryan founder are not all accorded historical veracity, especially those penned in a later period. But they also point to possibilities, events that could very well have happened, so we cannot entirely discount them. After all, there is always a kernel of truth in tales, however miniscule this may be. And in the absence of detailed corroborative information, this is all we have. But this is also the reason why Chandragupta and Kautilya are often touted as the country's first empire-builders, assembling their political spaces on the basis of broad religious and linguistic freedoms, and enabling subsequent heirs—or, at least, the first two—to slip easily into their seats and seamlessly wield the reins of Mauryan governance.

The fairly unanimous conclusion drawn by historians is that as Ashoka inherited an empire that extended over almost the entire subcontinent and even into the Karnataka region, it is very likely that all the major conquests had been made by his grandfather. He definitely controlled the Indus and Ganga plains, as also the far northwest—a formidable empire by any standards! In addition, Chandragupta's trans-Vindhyan conquests are indicated by Graeco-Roman sources. Plutarch notes that Sandrocottus overran and subdued all of India with an army of six lakh. The Junagarh inscription of Rudradaman suggests that Chandragupta's reach extended upto Saurashtra in Gujarat—and this very fact attests to his tremendous power; Saurashtra was virtually unconquerable and it was only the Mughal emperor, Akbar, who was able to emulate Chandragupta's feat, in this regard. We have already referred to Chandragupta's clash with Seleucus Nikator, the inheritor of Alexander's eastern provinces, and the territories he acquired thereby. All these indirect references indicate that Chandragupta was chiefly responsible for the massive extent of the Mauryan empire.

There is slightly more specific evidence with regard to Chandragupta and the south. A poem in the *Akananuru/ Ahananuru*, a classical Tamil poetry collection, written by a Sangam poet, Mamulanar, makes a cryptic reference to the Koshar achieving many successes against their enemies but being assisted by the Moriyas and their huge army to defeat the Mokur who stood out against them. The poet describes the Moriya chariots rolling across a swathe cut in the mountain for their onward march. Another poem by the same poet states that the warlike Vadugar formed the vanguard of the Mauryan army on its southern march. The word means 'northerners' and refers to the people of the Andhra-Karnataka region and to the north of the Tamil country. Reading between these random and somewhat disconnected references, the storyline is clear: the Mauryans actively interfered in the politics of the south, they had an alliance with a southern power called the Koshar of north Karnataka, and local troops of the Deccan formed part of the Mauryan army.

However, what usually excites most historians are the intriguing references in later inscriptions and Jaina texts that seem to connect Chandragupta to Jainism and, more specifically, Karnataka. The Jaina tradition speaks eloquently of the relationship between Chandragupta and the Jaina saint, Bhadrabahu. A severe famine in the Magadha area prompted Bhadrabahu to lead a Jaina migration southward (he predicted it would last twelve years); Chandragupta followed him as his disciple, later the chief one, and after an ascetic existence of some years on a hill in Shravana-belagola named Chandragiri (apparently in his honour), died of ritual starvation. An inscription of *c.* CE 600 links Bhadrabahu with 'Chandragupta *muni*' and there is other epigraphic evidence in the same vein.[6] (Subsequently, Ashoka is also connected to the area through his inscriptions, further corroborating this fact.)

Odd that the king would abandon his throne and people so precipitately but, as noted elsewhere, he was probably sick and tired of politics and its machinations, the endless strategising and plotting. Besides, Kautilya's general hysteria and paranoia would have tried the patience of a saint. Embracing the life of one could quite conceivably have appeared to Chandragupta as a more attractive option. And perhaps this was the only excuse for his leaving Magadha that Kautilya would accept, however unwillingly. Chandragupta is eventually supposed to have observed *sallekhana* or the Jaina ritual of death by starvation. Later texts mention this story, and if one adds the inscriptions in the Shravana-belagola hills of the period between the fifth and fifteenth centuries CE that mention Chandragupta and Bhadrabahu to this, one can speculate that there might be a historical basis to this persistent Jaina tradition that links Chandragupta to Karnataka.

With his death, though, we proceed into a rather shadowy phase of Mauryan history. Admittedly, Chandragupta was himself a somewhat elusive figure but there are so many legends and stories, as well as oblique and straightforward references to him, that he has captured the public imagination in a way that very few rulers of the past have managed to do. Television adaptations of his tale abound, highly satisfying sagas of revenge and vindication, with several blue-and-green-eyed Greek women thrown in for good measure. Whether these versions possess any modicum of historical truth is a different story altogether!

Chandragupta's son and successor, Bindusara, on the other hand, inhabits the peripheral realm of known Mauryan history despite clearly being a man of much charisma and a powerful ruler of a very large kingdom to boot. Why that should be so is ascribable to one of the most enduring and intractable mysteries of history and its writing whereby some figures slip easily into perpetual obscurity while others remain larger-than-life entities whose presence is faithfully recorded in every single narrative and historical reconstruction. All we can do is try to resurrect some of the former figures so that they rise, triumphant and phoenix-like, from the ashes.

And so, we shall put this into effect with Bindusara.

Notes

1. Deepa Agarwal, *Chanakya—The Master of Statecraft*, Puffin/Penguin, p.99.
2. See, for instance, R.K. Mookerji, *Chandragupta Maurya and His Times*, Motilal Banarsidass, 1966, rpt.1988, p.165.
3. Ibid., pp.178–179.
4. Charles Allen, *Ashoka—The Search for India's Lost Emperor*, Abacus 2012, pp.367–368.
5. If you want to engage with this turbulent and very exciting period in English history (basically, the Wars of the Roses and the Tudor saga) in a painless and enjoyable way, you could read books by Philippa Gregory and/or Conn Iggulden.
6. Mookerji, *Chandragupta Maurya and His Times*, pp.39–40. Later texts like the tenth century *Brihatkathakosha* of Harishena and the nineteenth century *Rajavalikathe* narrate the story of Chandragupta's ritual death by starvation. See Upinder Singh, *A History of Ancient and Early Medieval India—From the Stone Age to the Twelfth Century*, Pearson/Dorling-Kindersley, 2008, p.331.

9

BINDUSARA

The possibility of Chandragupta Maurya having married a Greek princess (probably the daughter of Seleucus Nikator, as noted earlier; but it is unclear, in the first place, whether he was the latter's son-in-law or father-in-law) has sent many writers of fiction into transports of delight. Endless storytelling opportunities present themselves, in this regard, particularly for those who are not really worried about historical accuracy and would rather focus on the enigmatic ruler being surrounded by one or many exotic green-eyed women and spawning an exotic green-eyed brood. Unfortunately, the actual facts of history are not always as romantic or alluring as one would wish. And so, the Mauryan narrative eventually shifts from Chandragupta, not to any of his probable half-foreign offspring but to Bindusara, his very Indian son.

The story of Bindusara is interesting precisely because nothing much is known about him. This is the usual fate of people in history sandwiched between two extremely well-known characters who have caught the public imagination in one way or the other. In Bindusara's case, he is stuck between his father, Chandragupta Maurya—whose mysterious identity and meteoric rise to fame has spawned several exciting and wildly imaginative tales—and his grandson, Ashoka, whose charismatic personality and enduring legacy have ensured that he regularly figures in the list of most remarkable rulers from around the world. Caught between these two, Bindusara appears as a mere apology—a postscript, as it were, to the goings-on in the Mauryan empire. You catch him peeping from the annals of history but disappearing just as fast so that you sometimes wonder whether he really existed at all. And, of course, his name is routinely mixed-up with Bimbisara's so that their two selves often meld in public memory into one confusing entity. (Bimbisara, of course, was the one who steered Magadha to political glory in the sixth century BCE and was the sinister Ajatashatru's father.)

So why did Bindusara disappear and is he worth devoting an entire chapter to other than in the interests of a sequential Mauryan narrative? Let us examine the evidence for ourselves keeping in mind the fact—reiterated earlier—that writers of historical narratives are notoriously selective when it comes to compiling lists of past rulers and their deeds. Some make the final cut and some don't—it is as simple and unfortunate as that! But, then, even early Buddhist sources are not particularly enthusiastic about Bindusara and are stingy with details on him. His interest in and/or preoccupation with the rival Ajivika sect might have had something to do with it. Conventional histories note that Bindusara ruled the Mauryan empire between around 297 and 273 BCE. But let us begin at the beginning—with the rather gory story of his birth.

As recounted in the previous chapters, Kautilya more or less dictated the course of Chandragupta's ascendancy to the Mauryan throne but continued to be jittery about the latter's hold on it. Admittedly, it was a tenuous one, at first—as was to be expected—but Kautilya honed suspicion to a fine art, purportedly seeing potential assassins and schemers lurking everywhere at court. His fevered imagination had Chandragupta strangled, stabbed and murdered in varied ways, and he soon became increasingly convinced that poison would be the chosen method of the dastardly (albeit hitherto invisible!) villains.

Accordingly, he began to inure his protégé to poison by dint of introducing small amounts of it in his food. Thus, when the actual assault happened (and Kautilya was sure it would), Chandragupta would be none the worse for it. Kautilya did not, of course, think it necessary to inform the king of his plan and the latter, blissfully unaware of these charming exertions on his behalf, continued to consume his daily poisoned meals. One day, he invited his pregnant wife, Durdhara, to share his food and the inevitable happened: the queen barely took a bite before falling, insensible, to the floor, her face turning blue. The attendants hurried to inform Kautilya and he burst in on the scene to find the king alternately wringing his hands and exclaiming aloud at why the meal had not affected *him* at all.

Kautilya was used to thinking on his feet. Snatching up a sword, he raced to the dying queen's side and—grotesque as this sounds—sliced off her head and cut open her womb, taking her unborn baby out into the world. As he did so, some drops of blood splattered the baby's forehead, thus conveniently solving the problem of a name for him—Bindusara (*bindu*/spot). At this point, there are several colourful textual versions that vie with each other in being increasingly bizarre. One claims that as the baby was taken out prematurely, Kautilya sealed him in an ewe's womb (or a succession of ewes' wombs) for some months till the whole tiresome process of cutting it open and taking him out was repeated. Once again, drops of blood splashed his forehead, hence his name. Others claim that the poison left a blue spot on his forehead, hence his name. Whichever way you look at it, though, Bindusara's seems to have been a very traumatic birth.

Nothing is known of Bindusara's childhood and youth but if we assume that Kautilya's strictures were adhered to, then being a prince in the Mauryan world could not have been an easy task. After all, as the venerable mentor warns, any royal family 'with undisciplined princes, will collapse under attack like a worm-eaten piece of wood'[1] and then he proceeds to expand on this theme. Accordingly, the strictest monitoring and regimen is recommended: a prince who is being groomed as the heir should not only learn words and numbers from the word go but also, at a later point, philosophy and the three Vedas 'from authoritative teachers', economics from the heads of governmental departments and the science of government from theorists as well as practising politicians,[2] along with observing some mandatory rituals—all this while, simultaneously, consorting with learned elders for maximum exposure to the merits of discipline. Thus, the prince was to be exposed to the rationale behind subjects *and* their actual working—a thorough indoctrination into the art of governance and administration, as it were!

And here is Kautilya's prescriptive daily regimen for the prince: the first part of the day was for training in the martial arts, specifically with elephants, horses, chariots and weapons; the latter part was for listening to histories and precedents; the remainder of the day and the night was for preparing new lessons for the next day, revising old lessons and listening 'repeatedly to things which he had not understood clearly'.[3] Not a single minute's let-up, then, in the young heir's schedule. Thus, with his body trained for battle and his brain crammed with learning, he could ascend the throne, in due course, as a worthy successor to his father. This is, presumably, the schedule that young Bindusara followed and the one that he would have imposed, in turn, on his chosen heir (although, as we will see, the lessons were focused on the entirely wrong person, in the latter case.)

Curiously, however, the sources are not unanimous on who succeeded Chandragupta to the Mauryan throne. Jaina texts note that he abdicated the throne in favour of his son, Simhasena. Another text refers to Chandragupta's successor as Amitraghata, or destroyer of foes, a generic title in itself but one that seems to be seconded by Greek sources, which use a similar name—Amitrochates. This is now seen as the Greek name for Bindusara. He himself makes an appearance in the records of the Mauryan empire in 297 BCE on his father's abdication of the throne.

Inheriting the massive realm must have been a bitter-sweet moment for Bindusara given that it was, quite conceivably, a logistical nightmare to govern, coupled with the fact that Chandragupta was at the other end of the country in Karnataka, where he eventually committed suicide. (Here, as noted earlier, it is tempting to speculate that Chandragupta's sudden fascination with Jainism that led him to renounce his throne and move to the opposite end of his realm might have, in part, been dictated by his being fed-up with Kautilya's endless machinations and manipulations—and, perhaps, a desire to not have his innards poisoned every single day, among other things!)

And to further complicate the historian's task, this is precisely the point where all the direct information dries up, leaving only incidental references to piece Bindusara's story together. There is evidence that Kautilya remained on the scene but this is not difficult to presume! After going to all those lengths to get Bindusara into the light, he would hardly have abandoned this untrained son of a beloved protégé to govern as he pleased. The Tibetan lama, Taranatha, in his *History of Buddhism in India* (CE 1608), talks of Kautilya as one of Bindusara's great lords who is supposed to have destroyed the nobles and kings of sixteen towns, and to have made his ruler the master of the entire territory between the eastern and western seas, which is seen as a reference to the Bay of Bengal and the Arabian Sea. Alternatively, some historians believe that this is an allusion to Bindusara's conquest of the Deccan, while others see it as indicating the suppression of a revolt.

In any case, Bindusara is credited for extending Mauryan control to Mysore. Tamil poets provide a very evocative description of the Mauryan chariots thundering across the land, their white pennants brilliant against the sunshine. So this, along with the fact of Ashoka inheriting a colossal empire, implies that Bindusara not only consolidated Chandragupta's acquisitions but also added to them in a significant way. At the time of Bindusara's death, almost the entire Indian peninsula—northern, central and eastern India, along with parts of Afghanistan and all the way up to Karnataka in the south—was under the Mauryan sway, apart from a few areas, such as Kalinga on the east coast, the Tamil kingdoms and Kerala. This was no small feat for an otherwise obscure ruler who has had no hold on the popular imagination!

Bindusara seems to have extended himself in ways other than territorial as well. Greek sources talk of his diplomatic relations with some kings of the west. Antiochus, the king of Syria (and Seleucus's son), is supposed to have sent an ambassador called Deimachus to the Mauryan court. Bindusara—in what would be construed as a distinctly undiplomatic move today—apparently requested Antiochus to buy and send him some sweet wine, dried figs and a sophist. This last petition must have confounded poor Antiochus but he seems to have recovered himself enough to send an exceedingly courteous response. He would send the wine and figs but not the sophist as Greek laws did not permit a philosopher to be bought. Presumably Bindusara wisely held his silence, thereafter. Incidentally, this desire of his has earned him a fair amount of reprobation. R.K. Mookerji, for instance, presumes, on the basis of this fig-and-wine request, that Bindusara was totally unworthy of the vast empire that his father had bequeathed him, heaps scorn on his 'easy-going disposition' and concludes, scathingly, that he 'can hardly be credited with any additions to the empire by his own conquests'.[4] The jury on this, though, could swing either way.

And here is something we must not forget: there would have been a palpable Graeco-Persian influence in the Mauryan court at this time, courtesy one of Chandragupta's wives (or Bindusara's, depending on who the original groom was), the princess of Seleucus Nikator's family. Given that Antiochus I, Seleucus's son, became the ruler of the Seleucid empire in 281 BCE, she would have been a formidable presence, at least until his death in 261 BCE. Bindusara is also supposed to have entertained Dionysius, the ambassador of Ptolemy II Philadelphos, the ruler of Egypt, but there is no evidence that he sent him a wish list of any kind.

Apart from this infuriatingly meagre evidence, there is a fragmentary inscription at Sanchi in central India, which has been seen as a possible reference to Bindusara, thereby suggesting a connection between him and this Buddhist establishment. However, before you jump to conclusions of the religious kind, there is also a story of a fortune-teller belonging to the Ajivikas, an ascetic sect of renunciation that was founded in around the sixth century BCE by one Makkhali Ghoshala,[5] who foretold Bindusara's son, Ashoka's greatness, perhaps indicating that the king favoured the Ajivikas—but we will come to this story by and by.

And now that we have come to Ashoka, we may proceed to examine the distinctly prickly relationship between father and son. There are several interesting, even curious, stories, in this regard, that dance in and out of the borders of historical fact but are worth recounting, nonetheless. The Buddhist *Ashokavadana* notes that Ashoka's mother was a queen named Subhadrangi who was the daughter of a brahmana of Champa, a well-fortified city near the Ganga, at the time, whose ruins are visible today on the outskirts of modern Bhagalpur in Bihar.[6] The story is a riveting one. It begins with a prediction made by some brahmanas to the beautiful Subhadrangi's father that she would eventually marry a king and bear two 'jewel-like sons'.

Incidentally, most stories in the ancient context commence with itinerant brahmanas uttering random prophecies and generally stirring up a lot of excitement, as a result. And, of course, beauty is a mandatory requirement for all young women who are the subject of such predictions. No story ever begins with a plain-looking girl who rises to dizzying heights! Anyway back to our story and the prophecy that concerns us: one of these worthy sons, so it went, would become a *chakravartin* (or universal ruler) with a mighty sway while the other would wander forth and fulfil his religious vows.

Subhadrangi's terribly excited father arrived in Pataliputra, daughter in tow, all set to make the prediction a reality. One can imagine poor Bindusara's bemusement, though, and his irritation at being confronted thus. Subhadrangi might have had a lovely face but he already had a harem, as well as a son, Susima, to succeed him. So there was no reason to expect that he would bound cheerfully off the throne and clasp her to his bosom. And now the story takes a very strange turn, indeed: Subhadrangi's beauty seems to have caught the eye of the other women of Bindusara's harem who, threatened by it, contrived to keep her away from Bindusara, while (and this is decidedly weird!) training her to become a barber! (This begs all sorts of questions. Whence this sudden wherewithal for the task? Were they all closet hairstylists, for instance?) And so, Bindusara went about his kingly duties, completely unaware that the newest recruit to his harem was honing her skills with hair to the point where she became a most excellent barber in time. He was given concrete proof, though, when she ended up in his chambers to groom his hair and beard—an appointment clearly arranged with much dexterity.[7]

Subhadrangi's instructors were impeccable: she was able to do her job so competently that Bindusara dropped off to sleep (much-needed, considering that he might have been following Kautilya's insane royal sleep regimen but the latter would have been horrified at this dropping of his guard!) and when he later woke, much-restored in body and spirit, magnanimously granted her a wish. Time for Subhadrangi to recite the grand prophecy and for Bindusara to retreat in horror at her proposition: how could a Kshatriya, such as he, make love to a low-caste barber woman? Time, then, for Subhadrangi to prop up the prophecy with practical details: she was a brahmana's daughter, the one who had tramped all the way from Champa to bestow her on the king. As history has repeatedly proven, rulers are nothing if not whimsical.

Bindusara promptly made Subhadrangi his chief wife and all was well except, of course, for the previous incumbent of the post and the others waiting in line who must have boiled in anger at their protégé turning rogue.

Much happiness and frolicking ensued with this royal union, culminating in Subhadrangi bearing Bindusara a son. Apparently, as soon as she set eyes on her baby, she is supposed to have exclaimed, 'I am now without sorrow!' And this is how Ashoka got his name, which literally means 'without sorrow'. Had Subhadrangi known how much sorrow her beloved baby would later unleash upon the world (at least for a length of time), she might have considered a totally different name but, as we all know, hindsight is perfect vision and does not help much in the present. She seems to have liked the name enough to confer a variation of it on her second son, Vitashoka (the ceasing of sorrow), also known as Tissa.

If we may fast-forward a little, it seems Vitashoka later abused his position as vice-regent under Ashoka until Ashoka persuaded (or forced?) him to become a Buddhist hermit, whereupon he became embroiled in a sectarian dispute—a tale bristling with treachery and mistaken identities—and was killed.[8] Incidentally, Subhadrangi is known by different names in different versions of her story. In one, that of the *Divyavadana*, she is Janapadakalyani—a real mouthful—and in another, she is Dharma.[9] The pivotal point, though, is that the original prediction worked but the one thing Subhadrangi could not have known, at the time, is that Bindusara would come to dislike his son heartily, creating all sorts of problems thereby.

Apart from having a cool head on her shoulders, as the story demonstrates, Subhadrangi also had a shrewd and pragmatic understanding of her royal husband's personality, as well as of political imperatives. This comes to the fore in another significant tale where she plays a leading role, along with an Ajivika mendicant called Pingalavatsajiva, who had been asked by Bindusara to examine his sons.[10] This was no random request—Pingalavatsajiva had the gift of scrutiny and was best suited to identifying Bindusara's successor. However, it seems that Ashoka, unwilling to be scrutinised and keenly aware of his father's dislike of him, kicked up a fuss. The *Ashokavadana* attributes Bindusara's hostility to Ashoka's rough skin and generally unattractive looks, at the time. In fact, in a recent fictional reimagining of Ashoka's life, he earns the sobriquet of 'crocodile' from his clearly sensitive step-brothers, owing to his pockmarked skin.[11] Subhadrangi, though, cajoled her beloved son into humouring his father and the net result was that as soon as Pingalavatsajiva's eye fell on Ashoka, he knew that he must succeed Bindusara to the throne.

At this juncture, the mendicant was caught on the horns of a dilemma. The troubled relationship between father and son was not exactly a secret, and inviting the royal wrath upon his head was pointless, even dangerous. Therefore, opting for discretion over plain-speak, Pingalavatsajiva revealed the truth in highly-obscure words, which, it must be confessed, must have greatly irritated Bindusara. The one 'who had the best mount, seat, drink, vessel and food', would become the next emperor, he said. This seemingly baffling pronouncement thrilled Ashoka to the core. Modesty was never one of his afflictions and so he was able to tell his mother the good news with total conviction: it was he who would succeed his father because he fulfilled all the requirements—the back of an elephant was his mount, the earth was his seat, his vessel was of clay, his food was boiled rice with curds and water was his drink.

Meanwhile, Pingalavatsajiva, who wanted to make doubly sure that he had been understood, contrived to meet Subhadrangi and told her the unvarnished truth. She promptly advised him to leave the kingdom for his own protection—if Bindusara made him spell out his prediction in clear terms, his head might very well part company with his body! Pingalavatsajiva did not tarry long; he rushed away from Magadha and only returned, it seems, when Bindusara died. The wise Subhadrangi, on the other hand, decided to remain tight-lipped about the whole affair and allow her husband to assume that the Ajivika mendicant had been babbling. It made no sense to dangle Ashoka's future greatness over Bindusara's head given their frosty relations or before her harem compatriots. Susima and his mother were alive and well, after all, and the last thing Subhadrangi wanted was to make active enemies in her own home. This time around, retribution might well go beyond hair-dressing lessons!

Stealth, secrecy, danger and coded words make for a satisfying tale, indeed. However, there are several other legends foretelling Ashoka's regnal glory in the textual tradition and differing versions of the same story in some cases. One notes that when he was in his mother's womb, the latter displayed a yearning for all sorts of odd things, which greatly puzzled Bindusara. Accordingly, he turned to the brahmanas of his court for help but they were equally bemused. Bindusara was at his wit's end when Janasana, an Ajivika known to the queen's family, stepped forward to unravel the signs and proclaim the unborn child in her womb as the future ruler of Jambudvipa (in this case, the emperor's realm but a reference to the country at large).

Incidentally, prophecies concerning Ashoka seemed to keep sporting an Ajivika motif. And as it happens, Ashoka, while on the throne, actively patronised the Ajivika sect, donating caves to them at Barabar near Gaya, remarkable for their polished interiors and glittering walls, and thereby bearing testimony to a lot of money having been invested in their creation.[12] And so, Pingalavatsajiva did not flirt with death in vain! The answer to why Ashoka and the Ajivikas are so entwined in legend depends on which end of the kaleidoscope you are peering into. This religion, in fact, completely vanished in time with no contemporary practitioners—a fate that none of its peer religions, such as Jainism and Buddhism, faced.

It seems that royal patronage to the Ajivikas extended all the way back to Ajatashatru, and the charismatic Makkhali Ghoshala, its founder, also managed to maintain cordial relations with the Buddhists and Jainas (the latter eventually souring when conversions to the Jaina faith started from within the Ajivika ranks!). Nayanjot Lahiri notes that although Ashoka's patronage of the Ajivikas was well-known, his motives thereof were unknown.[13] Therefore, it made sense to tie up these central figures in a significant way, hence the Ajivika stamp on prophecies concerning Ashoka, all of which were made several centuries *after* Ashoka and contained in the *Ashokavadana*, as noted earlier.

This, as Lahiri notes, is a fairly common narrative device when it comes to important figures in the Buddhist tradition—one, we may add, that was also borrowed by other textual traditions. Nothing really comes as a surprise, therefore: every central figure is well-accounted for—via heavenly portents and planetary configurations and mysterious signs conveyed by birds and animals—a long time before he (and it is always a 'he'; women figures aren't ever central nor is there any excitement surrounding them!) appears on the scene.

There are other tantalising suggestions in the textual

sources that hint at Bindusara's deep dislike for Ashoka. If true, this would have created endless complications for the future of the Mauryan dynasty and, particularly, for Ashoka at the time. There are differing versions of this hostility, though. Most sources agree that when Ashoka came of age, he was appointed the governor of Ujjaiyini. He might have held a similar post in the highly recalcitrant province of Taxila earlier or been sent there to suppress a revolt.[14] In any case, we know that he was given some sort of valuable administrative training during Bindusara's reign, which clearly served to strengthen his claim to the throne, at a subsequent stage.

Incidentally, Ashoka wasn't particularly unique, in this regard. If we fast-forward a bit through history, princes who had cut their teeth in rough areas usually managed to get the throne. The Mughal emperor, Aurangzeb, springs to mind. His father, Shahjahan, is rumoured to have disliked him in similar fashion and sent him to govern the unruly Deccan, whereupon the whole plan boomeranged on him and the newly-toughened Aurangzeb shoved him off the throne and imprisoned him.

Taxila seems to have had a critical part to play in the relationship between father and son.[15] The name itself was a Greek abbreviation of the original Takshashila, which, according to them, was the foremost city of Punjab. It is, in fact, a conglomeration of many sites pertaining to cities, with the ruins of Buddhist stupas and monasteries scattered around it. The people and the settlement of what is known today as the Bhir mound are the ones connected with Ashoka—and here it is the *Ashokavadana* that recounts its juicy details. It seems that Taxila, always a turbulent area, had risen in rebellion against Bindusara and he decided to send

Ashoka there to quell it. He gave him a pretty decent army for this purpose, consisting of a cavalry, elephants, chariots and infantry but—here's the catch—without any weapons.

The mysterious logic of providing a toothless army to his son to subdue a troublesome province was known only to Bindusara. If we are inclined to be charitable, we could presume a paucity of weapons in the Mauryan realm, which is why he could not provision Ashoka's army, in the first place. However, given that there are no known blips in the Mauryan power, at the time, or any known lessening of its hold on its massive territory, this seems highly unlikely. If we scrape the bottom of the barrel further, we could assume that the Mauryan blacksmiths had suddenly gone on strike or begun to suffer unaccountable fits of indolence. Both these are ludicrous assumptions. Bindusara might even have hoped that the very sight of the imperial army would strike fear in the heart of the Taxila rebels and cause them to give in. Yet, a mighty ruler such as him did not get to where he was by taking stupid risks and being delusional in military matters.

So the only plausible reason was that Bindusara *wanted* Ashoka to make a fool of himself in Taxila and, subsequently, crawl back to the capital with his tail between his legs. This would, then, effectively remove him as a serious contender to the throne. Crushed by his failure, his image irrevocably tarnished, Ashoka would retire to a life in the shadows and brood over what might have been. And Bindusara would get to choose his own successor, after all, without having to consider his odd son or the growing rumblings in his favour. In the light of what actually transpired, though, this was an eminently laughable proposition. The *Ashokavadana* throws a generous sparkling of magic—and divinity—over it all. It seems that when the obedient—and completely oblivious—

Ashoka was about to leave Pataliputra for Taxila, he was apprised of the situation by his apprehensive attendants. (One wonders why he did not think of inspecting his army beforehand, though!)

Ashoka, none deterred, apparently declared that if his merit was enough to make him king, weapons of war would appear before him. And lo and behold! As soon as the words issued from his mouth, the earth cracked open and sundry deities themselves brought forth the much-needed arms. Barely breaking his stride, therefore, Ashoka went off on his task. What happened, thereafter, is even more mysterious. It seems that when he arrived in Taxila with his fearsome army, which was bristling with (divine) weapons, not a single sword needed to be unsheathed because the people rushed out to welcome him, claiming that they had absolutely no problem with him or Bindusara but had been oppressed by 'evil ministers'.[16]

Now let us make it quite clear, at this juncture, that there is no corroborative record of Ashoka's campaign in Taxila nor does he breathe a word about it in his edicts, although the latter is in consonance with his complete reticence about his life prior to becoming king. (Why would he want to boast about the unsavoury steps he took to wrest power and his generally maniacal episodes of violence, when he is trying hard to convey an image of compassion and benevolence?) So we only have the *Ashokavadana*'s word on his armed-but-peaceful presence in Taxila, which, as Lahiri points out, rather conveniently ties in with his later textual representations as an 'iron-wheeled monarch' (*ayash-chakravartin*) who is supposed to have ruled Jambudvipa (India) with the threat rather than the actual use of the sword.[17]

However, the city of Taxila definitely bears many traces

of an association with Ashoka, so perhaps there is no need to be sceptical, in this regard. Lahiri, for instance, notes that its most impressive Buddhist monument was a stupa whose name, Dharmarajika, refers to Ashoka (it denotes a religious structure built by the Dharmaraja of the Buddhists, the emperor Ashoka). She also notes that the title by which Ashoka was known in his edicts, Priyadarshi, was used in an Aramaic inscription found at Taxila on a white marble pillar. That the word refers implicitly to Ashoka is clear from the message of non-violence towards creatures and obedience to the aged that is enjoined upon its readers.[18] This is a fortuitous reconstruction because this entire Mauryan episode has left no material trace and remains largely unconnected with the finds of the archaeological excavations at Taxila, painstakingly conducted by John Marshall of the Archaeological Survey of India (ASI) from 1913.[19]

So, quite clearly, Bindusara's grand plan fell on its head. That the prince was able to restore peace in Taxila without using a single weapon simply added another halo to his head and was recounted as yet another miracle in a life rife with them. There is no evidence of Bindusara's reaction, in this regard, but if our conjecture is true, he must have gnashed his teeth in private and wracked his brain for more ways to abase his son. To find more clues regarding this problematic relationship, we need to turn to the *Ashokavadana* again, which, obligingly, throws up more pointers. That Bindusara disliked Ashoka because of his ugly appearance is one of its claims, as noted above. Of course this creates the immediate impression that Bindusara was actually a very handsome man and felt affronted, in some way, that his son did not take after him in the looks department.

It could, equally, be the opposite case: perhaps Bindusara

was nothing much to look at and was, therefore, disappointed that his son was clearly going to perpetuate this legacy. Or could there have been some sinister palace intrigue in the making that prevented Ashoka from getting what he wanted? Whatever the reason, it seems that Bindusara wanted another of his sons, Susima, to succeed him but Ashoka was strongly supported by the Mauryan ministers. A minister named Radhagupta, who appears to have been Kautilya's protégé and/or relative, seems to have played a particularly pivotal role in resolving this impasse.

The *Ashokavadana* claims that Susima had slapped the bald head of Radhagupta's father in jest but this raised alarm bells in court over his obvious arrogance, making the ministers wonder what he would be like once he became king, hence the pro-Ashoka coalition. Meanwhile, Susima was sent to quell Taxila that had risen in revolt (again!) but a dying Bindusara recalled him, ordering Ashoka to take over the task. However, Radhagupta and the other ministers smeared Ashoka's body with red turmeric to make him appear too sick to travel but a little later, the latter appeared in complete royal regalia before Bindusara, demanding to be made temporary ruler. This apparently infuriated Bindusara so much that he vomited blood and died. We do not know if his deathbed scene was this dramatic but, all the same, Bindusara's death in 273 BCE precipitated a four-year succession conflict, involving copious quantities of blood and gore before the situation was resolved.

Kautilya rears his head again further on in Bindusara's reign. That he was retained by the latter for his services has already been noted but there is an eventual twist to their relationship that develops, engendered, in part, by mischief-makers at court and in part by Bindusara's alleged arrogance.

The story goes that the young and fairly lost Bindusara, who suddenly found himself king upon his father's abdication of the throne, begged Kautilya to stay on in court and guide him, which the venerable mentor agreed to do. However, after a point—and seeing Bindusara come into his own, he apparently retired by degrees from the hub of affairs.

The news of Chandragupta's death in far-off Karnataka was a bit of a body-blow to both—more so, one imagines, to Kautilya. After all, a significant part of his life had been devoted to Chandragupta's concerns and it is reasonable to presume that both were extremely close, even if the latter might have chafed at Kautilya's restrictions at times. Even if one imagines Kautilya writing away to assuage his grief (presuming he wrote the *Arthashastra* and at this very time!), he must have felt miserable and hollow, and, if the stories are to be believed, unwilling to continue with his duties as the prime minister.

At this juncture, there was no doubt in Kautilya's mind that Radhagupta would be the best fit—and he resolved to tell Bindusara so. Before he could act, though, Subandhu, another prime ministerial candidate and a stereotypical villain lurking around in the Mauryan court, struck—or, rather, blabbed. And the story he spilt into Bindusara's outraged ears was the one involving his birth and, therefore, the gory details of his mother's belly being cut open by Kautilya, leading to her death. Bindusara apparently flew into a right royal rage and demanded Kautilya's presence forthwith to explain himself.

The story goes that Kautilya, upon hearing this, was nonchalant. Once the dust settled down, Bindusara would believe *him*, after all, over any random gossipmonger. However, he was very disappointed in the king's credulity, of his being so impressionable that he instantly believed any rumours he heard. One imagines that Kautilya saw the empire he had so carefully constructed falling about his ears and ruing that he had not taught his second protégé better. He might, equally, have kicked himself for not divulging the dramatic circumstances of Bindusara's birth to him earlier. One suspects it was due to the fact that Kautilya appeared as the villain whichever way you saw it—for feeding Chandragupta bits of poison and making him inherently dangerous and/or slicing his wife's stomach open. One could, of course, argue that he was protecting both father and son but it was a deeply flawed argument, nonetheless.

Fortunately, there was a way out of all the stress and angst: Kautilya had been planning to renounce the world for a while now (Chandragupta's decision, in this regard, might very well have spurred his) and he felt this was the right time to take the step. He decided to ignore the royal summons and asked Radhagupta for his help—his possessions were to be donated and a cow-dung heap, which was to be his pyre, prepared for him to sit on and end his life. And so, while Bindusara was contemplating all sorts of horrible punishments for his mentor, the latter was calmly preparing to renounce the world. However, news, particularly of the bad kind, always travels fast and the city was soon agog, everyone waiting to see which way things would pan out. Predictably, the king was the only one left in the dark!

At this point, several things happened at once in the manner of all good stories. A messenger arrived from Kautilya to Bindusara, conveying his regrets at not being able to come before him. There were more pressing things to focus on, such as his own death. Before the dumbfounded king could react, an old woman rushed into the court, demanding to be heard and identifying herself as his old nurse who had cared for him since his birth. A bewildered Bindusara was now subjected to the same long story but with the facts turned the other way around in that his very birth and existence were attributable to Kautilya's quick thinking and courage. The blue dot on Bindusara's forehead was cited as clinching evidence. (She is also supposed to have sung Bindusara a lullaby that he recognised as *additional* clinching evidence!) By the end of her plea, Bindusara had rapidly revised his views and rushed out, chockfull of remorse, to apologise to Kautilya.

As it happened, though, he was too late despite his rushing wildly through the capital's streets to get to Kautilya's abode. The mentor of all mentors was already half-submerged by flames and although Bindusara apparently roared and wept and did his best to extricate him from the pyre, nothing worked. Some versions of the tale claim that he killed the treacherous Subandhu in his rage while others propose a gentler ending to the latter's story. And that, as they say, was that. Kautilya was presumably reunited with his beloved Chandragupta in a better place while a suitably chastened Bindusara appointed Radhagupta as his new prime minister, in deference to his mentor's wish, and went on with life and ruling. The Tibetan Taranatha adds a twist to Kautilya's end, though. Steering clear of any conspiracy angle, he attributes Kautilya's death to a disease that came on owing to the demoniac powers he possessed, and which he used to kill the kings and ministers of sixteen major kingdoms. We will not go down *that* path!

Would Ashoka have met his grandfather, Chandragupta? The answer is, yet again, an unclear one. According to one version, Ashoka evoked the latter's affection and admiration by his obvious intelligence and fighting acumen. Chandragupta's changing priorities, however, had him throwing his sword away and becoming a Jaina but Ashoka found and held on to this important weapon despite his grandfather's disapproval. It is more likely, though, that Ashoka was extremely young, probably little more than a toddler, when Chandragupta was around, so the sword incident could not really have happened. Or, perhaps, their paths did not cross at all!

Incidentally, Ashoka is credited by the Pali chronicles, *Mahavamsa* and *Dipavamsa*, with killing ninety-nine of his brothers and sparing just one, Tissa. That Bindusara had a hundred and one sons is stretching the limits of our credulity somewhat but that Ashoka indulged in some sort of bloodbath to get the Mauryan throne seems fairly plausible. In the *Ashokavadana*'s version of events, he apparently managed to become king after getting rid of the legitimate heir, Susima, by tricking him into entering a pit filled with live coals.[20] A highly unpalatable route to power but one that many contenders to the throne in ancient and medieval India adopted, employing different permutations and combinations of violence to grasp the reins.

And so, 'Ashoka the Fierce' takes his place on the Mauryan stage.

Notes

1. L.N. Rangarajan, ed. and trans. *Kautilya—The Arthashastra*, Penguin, 1992, p. 131, 1.17.22–27.
2. Ibid., p.119, 1.5.7–10.
3. Ibid., p.120, 1.5.11–13, 15, 16.
4. R.K. Mookerji, *Chandragupta Maurya and His Times*, Motilal Banarsidass, 1966, rpt.1988, p.39.
5. See, for instance, Basham, A.L., *History and Doctrine of the Ajivikas—A Vanished Indian Religion*, Motilal Banarsidass, 1951, rpt 2009.
6. Nayanjot Lahiri, *Ashoka in Ancient India*, Permanent Black, 2015, p.31; see also J.S. Strong, *The Legend of King Ashoka: A Study and Translation of the Ashokavadana,* Motilal Banarsidass, 1989,

rpt 2008, p.204. The *Ashokavadana* is considered part of the Northern Buddhist tradition, while the Sri Lankan chronicles, the *Mahavamsa* and *Dipavamsa* belong to the Southern tradition.

7. Incidentally, Bindusara's beard would have been a normal colour. There is no evidence that he dyed it orange, for instance, as did the kings of early Kashmir!
8. See Charles Allen, *Ashoka—The Search for India's Lost Emperor*, Abacus, 2012, pp.378, 386.
9. This was as per the Southern Buddhist tradition; Dharma's father was an Ajivika named Janasana. However, the northern tradition is more favoured, and it is Subhadrangi and her story that it focuses on. See ibid., p.373.
10. Lahiri, *Ashoka in Ancient India*, p.34.
11. I. Allan Sealy, *Asoca: A Sutra*, Penguin, 2021.
12. For a description of the caves, see Lahiri, *Ashoka in Ancient India*, pp.229-235.
13. Ibid., pp.37–38.
14. Ujjayini was the political and administrative centre of the province of Avanti. Also, if Taxila seems to have been in a state of continuous ferment, there are extenuating reasons. It had been fairly independent until the coming of the Mauryas and the latter's control might well have annoyed its people. And the Mauryas might not have been particularly diplomatic in dealing with this outlying city. See Romila Thapar, *Asoka and the Decline of the Mauryas*, Oxford University Press, 3rd edn, 2021, p.27. See also Lahiri, *Ashoka in Ancient India*, p.64, 73–74. Among Kautilya's recommendations for dealing with disaffected royal sons was to send them off to the frontier or some distant region where they might, hopefully, disappear. Perhaps Bindusara hoped that Ashoka would be swallowed up by Taxila.
15. Incidentally, this city lacked a drainage system, so was probably somewhat unpleasant to navigate! For more details of this sort and a detailed description of Taxila at the time, see Lahiri, *Ashoka in Ancient India*, pp.66–86. See also Upinder Singh, *A History of Ancient and Early Medieval India—From the Stone Age to the Twelfth Century*, Pearson/Dorling Kindersley, 2008, pp.265, 281 for details of the identification of Taxila by Alexander Cunningham and the city itself.

16. Lahiri, *Ashoka in Ancient India*, p.67; J.S. Strong, *The Legend of King Ashoka: A Study and Translation of the Ashokavadana,* Motilal Banarsidass, 1989, rpt 2008, p.208.
17. Lahiri, *Ashoka in Ancient India*, pp.67–68.
18. Ibid., p.68; B.N. Mukherjee, *Studies in the Aramaic Edicts of Asoka*, Indian Museum Calcutta, 1984, p.26.
19. Incidentally, this is the same John Marshall who is connected with announcing the discovery of the Indus Valley or Harappan civilisation but that is a different story altogether. See Nayanjot Lahiri, *Finding Forgotten Cities—How the Indus Civilization was Discovered*, Hachette/Permanent Black, 2005, rpt 2011.
20. See Allen, *Ashoka—The Search for India's Lost Emperor*, pp.189–190 for details of the artificial elephant and trick image of Ashoka that Radhagupta had thought up as part of the diabolical plan.

10

ASHOKA'S EARLY DAYS AS KING

Interestingly, Ashoka might very well have suffered the same fate as his father, Bindusara, and been relegated to the shadows of history had it not been for some eminently serendipitous discoveries that are regularly—and marvellously—made by clever people and that pump fresh blood, as it were, into the discipline. It is not as if he was entirely forgotten through the ages but living on in scraps of public memory and exerting a sort of covert influence is not the same as bursting into the public realm as a real flesh-and-blood character, which he did when the key to his voice was unlocked by James Prinsep, epigraphist and ardent Indologist.

So how did the (re)discovery of Ashoka come about and what did it entail? As with all genuine historical findings, its roots lay way back in time but we can sort of pinpoint it to the reign of the Mughal emperor, Jahangir, in the seventeenth century. An English traveller named Thomas Coryat, who had, incredibly, walked from England to Delhi, glimpsed, in 1616, a gleaming sandstone pillar soaring over the ruins of the Firoz Shah Kotla complex that had been built by Firoz/Firuz Shah Tughlak of the Tughlak sultanate in Delhi. Examining it at close quarters, he presumed that the inscription on the pillar was in Greek and, therefore, precipitately concluded that it pertained to Alexander of Macedon.

Matters remained as they were until John Marshall, who worked with the British East India Company and was later destined to become pivotal to the historical sphere in India as the first director-general of the Archaeological Survey of India (ASI), spotted an inscribed pillar in Bihar with a carved lion as its capital. Similar pillars were discovered in Allahabad, Nepal and other places—and similar writing found carved on rock faces as far west as Gujarat and as far south as Mysore. Excitement began to grow in historical circles, as is usual when a deep mystery is sensed. To add to the general fervour, James Todd, who had discovered the Girnar rock inscriptions (cited earlier), described how the massive rock had been virtually converted into a book with the aid of an 'iron pen', each inscribed letter being almost two feet high.

It was rapidly becoming clear that these messages were connected with some royal personage who probably controlled many regions in India and even beyond. Frantic research commenced from all quarters but neither the Puranic lists of kings nor the corpus of deciphered epigraphic material seemed to fit this nameless ruler, who, additionally, was using a script of 'pin men' to say something, which had no relation to either Gupta Brahmi or Kutila, the two known scripts that were identified by scholars as early forms of Sanskrit. Attempting to flesh out a mysterious and elusive figure who did not use an intelligible form of communication, and who seemed as vague and insubstantial as a shadow, was a baffling and frustrating endeavour but there were many enthusiasts who plunged headlong into the task. Yet destiny is notoriously capricious in its conferral of achievements, as we know, and so to James Prinsep fell the honour, in this regard—although he was already standing on the shoulders of giants, such as William Jones, for one, whose stellar work on the chronology of Magadha, and the synchronicity between the Greek and Indian sources of the time, had already unlocked huge parts of the puzzle.[1]

Arriving in India in 1819 as the Assistant Assay-Master of the Mint in Calcutta, Prinsep, a passionate scientist and inventor by training and inclination, instantly fell in love with the country and threw himself into the study of its past, while also designing sewers and bazaars, and an ingenious steam-powered mechanism to operate fans and musical organs—so that he could work and keep cool and enjoy music, at the same time—as well as using his artistic skills to capture his surroundings through a series of charming etchings (his delightful sketches on Banaras come to mind). While studying the coin collection of the Asiatic Society, of which he was a member, the 'pin men' caught his eye and he was fascinated, to put it mildly. Accordingly, he set in motion a mammoth enterprise—that of getting people across the country to make more tracings of similar inscriptions on rocks so that he could collate and study them. It was an eclectic crew that responded to his call, some of them being truly memorable—and idiosyncratic—personalities.

Take the case of Lieutenant Markham Kittoe who discovered an inscribed rock at Dhauli in Orissa in 1837. It seems he had had a skirmish with a bear, at an earlier point, and reached Dhauli only to find its fully-grown cubs staking claim to the area near the rock. Undaunted, Kittoe skulked about till dawn when he climbed to the rock and cut off two forked tree boughs so that he could stand on them to make his tracing of the inscription. The bears had presumably left by then but Kittoe had other woes in store for him. The bearer, whom he had tasked with keeping the boughs steady, fell asleep and slackened his hold whereupon Kittoe, absorbed in his task, made the cardinal mistake of forgetting his 'ticklish footing', lost his balance and pitched headlong down the Dhauli rock.

Fortunately for all concerned, he fell on his hands, receiving nothing more than a few bruises and a blow to his ego. Pausing to rest and reflect on the vagaries of fate—and, presumably, the animal kingdom—Kittoe then resumed his task, which was an inherently messy endeavour, involving smearing the rock face with printer's ink or a red colour, pressing a thin cloth over it, letting it dry and then slowly peeling it off so as to carefully preserve the tracing. Not a job for the ham-handed, this one, but the only workable solution when dealing with gigantic rocks and pillars that were over forty feet tall!

Nevertheless, Prinsep was not always able to obtain clear tracings from his amateur historians. The pillars in question were often broken or the rocks had developed cracks and, what is more, the inscriptions themselves had been slowly but surely fading over time, a span that we now know to be over two thousand years. Also, not all these enthusiasts treated the evidence with the same respect and caution. Take the case of Walter Elliot who seems to have defaced the Jauguda Rock Edict near Bhuvaneshwar in Odisha that he initially found in a pristine condition in around 1850. In 1854, after he left the area, it was discovered that he had tried to prise out the inscription from the rock by (according to the local villagers) throwing 'a quantity of hot tamarind juice and water' on it and then beating the rock with hammers, causing a large part of the inscribed portion to break off.

Elliot wasn't really identified and the question of the Jaugada vandal was eventually dropped but all fingers point to him as the prime suspect.

Undeterred by these bumps and glitches, though, Prinsep slaved away at his self-appointed task, studying the clues with dogged determination and loath to give up on this seemingly intractable mystery. For four years, he puzzled over the 'pin men' script in Calcutta's humid haze while most of his ilk disappeared into the hills for a respite from the heat. In 1837, a set of epigraphic tracings arrived from Sanchi in Madhya Pradesh, taken from the railings and gateways of a stupa and a fragmented pillar beside it. The pillar, apparently, had been uprooted and broken by a local zamindar to use as a sugarcane press.

Now before you raise your eyebrows at this, you should remember that most historical artefacts (at least, before they are dubbed as such) are treated with casual disdain by people all around the world—an aspect that enormously complicates the work of historians. Ancient pottery fragments are flung around in the interests of construction and will, quite often, pave the roads that you travel on. Epigraphs will often be buttressed by ardent etchings by modern-day couples, professing their love for each other or their valuable opinions about existence, such that the original material is obscured or damaged. People will lean lovingly on pillars to get their profiles shot and uploaded on social media, leaving their grubby prints all over the surface. And, of course, we should not forget that universal scourge of museums—the peculiar breed of people who, despite the express prohibition, will sneak in 'flash' shots of relics, undismayed by the likelihood of damaging valuable pieces of historical evidence, in the process. A stoic and stubborn species, this!

Let us return from our ranting to the tale of Prinsep, who, while viewing the Sanchi tracings, immediately realised that these inscriptions were shorter than most, ending with what appeared to be the same word of three letters—although these still remained largely impenetrable squiggles. Wracking his brain, he recollected the many donative inscriptions in Sanskrit that he had seen on temple walls and pillars in different places that recorded donations made by varied categories of devotees. The one word that always characterised these epigraphs was *danam* or 'the gift of'.

Working on the presumption that this was the last word in the Sanchi tracings, he identified three letters—D, N and M (or their equivalent). Eventually, the 'pin men' script resolved itself into what Prinsep called Ashokan Brahmi, written in Pali, an ancient language that existed alongside Sanskrit and used by the common people. Enlisting the help of scholars who could read the sacred Tibetan Buddhist texts, which used Pali, a light appeared at the end of this linguistic tunnel—these were inscriptions that recorded donations made to a Buddhist monastery in Sanchi by people who had lived two thousand years ago.

Prinsep promptly tackled the longer inscriptions and discovered to his joy that they all began with the same phrase *Devanampiye piyadassi raja hevam aha* (when transcribed into Sanskrit, *Devanampriya priyadarshi raja…*) or 'The beloved of the gods, Piyadassi raja declares…' Here was a huge Eureka moment—a king named Piyadassi was making a declaration to his subjects. The tone was benevolent, sometimes remorseful, usually caring. But there remained the mystery of his identity, helped very little by the speaker's offhand remark, off and on, that he was *raja magadhe*, indicating that he ruled Magadha but finding no parallel in any extant list of kings.

The tale is a long and complicated one, paved with tremendous hard work and fortunate discoveries that helped in putting the mammoth jigsaw together.[2] After collating all the information that was coming in not just as regards the inscribed surfaces but also other pertinent finds, and with key evidence provided by the Sri Lankan Pali chronicles, everything suddenly fell into place for Prinsep. His decipherment of the Brahmi script in question, his translations of the Sanchi and other donations and his identification of the Beloved of the Gods, Devanampiya Piyadasi, as Ashoka Maurya awed the historical world in general and his fellow Orientalists, in particular. Prinsep, on the basis of his translations, was even able to provide a rough chronology of events in Ashoka's rule that spanned the Kalinga war and his creation of the machinery of dhamma.

In Charles Allen's excellent narrative history of the 'discovery' of Ashoka in the nineteenth century, the atmosphere connected with it appears to be electric—and understandably so, charged, as it was, with the epigraphic evidence—facsimiles of the writings on rocks and pillars all over the country—that archaeologists, history-enthusiasts and others were sending in to the Asiatic Society of Bengal. There are all sorts of fascinating tales that form a part of the larger Ashoka quest, both of Prinsep's vintage and much later, such as Anton Führer being authorised in 1895 to cross the border into Nepal on an elephant to examine an inscribed pillar known locally as Bimasena ki Nigali (Bhim Sen's smoking pipe). It was discovered to be Ashoka's Nigali Sagar Pillar Edict, which, along with the one at Lumbini/Rummindei, were results of his royal tour in around 250 BCE.[3]

Nevertheless, with Prinsep's brilliant decipherment, Ashoka suddenly burst out of the darkness into the light, as it were;

thence commenced a fascination with this figure amongst historical circles that has not ceased till today. Painstakingly compiled compendiums began to emerge. Mention must be made, in this regard, of Alexander Cunningham's *Inscriptions of Asoka* (and here we must hasten to add that in historian-speak, which involves the addition of diacritical marks to aid pronunciation, this *is* the correct way to spell his name, along with the diacritical mark on the 's'—not Asoca, for instance, a recently-used version of it that, unfortunately, would end up being pronounced as Asocha, which is an unwarranted mangling of the original name!).[4]

Incidentally, Cunningham, himself the first director general of the Archaeological Survey of India (ASI), compiled the available epigraphs into the first volume of the *Corpus Inscriptionum Indicarum*, a Bible of sorts for anyone venturing into that period of history. The series itself is mandatory reading for any historian: it makes available all the epigraphic evidence of ancient India through different dedicated volumes. The one on Ashoka, though, had the added benefit of Cunningham's personal exploration of the Ashokan sites that preceded his compilation. Ashoka's epigraphs in the south were discovered later, though—they are not part of this volume.

Lest all this conveys the impression that we were, basically, waiting for the British to come and discover Ashoka, we must add that the onus did not lie on them. Nor did we know *nothing* about him until enlightenment dawned on us courtesy the history enthusiasts of the colonial era. As mentioned earlier, Ashoka was not just the focus of several chronicles, featuring in textual tradition down the ages, but also appeared in local legends from time to time, and was known to a select group of Indian scholars and Buddhist communities across Asia.[5]

In fact, as Charles Allen argues, the disappearance of 'Ashoka's Song', his resounding voice and persona, might have been intrinsically linked to his promotion of Buddhism and his consequent removal from historical records compiled over generations by those who felt threatened by it.[6] So Ashoka was not exactly a gift of the Englishmen to us; rather, they managed to nudge him out from relative obscurity into the public glare, there to remain while his extraordinary deeds captured the imagination of generation after generation and his epigraphs continue to be discovered to the present day, turning up fresh information to be considered and analysed.

And, of course, not all those connected with his resurrection were Europeans. The Indian archaeologist, Bhagwanlal Indraji, for instance, discovered Ashokan edicts in Maharashtra and Rajasthan in the late nineteenth century but for several insidious reasons intimately connected with language and power, did not get his due.[7] Ashokan epigraphs have been emerging with surprising and delightful frequency ever since—and in all manner of material contexts. A perusal of the exhaustive list provided by Nayanjot Lahiri, for instance, in her seminal work on Ashoka, *Ashoka in Ancient India*, attests to this.[8]

Thus, Ashoka's Maski inscription in Karnataka was chanced upon by a gold prospector in 1915 and his Gavimath edict (Karnataka, again) by the guru of a math in Gavimath in 1931. The most recent discovery, according to this list, was of the Ratanpurwa edict in Bihar in 2009. One suspects that further churning of the earth and digging-up of surfaces will throw up more significant finds for us to mull over and interpret. And therein, too, lies the secret behind Ashoka's popularity. Who can deny the attraction of this powerful historical figure whose story is still being put together in the manner of a very large jigsaw puzzle? One never knows what the next epigraph will reveal in this manifestly incomplete but fascinating tale!

Back to our original story and the point where Ashoka finally triumphed over rival contenders to the Mauryan throne. Having tasted blood, so to speak, Ashoka inaugurated his reign with displays of ill-temper and petulance, and a scale of violence that, if true, beggared belief. To begin with—and with chilling ingratitude—he apparently insisted that all the ministers who had supported him during the succession struggle undergo a loyalty test and then promptly killed five hundred of them because he found them wanting, in this respect. The details thereof are fairly convoluted but this is another classic cautionary tale of what happens when power goes to one's head.

Here is what transpired: it appears, or so the story goes, that the once-loyal team of ministers who had been instrumental in Ashoka's accession to the throne soon began to treat him with scorn and this was something that the arrogant king would not brook. Summoning the offending group, he issued a royal dictate—in order to prove their loyalty to him, they were to cut down every single tree that bore flowers and fruit while sparing those that were thorny. Now this was an entirely ridiculous proposition—thorny trees also bear flowers and fruit—but the whole idea was to blindly execute the order rather than to question its intrinsic logic.

However, the hapless ministers either could not understand how to go about the task or were confounded by its ludicrousness and so, despite Ashoka repeating his order thrice, they failed to carry it out. Accordingly, the young king personally chopped off their heads (which must have been an exhausting enterprise given their huge number). Incidentally, while you may well rail against Ashoka's cruelty, it is pertinent to note that the *Arthashastra* recommended regular tests for kings to appraise the loyalty—or lack of it—in their ministers, so there was nothing very unusual about this story, in that sense. It was just a part of prescribed state policy.

If this were not enough, though, Ashoka then turned his ire on some women of his harem who had insulted him. The story is an equally captivating and bloodthirsty one, and begins one day during the spring when Ashoka was strolling with his harem in a park in Pataliputra. In a mellow mood and stopping regularly to smell the roses, as it were, the king caught sight of a beautiful Ashoka tree in full bloom and tarried awhile to appreciate his botanical namesake. The more he gazed, the more his mercurial mind steadied, which caused him to become, all of a sudden, 'very affectionate' towards his women—a delicate turn of phrase for a roll in the hay, so to speak.

Unfortunately, though, the women of his harem did not enjoy caressing his rough-skinned body and were annoyed when forced to do so. Scouting about for ways to vent their frustration, they caught sight of the Ashoka tree that their king had so admired and, just like that, a brilliant plan of revenge slid into their minds. Accordingly, while the king slumbered, they chopped off all its flowers and branches, reducing it to little more than a denuded twig. When Ashoka got to know of this, the inevitable happened—he burned five hundred of the women alive as counter-revenge for maiming his precious Ashoka tree. (It is very tempting to think of the tree bemoaning its fate in the manner of Antonio in Shakespeare's *The Merchant of Venice*, thus: 'I am the unhappy subject of these quarrels', but that is neither here nor there!)

The *Ashokavadana* tells us that Ashoka's prime minister,

horrified at his sovereign's killings, prevailed upon him to appoint a royal executioner who could execute the king's bloodlust in his stead. After much research, a weaver boy named Girika the Fierce/Chandagirika from a Magadhan village was found to be the ideal candidate with the requisite amounts of ferocity that the job required and who obligingly offered to 'execute the whole of Jambudvipa' when questioned about his abilities by the king's men. It seems that on his request, Ashoka built a jail in Pataliputra, which was, in fact, an elaborate torture chamber where he amused himself by watching his various victims in the throes of great physical agony, while Chandagirika ran riot within its confines and with the king's blessing.

All in all, a thoroughly bloodthirsty, unpleasant character (both of them, in fact, but here we are referring specifically to Ashoka) with the means and the will to run amok, and unleash general havoc on his hapless attendants and subjects! Kautilya, had he been around, would have thrown a fit—and then some more!—at this callous disregard of the rules of royal etiquette by his beloved protégé's grandson. 'Watch your back', he would have warned with tight-lipped disapproval. 'This is *exactly* the sort of behaviour that creates enemies and beckons disaster.' But there was no one to rein Ashoka in or pour soothing and sensible counsel into his ears. He was, basically, a law unto himself. Incidentally, this torture chamber was tentatively identified by L.A. Waddell in the late 1800s in an ancient well (known locally as the *agam kuan* or bottomless well) outside Patna, whose long association with evil apparently ensured that nobody drank from it.[9]

The empire that Ashoka inherited in *c.* 268 BCE was a massive one. Fast-forwarding a little, the distribution of his inscriptions is a good indicator of its extent at the end of his own reign in 232 BCE. It included almost the entire subcontinent; in the northwest, it extended up to Kandahar in Afghanistan; and its eastern frontier extended to Kalinga (Odisha).[10] The only parts outside the Mauryan pale were the southernmost extremities, which were inhabited by the Cholas and Pandyas, according to Rock Edict 13 (however, Rock Edict 2 claims that these areas were occupied by the Keralaputras and Satiyaputras).[11] Before we get on with the actual details of Ashoka's story, it would be pertinent to note here that despite his later pacifism, Ashoka had complete control over his vast empire, which, unfortunately, went to pieces in the hands of his successors—an oblique indicator of the power and strength that he otherwise wielded at the helm.

There are several ways to approach Ashoka's story, which is a complex and multifaceted one—as befits a complex and multifaceted man. This was, after all, the only ruler in the ancient world to devise a way to speak directly to his people in every corner of his huge empire, making use of material that already existed in the form of rocks or creating further endurable ones, his pillars, on which to inscribe his thoughts and feelings and dictates. Clearly, this was a man of pure genius! He also ended, as Nayanjot Lahiri observes, 'a long phase of faceless rulers' though his inscriptions.[12] So even though, she notes, it is tough to write about Ashoka's life in a way that is consistent with modern biographical criteria, there are various ways to approach his story. And it is quite impossible to tell his tale without going back and forth in time and repeating oneself, and reiterating old and new connections.

So does one start with the Buddhism angle or the aftermath of Kalinga or his inscriptions in their entirety or go backwards in time from his memorialisation in the present?

It seems that we will have to mesh them all together to make any sense of it all! It would also be fair to remind the reader that if one intends to understand Ashoka, one needs to deal with the entire set of his major and minor rock edicts, and pillar edicts, as well as pertinent inscriptions, such as commemorative, donative and fragmentary ones, as well as a set of cave inscriptions belonging to his time in the Barabar hill caves in Bihar. As his messages were inscribed over several years, it is possible to trace his evolving personality and priorities through them.[13]

And of course, the mainstay of his story, the conflict he engineered at Kalinga in *c.* 261 BCE, where, ironically, he managed to horrify himself with the violence and devastation he had unleashed—and adopted (in his typical, whimsical way) a different path altogether. But we are anticipating ourselves a bit. Let us go back a little in the story to ask if Ashoka was really as bloodthirsty and terrible as he was made out to be. Was he, in fact, a normal, more-or-less sane person who was initially vilified? Or does the truth lie somewhere in between? Endless fascinating theories can ensue from this. For instance, did Bindusara sense the violence in his son, which is why he did not want him as the next Mauryan ruler? Or did Buddhist texts deliberately portray Ashoka in a dark light, as a violent degenerate, so as to later prove the colossal scale of his change? Looking back over such a massive span of time, it is difficult to pinpoint the truth but we can put together some hints and clues, and try to reconstruct it.

The *Ashokavadana* builds Ashoka's background with much care. Thus, in one of his previous births when he was a young boy named Jaya, the Buddha came upon him playing by the roadside. The little boy put a handful of dirt into the latter's begging bowl of his own accord and wished, as he did so, that he should become a king and a follower of the Buddha. The Buddha, touched and impressed by the boy's gift, smiled and this lit up the universe with rays of light. These rays re-entered the Buddha's left palm, signifying that the child before him would become a great emperor in his next life.

Accordingly, the Buddha told his disciple, Ananda, that this boy who had thrown a handful of dirt into his bowl would, in the course of time, become a great and righteous king who would rule his empire from his capital at Pataliputra. (The gift of dirt is seen as an explanation for his rough skin in this birth.) And so, Ashoka had a brush with divinity and was merely fulfilling his blessing by eventually becoming an exemplary Buddhist king. That his fame travelled well beyond the Indian subcontinent and endures till today is a matter of mortal contrivance, though.

So how and when did Ashoka fulfil this prophecy in its entirety by embracing Buddhism? Most popular accounts of his reign present him as distraught and broken after the battle of Kalinga, despite his being the victor, unable to digest the fact of his having caused so much bloodshed and destruction. This inner transformation leads him to eschew his previous *digvijaya* or conquest by war and adopt *dhamma-vijaya/dharma-vijaya* or conquest through dharma, thereafter. Buddhism apparently appears as a better, more viable alternative for him, at this point, and he devotes his entire life to following and spreading its tenets, the latter through his edicts and inscriptions addressed to the general public.

Yet right at the outset, we have several warring versions. Buddhist texts invariably present Ashoka as an evil character whose conversion to Buddhism was a sudden, transformative event. Interestingly, they make no mention of the Kalinga war itself. The *Mahavamsa* and *Dipavamsa* claim that Ashoka turned to Buddhism when his nephew, Nigrodha, who had become a monk at the age of seven, preached the doctrine to him. On the other hand, the *Divyavadana* points to the influence of Samudra, a merchant-turned-monk who had been subjected to the agonies of Ashoka's torture chamber but had remained unaffected. Incidentally, the Chinese pilgrim, Xuanzang, who visited India in the seventh century CE and whose account has been used as corroborative material for many key points of Indian history, supports this particular tale. The *Ashokavadana*, on the other hand, mixes both and speaks of Samudra, the twelve-year-old son of a merchant, as the person responsible for bringing Ashoka under the influence of the Buddhist dhamma.

Strangely enough, though, Ashoka's own inscriptions do not mention any of these incidents. You would think that if someone had played such an important role in a royal spiritual transformation of this scale, he would at least find mention in some official record or the other! But the whole affair remains somewhat shrouded in mystery. Yet Ashoka speaks very clearly through his inscriptions and so one should give credence to his voice. Ashoka's Major Rock Edict 13 speaks of the Kalinga war, which occurred in the ninth year of his reign, and implies that it had a pivotal role to play in his adoption of a policy of pacifism. Minor Rock Edict 1 also notes that Ashoka turned gradually, not suddenly, towards the Buddha's teachings.

More evidence of Ashoka's belief in Buddhism are provided by the Rummindei (Lumbini) and Nigali Sagar inscriptions. According to the former, Ashoka visited Lumbini, the birthplace of the Buddha, in the twenty-first year of his reign and worshipped there. He had a stone wall built around the place, installed this particular pillar to commemorate his visit and announced some tax concessions for the villagers.[14] The latter notes that fourteen years after his consecration, Ashoka enlarged the stupa containing the relics of Buddha Konagamana (a mythical Buddha, Kanakamuni) to double its size. Six years later, he visited this place and had the stone pillar in question erected.

And so, if you collate all this epigraphic evidence, you realise that Ashoka is not just confessing his personal faith in Buddhism but also making his deeds suit the words. However, there are more frustrating contradictions in store. The Pali chronicles claim that Ashoka convened a grand Buddhist council at Pataliputra, presided over by Moggaliputta Tissa, to cleanse the sangha of certain unacceptable practices.[15] And yet, the Ashokan inscriptions make no mention of this event, thereby provoking a flurry of explanations from scholars. Some claim that the Pali chronicles were inaccurate while others believe that a minor meeting of this kind might have occurred with which Ashoka had no connection. A third explanation is that there were, in fact, two councils, which the Buddhist tradition mistakenly merged into one.

Much is made of Ashoka's 'schism edict', in this regard, wherein he warns members of the Buddhist sangha against causing any division or dissension in its ranks ('It is my wish that the Sangha community may always be united.'). But it has also been argued that Ashoka only intervened in the affairs of the order to expel some of its disobedient members and not to counter some kind of doctrinal schism. Incidentally, three Schism Edict pillars have been found so far—at Sanchi, Sarnath and Kausambi—but there must have been many more.[16] Further evidence of Ashoka's Buddhist inclinations is provided by the remarkable twelfth-century text, *Rajatarangini* by Kalhana, according to which he (or someone with his very name but that is too much of a coincidence!) introduced Buddhism in Kashmir.[17] If, as was surmised, this Ashoka was the same as the third Mauryan ruler of the Puranic dynastic tables, then he was clearly powerful enough to impose his preferred religion on the largely Shaivite populace of early Kashmir.

In any case, that Ashoka had an abiding connection with the Buddhist sangha and its leading monks is a given, as also his unbounded generosity towards it, as seen through several legends. If one goes by the numbers provided by the Buddhist tradition—a mindboggling eighty-four thousand stupas and viharas were apparently built by him!—one might be forgiven for assuming that he spent a large chunk of his time in designing and sanctioning construction activities. But, remember, this was a sovereign who barely slept, going by his willingness to meet his officials at all times and, of course, Kautilya's royal spartan sleep regimen hanging over it all. Ashoka is also supposed to have gone on pilgrimage to all the major places connected with the Buddha and to have created signs there to guide future pilgrims. So he was clearly a fervent follower of the Buddha's teaching and to have been recognised as such by the sangha in general even if he did not ever become its formal member.

The question of who Ashoka's spiritual mentor was remains unresolved, though. The *Mahavamsa* claims it was Moggaliputta Tissa; the *Ashokavadana*, Upagupta; while others point to Yashah, the head of the Kukkutarama monastery outside Pataliputra, which plays an important part in his later life. Ashoka explicates his relationship with the sangha through his epigraphs. He seems to have drawn closer to it by degrees until a point when he throws himself heart and soul into its work so much so that Minor Rock Edict 3 at Bairat has him greeting the sangha, proclaiming his faith in it, and listing six Buddhist texts that he desires monks, nuns and laypersons to listen to and reflect upon. What the Buddhists of the time thought of his recommendations is a matter for conjecture. What is not, though, is that he had read and pondered over these stipulated texts; he would not be recommending them, otherwise!

What we also have incontrovertible evidence for, though, is the *Mahavamsa*'s assertion that Ashoka sent off a number of Buddhist missions at the end of the third Buddhist council—to the Himalayas, the northwest, Kashmir and Gandhara, central India, western Malwa, the western Deccan, Myanmar or southeast Asia, and Sri Lanka.[18] A very precise and thorough encompassing of his known world, this! Of the five monks despatched to the Himalayan region, two find mention on the relic casket found in Stupa no. 2 at the Buddhist monastic site of Sanchi in central India. And, of course, that the one sent to Sri Lanka was Ashoka's own son, Mahinda/Mahindra/Mahendra, is a well-known fact. Add to this the fact that Ashoka was the prime propagator of his own message of dhamma at home—and you have a clearly indefatigable, if dhamma-obsessed, person on your hands.

Self-righteously replacing his pleasure tours (vihara-yatas) with dhamma tours (dhamma-yatas), he declares that the latter has made him happier than anything else. And he obviously enjoyed meeting people: these tours involved conversing with and interrogating the latter about dhamma, as also bestowing gifts on them—rather in the nature of an ancient quiz show with prizes except that this one was conducted at random places all over the realm and with anyone who showed up (and they must have shown up in droves!). More notably, these dhamma-yatas were also a great way for him to gauge public opinion and check up on local officials. Also, with such a huge empire, it was necessary for him to visit rural areas (in fact, he was probably the first Indian ruler on record to appreciate the importance of the rural population) and outlying regions to let the people know he was around and generally keeping an eye on things.[19]

Also, Ashoka, the politically sagacious, rather adroitly kept the definition of dhamma fluid to suit his purposes. It was, basically, non-violence towards all living beings, truthfulness, compassion, respect towards one's parents and so on but, as B.N. Mukherjee points out, the Greek and Aramaic inscriptions (alluded to elsewhere) display some intriguing variations.[20] The Greek inscription in Kandahar, for instance, talks of the subjects' devotion to the king's interest as being an important part of dhamma—a significant addition. And neither do the Greek or Aramaic inscriptions talk of the attainment of heaven as a goal/result of following dhamma, which the Prakrit inscriptions mention ad nauseum. What they do reveal, though, along with some of his later edicts, is that dhamma was increasingly becoming the single thought in his mind to the exclusion of all else.

Ashoka was, in addition, somewhat delusional (or extremely hopeful, depending on which way you view it) on the manner in which he had changed the lives of his subjects through its propagation. Take the case of the bilingual Shar-i-Kuna inscription, for instance.[21] Incidentally, he is King Piodosses in the Greek portion and 'our lord Prydrs the king' in the Aramaic—examples of the often-delightfully whimsical ways in which names are cheerfully borrowed from a source and mangled, thereafter, so that historians are routinely confounded when they encounter them. The Greek part notes that from the moment the king made his 'doctrine of piety' (*eusebeia*) known, 'everything thrives throughout the whole world'.

Everyone took their cue from him: all hunting and fishing ceased, while the 'intemperate' became temperate and respectful—and there was every reason to believe they would continue to behave thus in the future and, therefore, 'live better and more happily'. The Aramaic part, which substitutes 'truth' (*qyst*) for the Greek piety, makes more grandiose claims: ever since the king's campaign, 'evil has diminished for all men', 'all hostile things' have disappeared and 'joy has arisen throughout the whole earth'. This, as you can imagine, must have bewildered the denizens of the area who might or might not have witnessed this radical transformation in their lives despite the edict's insistence on it.

And as you can further imagine, the question of what Ashoka's dhamma was really all about has bewildered most historians over the years. Some say it was a sort of universal religion (and we can draw parallels with the Mughal emperor, Akbar's invention of Sulh-i-kul, in this regard). Others say it was a form of raja-dharma (a king's dharma), melding the political and moral principles of the Buddhist and Brahmanical traditions. To complicate matters, it has also been seen as a simplified version of the Buddha's teaching for the laity (upasaka dharma) or even (and this might cause total bewilderment!) an amalgam of all these things. Romila Thapar, for instance, says that dhamma was a political or ideological tool used by Ashoka to draw his huge empire closer together.[22] It was a practical concept that, in her view, failed to unite the people. She also cautions against viewing him as a 'monster of piety', which is what the Buddhist sources would have us believe, a picture that is not really endorsed by his epigraphs, too.

The Buddhist core of Ashoka's dhamma, though, is undeniable: the constant and forceful reiteration of ahimsa (the *Arthashastra* also mentions it but more as a glancing reference), and the resonances of Buddhist teachings and ideas in the edicts are a case in point. Add to this the fact that Ashoka started his dhamma-yatas after a visit to Bodhgaya, the intensely Buddhist sculptural motifs attached to his pillars (a specific and telling instance, among others, being the elephant, symbolising the future Buddha, appearing on rocks bearing the dhamma edicts) and Buddhist remains being found near many Ashokan pillars[23]—and you have a distinct link between Ashoka, his dhamma and Buddhism.

Having said that, one should note that Ashoka, while inventing his own special creed, may have been heavily inspired by the Buddhist dhamma but went way beyond it in terms of its content and the manner in which he used it. Upinder Singh, for instance, points to his insistence on mutual respect between people of different beliefs and the fact that the dhamma-mahamatas were to concern themselves with *all* sects, as well as his phrasing and usage of dhamma-vijaya or conquest through dhamma as clues to his being a true 'innovator' who used his personal feelings and professional compulsions to come up with his masterful strategy of religious/ethical governance.

And now, we may turn to Kalinga, the event that started it all and the watershed in Ashoka's life.

Notes

1. His resolution of what Charles Allen calls 'the Palibothra-Pataliputra-Patna puzzle' resulted in his breakthrough identification that 'Chandragupta, who, from a military adventurer, became the sovereign of Upper Hindustan…was none other than that very Sandrocottus who concluded a treaty with Seleucus Nicator'.

From there, he was able to postulate a verifiable chronology for the Mauryans. See Charles Allen, *Ashoka—The Search for India's Lost Emperor*, Abacus, 2012, pp.67–68.

2. For details, see ibid., pp.153–181.
3. For details, see ibid., pp.310–313.
4. Alexander Cunningham, *Inscriptions of Asoka—Corpus Inscriptionum Indicarum Volume 1*, Indological Book House, 1877, rpt 1961. See also I. Allen Sealy, *Asoca: A Sutra*, Penguin, 2021 and Nayanjot Lahiri, *Ashoka in Ancient India*, pp.15–16.
5. The *Ashokavadana*, for instance: we have already spoken about this work of nearly 10,000 verses, considered a part of the northern Buddhist tradition, and the fact that it was written much after Ashoka's time. See also ibid., p.15.
6. Allen, *Ashoka—The Search for India's Lost Emperor*, pp.xiv-xv.
7. Lahiri, *Ashoka in Ancient India*, Permanent Black, 2015, pp.16–17.
8. Refer to the note above.
9. The well was adjacent to the Hindu temple of Shitala Devi, the goddess of smallpox, also the site of some Mauryan yakshi fertility goddesses. For details, see Allen, *Ashoka—The Search for India's Lost Emperor*, pp.318–319. Waddell claimed that the yakshi pillar he found here led him to the village of Kumrahar (cited earlier as having significant Mauryan remains) and his pioneering investigations there.
10. To put it simply—from Afghanistan to Karnataka and from Gujarat to Bengal with the provinces spread out over thousands of kilometres—quite clearly, an enormous realm.
11. Ashoka did not conduct any campaign in the south to include the entire peninsula in his empire. This made practical sense: as long as the southern kingdoms were on friendly terms with him and received the dhamma-mahamatas, he could let them be. Tamil literature shows that the Mauryans were already regarded with awe in that area. See Romila Thapar, *Asoka and the Decline of the Mauryas*, Oxford University Press, 3rd edn, 2021, p.211.
12. She notes that they represent a 'historical daybreak'. See Lahiri, *Ashoka in Ancient India*, pp.3, 7.
13. This, in fact, is one of Lahiri's priorities in her book—to examine his 'shifting mental horizons' as expressed through his inscriptions and which have not received due attention. See ibid., pp.9, 22.

14. This, incidentally, is the only Ashokan inscription that makes a precise reference to taxation. For more details of the terms used and the record's implications, see Thapar, *Asoka and the Decline of the Mauryas*, p.85. See also Lahiri, *Ashoka in Ancient India*, p.243: she notes that this is probably the earliest documented example in south Asia of a political patron using a sacred landscape to announce revenue concessions, so memorialisation is combined with an overt expression of political power.
15. The first Buddhist council was held at Rajagriha right after the Buddha's death while the second one was at Vaishali a hundred years later. And so, the one at Pataliputra was the third in the series.
16. See Allen, *Ashoka—The Search for India's Lost Emperor*, p.244. It seems he summoned the Buddhist monastic community to the Kukkutarama monastery and this ended with the expulsion of recalcitrant members and a council to codify laws, followed by a proselytising programme where missionaries were sent all over the place, including Prince Mahendra to Ceylon. This is one version, unsupported by his edicts and the northern Buddhist tradition. See p.386.
17. Xuanzang confirms the strong tradition linking Ashoka with the Kashmir valley. Together with the evidence in the *Rajatarangini*, he is recognised as ruling a large empire, and as the builder of stupas and monasteries. See Lahiri, *Ashoka in Ancient India*, pp.303–306 for his association with Kashmir in varied literary sources right up to the Mughal emperor, Akbar's time. In fact, she adds that the several mnemonic ways in which Ashoka was remembered from his death in the third century BCE to Akbar's time around 1,700 years later show that his existence was never really forgotten. Also, she argues, if his image as a Buddhist ruler is clear to us, it would have been clear to his subjects as well—a fallout of how he fashioned his image.
18. For details, see Upinder Singh, *A History of Ancient and Early Medieval India—From the Stone Age to the 12th Century*, Pearson/Dorling Kindersley, 2008, p.351.
19. See Thapar, *Asoka and the Decline of the Mauryas*, pp.202–203.
20. Singh, *A History of Ancient and Early Medieval India*, 2008, p.354.
21. Ibid., p.355; B.N. Mukherjee, *Studies in the Aramaic Edicts of Asoka*, Indian Museum Calcutta, 1984, p.33.

22. Singh, *A History of Ancient and Early Medieval India*, pp.354–355; Thapar, *Asoka and the Decline of the Mauryas*, pp.22, 136–181. Rock Edict 4 at Erragudi implies that the change in his priorities could be traced through a transformation in sound: the sound of the war drums versus the sound of dhamma or morality being proclaimed (*bherighoso aho dhammaghoso*). See, for instance, Lahiri, *Ashoka in Ancient India*, pp.194–195.
23. They possibly marked the sites of stupas and monasteries that Ashoka built, implying a link between his dhamma and Buddhism. See Singh, *A History of Ancient and Early Medieval India*, p.356. See also A. Ghosh, 'The Pillars of Asoka: Their Purpose', *East and West*, New Series 17 (3-4), pp.273–275.

11

KALINGA

Kalinga is so pivotal to Ashoka's story that it warrants a chapter all to itself. It is, of course, also a key event in the larger Mauryan tale but what makes this entire episode stand out in terms of historical narratives is that it is the only instance when the victor laments his triumph; where instead of indulging in chest-thumping and bragging—completely justified under the circumstances—he mourns his deed and, furthermore, ensures that he records his 'mistake' for posterity in every which way, on durable materials that will survive to speak of it long after he is gone. There are no parallel precedents of this sort in Indian or world history, for that matter, which makes Ashoka's behaviour in the aftermath of the Kalinga war pioneering in every sense of the term.

Rather, the opposite prevailed—one has only to take a look at the Allahabad pillar inscription of the Gupta ruler, Samudragupta, or the Aihole inscription of the Chalukyan ruler, Pulakesin II, to know what eulogies constructed around military victories are all about and why they were inextricably connected with any ruler's glory. Ruing the bloodshed caused by battle is a popular poetic theme (although the glory associated with the latter is most-often highlighted) but Ashoka's penitence and his desire to be remembered through the ages for this one 'failure' rather than his several other triumphs makes his personality even more intriguing than ever—a quixotic mix of humility and arrogance, of self-effacement and confidence, of acid honesty and candidness laced with boastfulness. What a challenging case study for a modern-day psychologist—and almost certainly an enigma for his peers!

But let us begin at the beginning. Ashoka's desire to bring every bit of the land under the Mauryan yoke was completely understandable. Kalinga, on the eastern coast (in what is now part of modern Orissa and Andhra Pradesh), and lying strategically between the Mahanadi and the Godavari, was a key point in the sea traffic between Vanga (Bengal) and the south. Moreover, it was one among the recalcitrant, untidy parts of the country that still held out and by virtue of doing so, taunted him and his ambition of supreme control. In desiring Kalinga and complete power, Ashoka was adhering to the time-honoured dictates of rulership in the ancient world, memorably endorsed by great Greek writers like Herodotus and Homer, for instance: to go forth and conquer was the first and foremost rule for any ruler worth his salt, and if you were just going to loll about on your throne and stay content with the territories you already possessed, then you were a sad apology for a leader. All around him—if one can stretch the dates somewhat—great rulers were scrambling up and down their realms, positively aching to conquer new dominions and carve places of honour for themselves in the annals of history thereby. What was happening in Rome and Persia and Macedon were cases in point.

More importantly, this conquering lust was also perfectly in tune with what the *Arthashastra* prescribed. Kautilya's world was one of constant challenges posed to and for thrones in an interminable wrangle for power. The idea was to keep expanding your realm through strategically-conquered territories and to continue doing so for you couldn't ever rest on your laurels. The alternative was too horrific to contemplate: loss of dominion and inevitable enslavement. So war was welcome, even necessary. And, of course, let us not discount the ubiquitous, overweeningly male desire for acquisition—something that underlay the very definition of masculinity. You are a powerful king? Well, then, prove it. How much land and goods and women can you acquire? How else do you justify being on the throne?

Nayanjot Lahiri provides the perfectly apposite example of the Assyrian king, Ashurnasirpal II, in this regard.[1] In around the ninth century BCE, one of his minor campaigns won him a booty that included forty chariots with men and horses, four hundred and sixty horses, a hundred and twenty pounds of silver, a hundred and twenty pounds of gold, six thousand pounds of lead, eighteen thousand pounds of iron, a thousand vessels of copper, two thousand heads of cattle, five thousand sheep, fifteen thousand slaves, and the defeated ruler's sister. And if this was the result of one of his smaller campaigns, it boggles the mind to consider what he might have secured from one of his major ones.

Ashoka went about planning for the Kalingan campaign with the usual close attention to detail and logistics that such a military undertaking warranted. This involved a careful assessment of Kalinga's forces, as also an understanding of its terrain. Winter, the optimal season for launching an attack, was when the Mauryan forces set out. Ashoka does not mention the size of his army in any of his inscriptions but we can muster a fair picture from what we know of his ancestors' military campaigns. As with Chandragupta's forces—and later, Bindusara's—Ashoka's army definitely had archers, foot-soldiers with spears, army commanders and horses and elephants, among other fighting units. As noted earlier, elephants were considered one of the most effective weapons of destruction in any fighting force in the ancient world not only on account of their size and fearsome build but also the simple fact of their ability to run amok on the battlefield, killing more enemy soldiers at one go than, say, an entire platoon of foot-soldiers could manage. Buttressing their destructive potential was the usual ammunition of maces, swords and massive stone catapults, among others.

In the six or so weeks that it would have taken this army to progress from Pataliputra to Kalinga, it would not be fair to assume that the Kalingan force sat quivering and quaking and waiting for doom to descend on its head courtesy the famed Mauryan force. The description of the numbers that eventually died, in Ashoka's Rock Edict 13 (mentioned earlier), suggests that the Kalingan force was considerable in size. And although the resounding victory was Ashoka's, 'defeat', as Lahiri eloquently phrases it, 'is snatched from the jaws of victory'.[2] All conventions of state propaganda are contravened and the triumph is recorded as a disaster, whereby 'the emperor weeps when he ought to swagger'. This, in Lahiri's view, is 'a staggering reversal of the very conception of kingship', associated, as mentioned earlier, with self-aggrandisement and boastful claims, with military triumph being seen as synonymous with manhood and masculinity, the underlying essence of a king.

While we are on the subject of gender identities, one is tempted to make a diversion here and note that there is a category of 'warrior queens' or *virangana* in history of which much is made because these women rulers fought battles like their male counterparts and thereby expedited their acceptance into society as honorary males. Therefore, they are viewed as largely non-threatening to the patriarchal order as opposed to, say, a ruling queen like Didda of Kashmir (CE 980/1-1003) who does not wage actual battles on account of her lameness but rules very well and capably in other ways. There is a whole lot of confused speculation on whether she was a woman or, in fact, a man on account of her ambition and general ruthlessness. So whether military triumph is essential to the identity of powerful women or not remains a contentious issue that most historians try to skirt around the edges of or conveniently ignore altogether.

Back to Ashoka and his astonishing volte-face. If one looks long and hard into the Indian past, there *is* a sort of lukewarm parallel that can be made with a traditionally chest-thumping context and its completely unexpected reversion thereof. This pertains to the *Uttara-ramacharita*, written by a poet, Bhavabhuti, in the eighth century CE in the court of Kanauj. Those familiar with the tale of the epic *Ramayana* will know that its writer, Valmiki, portrayed Rama as so ideal a king that he did not bat an eyelid when he exiled his pregnant wife, Sita, on the basis of some scurrilous rumours regarding her chastity. After all, his duty towards his subjects was paramount—indeed, the very essence of ideal kingship—and if he had to sacrifice his personal desire at the altar of kingly obligation, so be it.

Bhavabhuti turns the epic on its head in his magnificent reinterpretation: Rama wanders around in a frantic state, bitterly chastising himself and his precipitate decision, and calling himself a murderer for visiting such an awful fate upon his wife. He would do anything, he declares, to recall his decision and bring her back to court, and he laments the fit of madness that provoked it, in the first place. At one point, he even looks sarcastically at his arms and says they should be lopped off because they belong to a killer and were the architects of his order, so to speak. So here is a king who rues his royal order, is desperate to revoke it and has no qualms in critiquing his own actions. Admittedly, Bhavabhuti's version has not gone down well with diehard *Ramayana* admirers who would rather stick to the original portrayal of the strict, austere king rather than one who, in fact, cares deeply about his woman, and would not mind angering and alienating his people if it meant he could have her back.

Incidentally, Bhavabhuti's other path-breaking work, the *Malati-madhava* (again, a retelling thereof and a completely charming one besides), features a remarkable woman protagonist, the Buddhist nun, Kamandaki, who completely subverts all feminine stereotypes of helplessness and passivity by ruthlessly manipulating all the (largely male) characters and calmly achieving what she had set out to at the beginning. As you can imagine, Bhavabhuti and his works were not particularly successful—either during his time or later—and although much has been made of his beautiful prose and his excellent metaphors and so on, no one exactly points to him and says, '*There* is an example of a gender-sensitive writer, one much ahead of his times!' Writers of his ilk have always enjoyed an odd sort of reputation where there is some amount of tentative, barely-there acknowledgement of what lies at the core of their texts but a sheepish and insistent focus on everything else besides. And Bhavabhuti, when it comes right down to it, has committed the worst of the cardinal sins—to tamper with sacrosanct material and provide his own slant to it, which will always (whether then or now!) have the orthodox up in arms and snarling in fury.[3]

There is a sort of similarity that can be construed with the Ashokan context whereby you expect a certain amount of male bravado and vainglory in a particular situation but are stumped by the exact opposite—an outpouring of penitence and contrition, a regret so loud that it borders on the maudlin. Bloodshed in the context of battle, as noted earlier, was nothing unusual in the ancient world. Hordes were regularly decimated by one conqueror or the other in their attempts to enlarge the realms they ruled over. But picture for one instant, if you will, one of these very men standing on the battlefield, battered in body, perhaps, but the implications of his triumph just beginning to sink in. The pride is tangible; so is the reek of blood and fear and the stomach-churning sight of disembowelled bodies. Strong men have been felled by less. After all, who can possibly quantify the exact, defining moment when a person's mind goes into complete reversal?

Literature is rife with examples of people pulling back from the brink of goodness or wickedness due to some trigger or the other. In Ashoka's case (and if we go by the sense of his confession, the only surviving contemporary account of the calamity), the tramp of over 900 km from Pataliputra to Kalinga, which was meant to be a martial pilgrimage of sorts, suddenly turned into the worst sort of excess that he could perpetrate, the ultimate horror, the sublime defeat—and, thus, to the realisation that his remorse needed to take a much larger form than a mere sentiment.

This seismic shift within him caused him to take a second birth, as it were—as a caring, benevolent king for whom his subjects' welfare and happiness was paramount. That he turned to the Buddhist principles in his hour of grief is not unusual or surprising—and in saying so, we are according more agency to his Buddhist wife, Devi, than otherwise acceded. It is well within the bounds of possibility that he had more than a nodding acquaintance with the religion's tenets through her. One suspects, though, that even if this was expressly recorded, at the time, it would be brushed aside. A woman behind such an earth-shattering transformation? Perish the thought!

What, after all, explains Ashoka's extreme reaction to the Kalinga war? Several explanations have been offered, in this regard, but they are all inadequate or incomplete in one way or the other. Attributing it to his active participation in the fighting does not hold muster because he was already inured to violence—that is, if we believe the stories regarding his early days on the throne. So there was clearly something unusual about the Kalinga war, something that removed it from the usual run-of-the-mill clashes and placed it in a separate bracket altogether.

Upinder Singh's musings are very helpful, in this regard. She wonders whether there were changes in the nature of warfare, at the time, involving higher levels of military deployment, higher casualties and mass deportation of captives, perhaps even of non-combatant citizenry.[4] By extension, she points to the 'rhetorical numbers' mentioned at the beginning of Rock Edict 13 (Ashoka's 'Kalingan edict', if you will) as implying that it was one of the most massive and brutal campaigns in ancient Indian history, with its scale of devastation turning the king's own stomach.[5]

Alternatively, could Ashoka have lost someone dear to him in this war? The loss of a son or a close friend could have forced him to stop and consider what he had done. Or the wheels of change might already have been turning in his mind: he may have become more sensitive to violence the more he heard about the Buddha's lessons, impelling him to make this powerful anti-war proclamation whereby in his future political philosophy, war and military victory had no place in the moral empire that he sought to build (although he *would* take action against rebellious forest people, for one, if they provoked him—which we will come to later. There is no mention of pain or suffering stemming from a possible conflict here!). These are not mere words or a fleeting, intangible feeling; Ashoka follows it up with highly concrete action.

In Singh's interesting view, while Ashoka's reaction to the Kalinga war is seen as remorse (*anusochana*/*anutapa*), the tone of Rock Edict 13 veers, instead, towards grief and a subsequent firm resolve. Also, despite his expressing his sorrow at the war's aftermath, he does not seek forgiveness from anyone, although he is careful not to display his feelings in Kalinga itself (or at Sannati in Karnataka, another place that experienced his army's impact), perhaps from a combination of empathy, shame and practicality.[6] Therefore, in Jauguda and Dhauli (also in Odisha), the rock edicts bear instructions to the mahamatras to execute his instructions regarding the people's spiritual welfare so that the denizens of Kalinga may live in mutual peace. Meanwhile, that he is like their father and cares for them like his children is the message (inscribed on Rock Edict 2 for people of 'unconquered territories') that Ashoka intended for those who lived south and east of Kalinga, whose lands he had yet to conquer. Although he had brutalised Kalinga itself, he wanted them to understand that he was a changed man with a different weapon of conquest.

Accordingly, Rock Edict 13 announces the deployment of the metaphor of victory for a new purpose—that of dhamma-vijaya or victory through dhamma. And success immediately follows: Ashoka claims to have won precisely such a victory in the realm of the Greek king, Antiyoka (Antiochus II Theos of Syria); in the kingdoms of Turamaya (Ptolemy II Philadelphos of Egypt), Antikini (Antigonus Gonatus of Macedonia), Maka (Magas of Cyrene in north Africa) and Alikasudara (either Alexander of Epirus or Alexander of Corinth); and in the dominion of the Cholas and Pandyas in the south, stretching all the way to Tamraparni (Sri Lanka).[7]

Within his own realm, the same satisfying result was apparently seen among the Yavanas, Kambojas, Nabhakas, Nabhapanktis, Bhojas, Pitinikas, Andhras and Pulindas (the first two were in the northwest; the Bhojas, Andhras and Pulindas were in the trans-Vindhyan region; the rest are tough to identify). Irrespective of whether this was Ashoka patting himself on the back in a somewhat delusional manner, Singh notes that it refers to a highly unusual and unprecedented sort of interaction with other kingdoms. It overturns the conventional templates for warfare and diplomacy.

In her search for possible parallels, Singh draws an intriguing one between Ashoka (and his Rock Edict 13) and the Achaemenid ruler, Cyrus, whose inscription on what is called the Cyrus Cylinder describes his conquest of Babylon in 539 BCE. Cyrus claims Babylon with, it seems, a bloodless ictory, declares himself a universal emperor and holds forth n the necessity of military campaigns, having established ace after a successful military career. The similarities are ricted to, broadly, the description of a notable huge military paign and the idea of a universal empire.

ere are the dissimilarities: Cyrus describes a bloody s a bloodless one while Ashoka talks of the death and h caused by his; Cyrus fights several battles and dubs universal emperor while Ashoka fights one battle (as far as we know!) and adopts this very sobriquet on account of his propagation of virtue. Singh also points to a lukewarm similarity between Ashoka's idea of righteous warfare and that of the Mohists in ancient China (between the fifth and third centuries BCE) who advocated disarmament. He was, quite obviously, therefore, in a league of his own![8]

The mainstream Buddhist textual tradition is very well-crafted with regard to Ashoka's transformation because the juxtaposition of the pre-Kalinga Ashoka's cruel and sadistic deeds with his drastic change in personality and motives post-Kalinga makes the event even more startling, dramatic and memorable. The violently ruthless emperor abruptly transitioning to a wisely compassionate ruler is a visceral moment; shocking, even, in its intensity. The stage is, therefore, carefully set for Ashoka to step forward and play his part as the ideal Buddhist ruler in the *Ashokavadana* (which, incidentally, does not hint at either pacifism or the renunciation of war while discussing his life!). A somewhat different picture of Ashoka's change emerges in the Sri Lankan Buddhist texts, one in which his early regnal years saw a spiritual yearning in him. Here, the narrative is crafted with equal care to demonstrate the inherent superiority of his Buddhist spiritual preceptor—Ashoka's eventual choice. This is why he turned to Buddhism in the first place, so the tradition implies. Otherwise, he might as well have opted for Jainism with its broadly similar precepts.

If we go by the *Dipavamsa*, then (whose version is tolc in relation to his son, Mahinda/Mahendra, who brought th Buddhist tenets to Sri Lanka), Ashoka, seized by an inn restlessness, began to scout about for a way to assuag soon after he ascended the Mauryan throne. Mahinda apparently ten years of age when his father killed his brothers and presumably indulged in further bloodbaths for four years until he finally became the king. (The *Mahavamsa*, incidentally, makes only a coy reference to his initial cruelty but the writing on the wall, in this regard, is quite clear.) Thereafter—and clearly at a loose end—he honoured the Pasandas for three years,[9] a term that covered a motley crew from different religious sects and ascetic persuasions. There was a catch, though—in return for the pampering, they needed to answer 'an exceedingly difficult question' that Ashoka posed to them. What this question was is, annoyingly, passed over by the text that, instead, confines itself to the inability of the examinees to answer it.

Enlightenment eventually came to the frustrated Ashoka in the form of a young Buddhist monk, Nigrodha (referred to earlier), whose very demeanour impressed the former. Drawn to this serene yet fearless man, Ashoka proceeded to lap up his sermon on earnestness ('the way to immortality', in his words, indifference being 'the way to death'), and made him a donation on the spot of large quantities of silver and a daily rice ration. And so, Ashoka's switch to Buddhism, when it happened, was as easy as that and did not involve battlefield repentances or gory scenes or anything larger-than-life—or so the text implies. It also helps that the first set of edicts issued by Ashoka gives us the gist of Nigrodha's lecture and the importance of zeal, which the emperor is said to have realised in slow stages. Romila Thapar agrees: his was not a case of 'a somewhat eccentric or overnight conversion', she says.[10]

Lahiri argues, however, that Ashoka's transformation had very little to do with the spiritual realm.[11] It was a common kingly pursuit that became the starting point of his metamorphosis: war and conquest, as noted above, were mandatory requirements for any successful ruler,[12] involving, as they did, economic considerations. Thus, by undertaking them—and thereby adhering to the *Arthashastra's* dictums for kingship—Ashoka would be able to promote his own undertakings 'concerning forts, water-works, trade routes, settling on waste land, mines, material forests and elephant forests, and to injure these undertakings of the enemy.' It was in this spirit and with these imperatives in mind that Ashoka planned and undertook the campaign to conquer Kalinga. His response, in its aftermath, was also part of the strategy of kingship except that he chose to reinvent it altogether: a compassionate and caring king emerges and proclaims this aloud for the world (or rather, *his* world) to hear for the first time. Also, his assertion is underlined with cold, hard evidence.

And in both these things, he had no parallel.

Notes

1. Nayanjot Lahiri, *Ashoka in Ancient India*, Permanent Black, 2015, pp.113–114.
2. Ibid., p.117. The exact location of the clash remains unknown. Lahiri speculates that it was in the zone stretching from Jajpur to Ganjam. See pp.220–221.
3. For an analysis of his books, see Devika Rangachari, *Invisible Women, Visible Histories—Gender, Polity and Society in Early Medieval North India (7th to 12th Century AD)*, Manohar, 2006, pp.302–321.
4. Upinder Singh, *Political Violence in Ancient India*, Harvard University Press, 2017, pp.270–274.
5. Incidentally, Rock Edict 13 is at Girnar, Kalsi, Mansera, Shahbazgarhi and Erragudi.
6. Could it also be that he cared deeply about his image, so he made sure that his remorse was elevated to dramatic levels such that the people would forgive him and eventually consider him blameless? Possible but unlikely, though! On Ashoka's conquest

of Sannati and the tenuous evidence thereof, see Lahiri, *Ashoka in Ancient India,* pp.216–217.

7. Their dates are as follows: Antiochus II of Syria, 261–246 BCE; Ptolemy II Philadelphus of Egypt, 285–247 BCE; Antigonus of Macedonia, 276–239 BCE; Magas of Cyrene, *c.* 258–250 BCE; Alexander of Corinth, 252–244 BCE; and Alexander of Epirus, 272–255 BCE. See, for instance, Romila Thapar, *Asoka and the Decline of the Mauryas*, Oxford University Press, 3rd edn, 2021, p.51.
8. Nayanjot Lahiri, however, notes that the closest parallel to Ashoka in the west was perhaps Constantine, the Roman emperor in the third century CE, who espoused the relatively new religion of Christianity, sometimes described as the imperial state changing into the sacred state. Theirs were 'massively influential monarchical conversions' and a comparison between the two personalities would be fruitful. See Lahiri, *Ashoka in Ancient India*, p.136.
9. Ibid., p.109. See also H. Oldenberg, *The Dipavamsa: An Ancient Buddhist Historical Record*, Asian Educational Services, 1879, rpt 1982, p.148.
10. Thapar, *Asoka and the Decline of the Mauryas*, p.2.
11. Lahiri, *Ashoka in Ancient India*, pp.110–117.
12. See, for instance, L.N. Rangarajan, *Kautilya—The Arthashastra*, Penguin, 1992, p.636.

12

ASHOKA'S EDICTS

'BEHAVE YOURSELVES OR ELSE' AND OTHER MISSIVES

Many things are revealed by Ashoka's edicts as regards their inscriber and are all intrinsically important to the reconstruction of history but the non-history-enthusiast would baulk at the idea of dissecting and discussing each and every one of them. And so, in order to keep the general readers' eyes riveted on this page, we will take up only the most interesting ones. However, for those who like comprehensive lists and who might, therefore, fear that this approach is sketchy, there are several excellent works (provided in the references), that they could consult, which will give them a detailed analysis of Ashoka's words.[1]

Incidentally, where edicts are concerned, the omniscient Kautilya had already provided a template. He holds forth on the ideal one, which, quite apart from the framing of content, should, ideally, contain 'sweetness' by using 'pleasant' words, 'dignity' by 'avoiding vulgarisms' and 'lucidity' by using well-known words.[2] Defects to be avoided, at all costs, include 'absence of charm' through poor surfaces or handwriting, contradiction and confusion. However, Ashoka, with his thoroughly original approach to things, would not have bothered much with these dictates. Choosing lovely words was not particularly at the top of his mind while he framed the content of his edicts and he *was* inclined to be repetitive, at points. Nevertheless, his message came through loud and clear—and that, in the end, was what really mattered.

In Upinder Singh's view, Ashoka, while powering a new attempt at imperial communication, was not really trying to speak directly to his people.[3] The audience for his edicts was three-pronged: the direct audience or the senior administrative officials, the indirect audience or the emperor's subjects who would receive his message through various intermediaries, and the future audience or posterity. The last one is an interesting thought. Immortality is, presumably, a compelling human desire and there is no reason to believe that Ashoka was immune to it. However, seeking to achieve it in the manner and scale in which he did is evidence, indeed, of his genius, one totally unprecedented for the times.

The majority of Ashoka's inscriptions are in the Prakrit language and the Brahmi script.[4] There is a special sort of thrill that you experience if you happen to be a student of history and are taught the Brahmi script, and can actually decipher his epigraphs for yourself. The squiggles cease, all of a sudden, to be mystifying and arbitrary, and it feels very much as if you have cracked an ancient and difficult code to an impenetrable mystery. Which, of course, is exactly what this is in relation to the past! The adroit Ashoka does vary the script, though, when it makes sense to do so given the enormous range of his empire and the varied scripts and languages in use. Thus, for instance, the epigraphs at Mansera in the Hazara district and Shahbazgarhi in the Mardan district of Pakistan are in Prakrit but in the Kharoshti script. Greek and Aramaic are employed in a few other inscriptions, either separately or together.

A bilingual record, in this regard, was found at Shar-i-Kuna near Kandahar in southeast Afghanistan, while two Aramaic ones were discovered at Laghman in east Afghanistan and one at Taxila. Furthermore, a Prakrit-Aramaic inscription was also found at Kandahar. So not only does Ashoka embark on this pioneering path but he shows himself capable of employing linguistic innovation as well whether or not he is conversant with the language or script in a particular region. He varies the content and material, too. Of the rock and pillar edicts, the two main categories of his staggering body of evidence, there are fourteen of the former and six (seven, in one case) of the latter with minor variations in the sets of inscriptions that they bear. Additionally, there are minor rock edicts, minor pillar edicts and cave inscriptions—a chronological sequence from earliest to later.

Spare a thought for the Ashokan scholar who must needs be conversant with where and on what these were inscribed, and when and what they said, and how variations of the same content are visible across the records—for Ashoka alternatively confesses, preens, laments or orders through these, his mouthpieces.[5] Finally, there are variations in locales as well. We cannot pinpoint the exact number of inscriptions that Ashoka inscribed in all—the Chinese pilgrims, Faxian and Xuanzang, for instance, refer to pillars at places where they do not exist today.

However, what we do know is that the major rock edicts are usually located along the borders of his vast empire. The major pillar edicts are overwhelmingly located in north India, while the minor rock edicts are distributed all over, notably in the Andhra-Karnataka area. Ashoka's epigraphs were largely placed along ancient trade and pilgrimage routes—aiding maximum visibility and consequent dissemination. Some of them were also located at important Buddhist monastic sites, such as at Sanchi, and some in the south notably abutted a gold-mining area.[6]

But it is Minor Rock Edict 1 (at Rupnath) that spells out the entire process of this logistical exercise. Issued slightly over a couple of years after Ashoka's spiritual transformation, the emperor confesses to not having been particularly zealous, in this regard, in the initial stages until he drew closer to the sangha, and realised that rich and poor alike—and even those beyond the empire's borders—could attain heaven if so desired with precisely the same sort of zeal. Now what this seemingly intangible *zeal* entails has been covered, in lesser or greater detail, by several epigraphs—and we will come to it in due course.

Suffice it to note here that his increasing preoccupation with explaining and propagating dhamma seems to have been a fact from when he first started issuing inscriptions on this issue twelve years into his ascension (as noted in Pillar Edict 6, for instance) until the very end of his reign. In this particular epigraph, though, Ashoka confines himself to the manner in which he is sharing his Eureka moment with his people. Addressing his officers, he says: 'And you must cause this matter to be engraved on stone whenever an opportunity presents itself. And, wherever there are stone pillars here in my dominions, this should be caused to be engraved on those stone pillars.'

Nothing Ashoka does is ever ordinary or derivative; therefore, the brilliant thought that has gone into constructing his plan is also very evident in this epigraph, although, for the moment, it remains understated. And since he also does not do anything by halves, the logistics thereof are thorough and impeccably devised. Continuing to address his officers, he says: 'And, according to the letter of this proclamation, you must despatch an officer to go everywhere, as far as your district extends.' The fact that he has not been lolling about on his royal couch and idly concocting grandiose schemes is also smartly slipped in by him: 'This proclamation,' he declares, 'is issued by me when on tour. Two hundred and fifty-six nights have been spent on tour.'

The impression he successfully conveys thereby is of a leader who is never off duty, who cares for the spiritual salvation of all the people within his realm—and even the ones beyond—even while he is tirelessly transacting state business all over. And so, that he is exerting himself physically and mentally on everyone's behalf is crystal clear. Ashoka, thus, reels the people in with his words, binding them even more firmly to him and the Mauryan empire at large—an original, somewhat quixotic but thoroughly praiseworthy interpretation of rulership.[7]

Assuming, though, that all Ashoka's subjects were literate and could wander around reading his missives with ease is a bit like putting the cart before the horse. Few people would have known how to read and write at the time, and the astute emperor was well-aware of this simple yet crucial fact.[8] So the instructions to his emissaries were twofold: find suitable, preferably striking, surfaces to inscribe his messages on but also make arrangements for the oral dissemination of the latter. The messages themselves were carefully composed so as to give the overall impression of Ashoka chatting with his people rather than commanding them in a distant manner—inasmuch as a grand royal figure could be expected to natter away!—which is why many of the edicts begin with the phrase, 'Thus speaks Devanampiya Piyadasi' (the Sanskrit Devanampriya Priyadarshi, or Beloved of the Gods whose gaze is affectionate), the sobriquet that he adopted for the express purpose of communicating with his subjects.

Incidentally, Kautilya, in his infinite wisdom, had already recommended the use of a qualified writer/*lekhaka* in administrative processes who would listen to the king's orders and transcribe them. The post required a decent handwriting, an ability to compose on demand and the eye to decipher all sorts of writing—and, presumably, the incumbent, particularly in Ashoka's time, must have had to work all hours to meet his royal employer's insatiable needs!

The procedure of oral communication itself was not as simple as it sounded. Separate rock edicts indicate that they were read out to the people on certain auspicious days, such as the full moon days of specific months and so on. This was, in all probability, a momentous occasion every time it was carried out. Imagine, if you can, a scenario where an entire community of people in a village or a hamlet or a town gather around a mysteriously-inscribed part of their landscape at a pre-assigned time of the day in answer to a summons by their ruler's representative, who, then, proceeds to read out the missive in sonorous tones to an audience that is agog with excitement and anticipation.

Subsequently, the air would be thick with questions and explanations and, of course, the thrill of having had a conversation, so to speak, with the emperor himself. Crowds would continue to gather around the carved surface for days afterwards and curious fingers would trace the letters while the educated ones would obligingly decipher them—all permeated, quite possibly, by a hushed air of reverence. There is something quite cosy and empowering in being included in your leader's plans and no one who came across these direct messages from the emperor would have remained unaffected by them. Their precise reactions, though, find no documentation.

Therefore, as is fairly obvious, the dhamma mahamatas (dharma mahamatras), the elite group of people that Ashoka created for this express purpose, had to be several things at once—keen purveyors of the terrain who could spot perfect, durable material to be inscribed upon; storytellers of sorts who could gather crowds around them and convey Ashoka's ideas in an engaging yet pithy manner; and indefatigable and gregarious travellers who were willing to accost all sorts of people within the realm and spread the gist of the emperor's new philosophy to them. In fact, Rock Edict 5 commands them to spread dhamma not just within the Mauryan kingdom but also among the border people, such as the Kambojas and Gandharas.[9] The latter might not have been the most welcoming kind of audience but the dharma mahamatras, by definition, were nothing if not intrepid.

In these days of fervent and frantic social media communication where messages are consumed almost as soon as they are posted and then promptly become redundant, it is easy to overlook the magnitude of Ashoka's endeavour. He was attempting—and, eventually, perfecting—a form of mass communication in the absence of the tools that we take for granted today. No technology, no replication aids, not even, perhaps, a constant supply of durable material on which he could scribble his notes at all times—and yet Ashoka pulled off this magnificent feat so successfully. Also, as Nayanjot Lahiri so pertinently points out, each of his messages to his varied administrators all over the empire was in a more or less identical form since he wanted to convey the same image of himself to all his subjects.[10] There was to be only one voice echoing across the Mauryan realm.

This was how the machinery swung into action: ideas for the content of the messages would have struck Ashoka at different points of time, whereupon he would have had them composed by his scribes and sent to princes governing various administrative centres, who, in turn, would have sent them on to the officials under them to disseminate further within their provinces. And we happen to know this through an inscribing mistake or 'ancient error', as Lahiri aptly dubs it, which, as it turns out was a fortuitous one, enabling the demystification of Ashoka's intricate logistics.

Three versions of an edict found near each other in the Chitradurga district of Karnataka (at Brahmagiri, Siddapura and Jatinga-Rameshwara) contain greetings and instructions from the provincial head, all of which have been faithfully transferred onto stone. Each of them notes that the prince or aryaputra, probably one of Ashoka's sons, and the officials or mahamatras from Suvarnagiri, the southern provincial capital, conveyed their wishes for the good health of the mahamatras at Isila—and this is followed by the pertinent content, which resembles that of Ashoka's other missives.[11] Clearly, therefore, the mahamatras at Isila had the edict inscribed in exactly the same form as they received it, following it to the letter, as it were, and mistakenly replicating the cheerful address at the beginning.

Lest you form the impression that some of these provincial minions and engravers were not the sharpest minds, let us just note in their defence that they have more or less vanished from the pages of history—and this is completely ironic given that they are the ones who actually gave Ashoka his 'voice'. It is not enough that Ashoka had these epiphanies; someone—or many someones—had to get them across to the hoi polloi, after all. And the fact that the messages have stood the test of time in every which way shows that they did a competent, even brilliant job of inscribing them. Yet, they hover, like most other ostensibly 'peripheral' characters, in the shadows of history and it is not just a matter of digging around for them and finding evidence. They have been lumped together, predictably, in one amorphous group and are talked about in much the same manner as the 'builders' of the pyramids of Egypt or the Taj Mahal in India—an anonymous body that we cannot or will not tell apart from each other.

There are, however, some rare and notable exceptions with regard to this faceless tale and the first of these pertains to the three supposedly 'faulty' messages, mentioned above. A person called Chapada, who might be the scribe who prepared the transcript or the engraver (the former is more likely given that several engravers might have worked on the engravings), signed his name on all three texts. Furthermore, he used the Kharoshti script, written from right to left, and popular in the Gandhara area and north-west India, for this purpose. This could well have been Chapada's private swagger, an indulgence he allowed himself to demonstrate his familiarity with varied scripts. Alternatively, he could have been indicating his connection with the areas near Afghanistan. Either way, his presence is literally set in stone, the signature chiselled into the rock along with Ashoka's message. And so, he goes down in history as the only writer-clerk working in the Mauryan administration whom we know by name.

Another scribe clamoured to be known, in a manner of speaking, by ensuring that he deviated considerably from the other styles employed in most Ashokan engravings.[12] The engraver of the Erragudi edict in Andhra Pradesh, this gentleman tackled his task in a rather eccentric and whimsical manner. He starts off with a bi-directional or boustrophedonic segment, the somewhat pompous word that describes a form of writing related to ancient Greece wherein the lines proceed from right to left and left to right instead of following a single direction. Perhaps the intention, yet again, was to show a general dexterity with scripts so that fellow-engravers could gnash their teeth in envy.

But then, he suddenly does the equivalent of throwing up his hands, abandons this style altogether, and then squeezes the rest of the text into the available space so that it can hardly be read at all, probably having caused his interpreters to gnash their teeth in anger instead. One can picture them peering at the words in frustration and attempting to make sense of them to their audience who probably regarded the engraving as a marvellous piece of art rather than a somewhat incomprehensible and garbled epistle.

And let us not forget the stellar contribution of the local officials and administrators in one important respect quite apart from their cumbersome work of transmitting the imperial messages all over the realm. Ashoka, for all his political shrewdness and sagacity, fondly—and naively—believed that the populace would recognise him by his titles alone. Now Devanampiya and Devanampiya Piyadasi sound very grand and glorious and exactly the sort of sobriquets that an emperor should adorn himself with but Ashoka's subjects were not exactly going around coyly referring to him as 'the one beloved of the Gods' or 'the one who looks at us affectionately'.[13] And yet, Ashoka persisted in wording his messages as emanating from this titled source ('Thus speaks Devanampiya'...and so on in similar vein).

Here is where some of the provincial officials stepped in to dole out some much-needed pragmatism. They did not share Ashoka's delusion and did not see the point in spreading messages that had an air of mystery clinging to them, however romantic or enticing this might have seemed. What they did was eminently simple: they added Ashoka's name to his messages so that it would be amply clear to the people that they were being addressed directly by their ruler. So, for instance, in Maski in Karnataka and Gujjara in central India, he is mentioned by name as 'Ashoka' and 'Ashoka-raja', respectively. And years down the line, this was one of the crucial pieces of evidence that aided in the resurrection of Ashoka and this crucial part of Mauryan history.

Ashoka's fascinating story can be approached from any of the pieces of evidence he left behind but let us start with the very heart of the tale: the Shahbazgarhi version of Rock Edict 13 because this is the one that tells us how the transformation from Ashoka the Fierce to Ashoka the Benevolent happened. It also has his changed philosophy of life in a nutshell. *And* it contains a rap on the knuckles, a veiled warning, as it were, to all those who do not toe his line. All this is in the third person (he varies between the first and third person in his inscriptions so he appears passionate and aloof, in turn). In this particular record, he holds forth on the thoughts and policies of Devanampriya Priyadarshi for all the world as if this were an interesting person whom he had encountered and whose tale he wants to tell.

The emperor begins with the war against Kalinga eight years into his reign and the devastation it caused ('One hundred and fifty thousand in number were the men who were deported thence; one hundred thousand in number were those who were slain there; and many times as many those who died.'). He then talks of his horror and remorse at the destruction wrought by him ('...now that the country of the Kalingas has been taken, Devanampriya is devoted to the pursuit of dhamma, the love of dhamma, and to instructing the people in dhamma. This is the repentance of Devanampriya on account of his conquest of the country of the Kalingas. For the slaughter, death and deportation of people that take place in the course of conquering an unconquered country is considered very painful and deplorable by Devanampriya.'). So he rubs in two facts here: first, that he has conquered Kalinga, which had previously remained outside the Mauryan pale, an important fact that requires a double iteration; and second, that he rues the bloodshed this conquest involved.

Ashoka then launches into a very perceptive and reasoned criticism of war, and the suffering it inevitably causes to all and sundry ('...all these suffer injury or slaughter or deportation of their loved ones;...this misfortune too becomes an injury to their own selves'). This is why dhamma-vijaya or conquest by dhamma, which he has patented, is the best conquest of all. But it isn't all sweetness and roses here—Ashoka cleverly inserts a strong warning into this deceptively mild, almost-rambling message: the recalcitrant forest people (*atavi*) and their chieftains had better behave themselves or face the consequences thereof ('And they are told of the power to punish them which Devanampriya possesses in spite of his repentance, in order that they may be ashamed of their crimes and may not be killed.'). Sugary words do not hide the significant fact that Ashoka still possesses the military means to subdue and punish, and has no qualms about using them, if need be.

So who are these forest people and why was it considered necessary to warn and/or subdue them? The *Arthashastra* includes a range of groups within this overreaching category—savage, essentially wild tribes; trappers; wanderers; forest chiefs and their ilk; people with criminal tendencies and so on—

and in its typical style, recommends that spies disguised as hermits be used to nose around the territories of these forest people. The relationship of tribes and forest dwellers with power centres has always been a problematic one through history and the additional problem is that one has to tease out references to them from sources that generally view them with distaste and suspicion. Aloka Parasher-Sen, for instance, says that no matter how powerful an ancient empire might have been, it would have encountered problems with regard to containing diverse ethnic populations.[14]

Thus, in the Mauryan period, the imposition of new forms of political, economic and ideological dominance on the forest people, and the need to keep them beneath the Mauryan heel while also assimilating them led to a change in the earlier attitude of keeping them strictly away from imperial territory. It was a dilemma, though, because the forest people and the resources under their command (such as timber, minerals and elephants) were immensely valuable to the state and could not be dispensed with altogether. The *Arthashastra* offers an entirely practical solution: use them as troops, spies and assassins instead.

Ashoka's stern warning begins to make sense in the light of this information. He is ordering them to repent for their misdemeanours and to watch their step; they are not to expect forgiveness for what cannot be forgiven. At the same time, there are other tribes like the Pitinikas and the Andhras who apparently follow dhamma, so this rap on the knuckles was clearly meant for all other recalcitrant tribes within the empire who should not mistake Ashoka's newfound spiritualism and pacifism for military weakness. The empire and its strength are still his priority; he will do whatever it takes to keep this intact—sort of reminiscent of a schoolteacher who appears to be initially mild but could, equally, lash out with reprimands and punishments when provoked.

The emperor's internal compulsions might have changed but his eye is on everything (much like Sauron in *The Lord of the Rings*!)—and Ashoka makes a point of distinguishing himself from his predecessors, in this regard. This is not the scrutiny of the unforgiving taskmaster but, rather, the watchful gaze of a leader for whom his subjects' affairs are paramount and to which he intends to respond with alacrity. To this effect, Rock Edict 6 at Girnar claims that in earlier times, state business and the reporting of incidents did not take place round-the-clock but this is where Ashoka has effected an important change whereby he will attend to his people's affairs at all times and anywhere.[15]

Reporters or *pativedakas* were posted all over the Mauryan realm with specific instructions to report to Ashoka on the doings of his people irrespective of his own engagements at the time: 'whether I am eating or in the harem or in the inner apartment or even in the cowpen, in the palanquin, or in the parks…And, if there is a dispute, or argumentation that arises in the council regarding any donation or proclamation I have made verbally, or in connection with an emergent matter which has been delegated to the *mahamatras*, it must be reported to me immediately, anywhere, at any time. Thus have I ordered.'

Not only is he quite categorical on the issue, he also outlines his highly-altruistic motives thereof with, of course, an oblique pat on his own back. 'For,' he declares, 'I am never content in exerting myself and in despatching business. For I consider it my duty to promote the welfare of all men…There is no duty more important than promoting the welfare of all men. And whatever effort I make is made in order that I may discharge the debt which I owe to all living beings, that I may make them happy in this world, and that they may attain heaven in the next world.' And then, he adds a strong dose of pragmatism to the mix: what underlies his duty to promote his people's welfare is 'exertion and prompt dispatch of business', and that while he wants his successors to conform to the same noble motive, 'this is difficult to accomplish without great effort'. He is already probably aware that his sons and grandsons might not share his passion and zeal, and this mammoth endeavour that he has undertaken will, inevitably, falter and fall by the wayside in their hands. Which it did!

Other strictures abound. In a separate rock edict (and as cited earlier), Ashoka appeals to the unconquered people on his borders not to fear him but to follow dhamma as espoused and encouraged by his dhamma-mahamatas. And then, there is Pillar Edict 5, which bans the killing of many species of animals twenty-six years into his reign (parrots, geese, bats, queen ants, terrapins, boneless fish, tortoises, porcupines, the rhinoceros, doves 'and all quadrupeds which are neither useful nor edible', to name a few quaint categories). How he determined this somewhat variegated list is a mystery. One can almost picture him strolling among his gardens and woods, contemplating each creature that scuttles across his path, and then leaning over the water bodies to examine their depths for more.

There are also intricate injunctions against animal castration and branding, as also hunting and fishing, on particular days. Furthermore, 'forests must not be burnt either uselessly or in order to destroy living beings'. 'Yes!' you might crow. 'Here is an ancient environmentalist par excellence, perhaps one of the earliest!' Yet picture to yourself, if you will, the bafflement of the very same forest people who must not apparently hunt or fish—their staple—or move a finger in the forest without inviting the wrath of this mercurial ruler upon their heads. But here we have a potentially classic clash between theory and practice, one of the perennial problems of historical reconstruction: did they, in fact, stop everything and live on love and fresh air alone or was Ashoka's ban more of a boast than anything else?

Ashoka definitely seemed to be obsessed with non-violence and viewed it as extendable to all living beings within his purview. Rock Edict 1 encapsulates his attempts to curb violence towards animals in sacrifices, festivals and, more pragmatically, in the royal kitchens.[16] No more gory hunting-and-feasting scenarios where the cooks laboured to convert fresh kills into palatable fare. All pleasure tours (largely for hunting) were replaced by dhamma tours, which were every bit as worthy as they sounded. Rock Edict 2 takes Ashoka's concern for animals a step further with a welfare package for them: the provision of medical treatment, the planting of herbs and trees, the digging of wells. However, it is Pillar Edict 5, issued in the twenty-seventh year of his reign, that clearly spells out his policy towards them (in a nutshell, 'the living must not live on the living'), and which, therefore, is remarkable and pathbreaking in itself.

Among a series of commands in this epigraph is the injunction against killing female goats, ewes, pregnant sows and animals less than six months old; animals that were earlier hunted in elephant forests; and the impaling and killing of fish in fishermen's preserves on certain days, as mentioned earlier. Husk containing living animals could not be burnt and living beings, in general, were not to be fed with other living beings. For those of you envisioning a halcyon Mauryan world where animals flitted and flew and scampered and swam without a care in the world, here is a bit of a reality check—Ashoka and his officers could not possibly have run up and down the realm ensuring this! What would have happened, in all probability, is a lessening of violence towards them but not the elimination of it altogether. A laudable step, nevertheless, and one that animal rights groups are still struggling to enforce, so you can appreciate the farsightedness of Ashoka's measures.

So is non-violence the sole constituent of Ashoka's dhamma? It was definitely key to it but dhamma itself, as understood and preached by the emperor, also embraced general themes of good conduct and social responsibilities.[17] It, therefore, encompasses courtesy to those who serve you; respect towards those older than you (particularly your parents); restraint in your dealings with living beings (here is where the non-violence comes in); and generosity towards friends, relatives, shramanas (Buddhist monks)[18] and brahmanas. It is also vastly superior, claims Rock Edict 9, to redundant rituals performed during sickness or marriage or travel, for instance—and here Ashoka shakes his head in sorrowful displeasure at women, who, it seems, are largely guilty of this.

And here is one of the critical aspects of Ashoka's dhamma as he saw it: the practice and accordance of mutual respect between different sects and religious communities. In our current context when religious groups seem to have nothing better to do than hurl invectives at each other and routinely vitiate the atmosphere, this comes as a breath of fresh air. Given the power Ashoka wielded and the vast resources at his command, he could have forced Buddhism down the throats of everyone in his massive realm if he had so desired—and that would have meant almost all of the country—but he showed restraint at the height of his strength by taking a step back and considering the motley crew of sects under him. So dhamma, clearly, did not mean the promotion of a particular sect to the detriment of others. Rock Edict 12, in fact, notes that Ashoka did not want his subjects to go around shrilly praising their own religions and lambasting others. As Rock Edict 7 succinctly puts it: '...all religions should reside everywhere'.

But this was not even 'antagonistic tolerance'—that elegant, almost-fashionable phrase composed to explain situations when the adherents of two or more religions glower at each other while they go about their lives without actually going so far as to murder each other due to practical considerations, despite occasional inner urges to do so.[19] Lest you consider this a modern construct, let us hasten to add that this was something that had been practiced more or less all over the world in varied religious contexts and time periods and, most probably, since the beginning of civilisation. After all, you can only get so far by chopping off the heads of your opponents and shouting yourself hoarse about the merits of your own form of worship. Pragmatism usually rules in any context and so, the realisation that more was to be gained by just getting along, whatever annoyances this entailed, was quick. You might build huge religious structures to dwarf the others and you might play your religious songs at the highest pitch to drown out contending noises but you still need your neighbour and their trade if your economy is to function with a modicum of convenience. Hence, the beauty of this term—and its practice.

Ashoka's plea, though, was something more besides, a request (or command, if you chose to interpret it that way) to be proactive in that his people were to make an attempt to understand the dhamma of others, so that the different essentials, in this regard, could be promoted together. Everyone had a dhamma: his was to promote the welfare of his people, and ensure their happiness in this and other worlds, as Rock Edict 6 notes. Then, of course, there are the specifics thereof, amply illustrated by Rock Edict 2: providing medical treatment and succour, digging wells, planting beneficial herbs and so on not just for humans but for animals, too. He, thus, differentiates himself from every other preceding ruler in one stroke—none of the latter had bothered to consider the four-legged world before in their welfare measures, however enlightened they claimed to be.

So now we come to what the edicts *do not* mention—his parents or his worthy royal predecessors, his being part of the Mauryan line, the manner in which he got the throne and his earlier rumoured excesses—or any guilt thereof. If we get into Ashoka's shoes, however, this is understandable. If you have run riot in your younger days and violated the law of primogeniture (by which the oldest son inherits the throne), got rid of several people on the way and then indulged in a bloody campaign of revenge, you do not necessarily want to proclaim this to the world at large, especially if you are now a responsible ruler who is seeking to unite your vast realm. Yet Ashoka's silence on his early days becomes all the more resounding when we consider how voluble he is post-Kalinga. None of his epigraphs contain his lineage—an almost mandatory requirement in most royal records—or that of his queens. It is almost as if family and relatives do not matter to him; his new royal policy and state imperatives do. He chooses to record only what matters to him, not what traditional policy dictates. Here, too, he is a pioneer.

And how does Ashoka compare with Kautilya, the two political stalwarts par excellence? Both spoke through their strictures although the media they chose to disseminate them was, admittedly, different—epigraphic and textual, respectively. Upinder Singh speaks of the startling similarity between them despite their deceptively different approaches.[20] For a start, both believed in what is termed benevolent paternalism, much like a kindly father holding their child's hand and helping them navigate this world and the one beyond. Their concern for animals is, oddly enough, another issue that links them. However difficult it is to imagine Kautilya casting a benign eye on anyone, let alone four-legged creatures, it is, in fact, true and the *Arthashastra* provides extensive evidence on his concern for their welfare. There are regulations for protecting wildlife and on grazing, punishments for cruelty to animals, a list of a veterinarian's responsibilities and so on.[21]

However, while Ashoka is viewed through the ages as a remarkable king who decided to eschew war and violence at the height of his triumph, and devoted his life to propagating dhamma and non-violence among his subjects, Kautilya propagated realpolitik whereby the ends justified the means, involving a moral lapse or two along the way, and the ruthless pursuit and acquisition of power, where subterfuge and killing were par for the course. Also, for Kautilya, political integration required conquest and centralised administration whereas Ashoka's edicts seem more akin to a flexible one, where the local was governed through adjustments and concessions. In fact, non-violence and mutual respect may have been the most practical mode to run a huge, subcontinental territory—proof that ideas of governance always grow out of the exigencies of the times.

And the enormous sprawl of the Mauryan realm *would* have thrown up all sorts of ruling challenges, ones that Ashoka ably combatted despite giving the impression that his priorities lay elsewhere.

Notes

1. See, for instance, Charles Allen, *Ashoka—The Search for India's Lost Emperor*, Abacus, 2012, pp.352–353. Also, the Appendix (pp.405–425) contains a translation of Ashoka's Rock and Pillar Edicts. See also Romila Thapar, *Asoka and the Decline of the Mauryas*, Oxford University Press, 3rd edn, 2021, pp.376–396. For another excellent survey of the sites and content of Ashoka's inscriptions, see Nayanjot Lahiri, *Ashoka in Ancient India*, Permanent Black, 2015, pp.308–317. Also, Upinder Singh, *A History of Ancient and Early Medieval India—From the Stone Age to the 12th Century*, Pearson/Dorling Kindersley, p.327.
2. L.N. Rangarajan, ed. and trans., *Kautilya—The Arthashastra*, Penguin, 1992, pp.184–185, 2.10.6–12; 57–62.
3. Upinder Singh, *Political Violence in Ancient India*, Harvard University Press, 2017, p.44.
4. Prakrit was spoken in Magadha, the language of the people at large. Sanskrit, on the other hand, was the language of culture and erudition. For details of the languages and scripts of the time, see, for instance, Allen, *Ashoka—The Search for India's Lost Emperor*, pp.426–427. See also Thapar, *Asoka and the Decline of the Mauryas*, pp.xxxix, 277–287. Prakrit transcended political boundaries and most religious affiliations.
5. We are including, in this corpus, a donative edict of Karuvaki, one of Ashoka's queens, inscribed on the Allahabad-Kosam pillar, which we will come to later.
6. This pertains to the Hutti and Kolar gold mines in Karnataka. See Thapar, *Asoka and the Decline of the Mauryas*, pp.274–275. For a detailed analysis of the geographical locations of the edicts, see pp.350–362. For a discussion on Maski, for instance, and its connection with gold mining, see Lahiri, *Ashoka in Ancient India*, p.146. See also pp.260–262 for a discussion of the pillar edict sites. Lahiri points out that while Ashoka's fourteen major rock edicts were issued over four years, the six pillar edicts were engraved like 'a single prearranged bunch' from Haryana to Bihar and at around the same time. As the pillar edicts are mostly in north India, she also looks at fauna at sites excavated there to check the efficacy of Ashoka's anti-animal-slaughter measures. See pp.275–276. For a discussion of the rock edict sites, see

pp.177–181. Incidentally, Girnar is the most arresting example of the rock edicts being simultaneously engraved at one place, creating 'one long sermon'. For further details of Girnar and the excavations there, see pp.189–191, 203–214.

7. Opinions differ, though. Charles Allen, for one, says Ashoka's words may be heartfelt 'but they are naïve, incoherent and egotistical'. See Allen, *Ashoka—The Search for India's Lost Emperor*, p.381.
8. The literate groups would have been the brahmanas, Buddhist monks, officials and some other professionals who required writing. On the subject of writing and literacy, see Thapar, *Asoka and the Decline of the Mauryas*, pp.283–287.
9. They were, in fact, deployed everywhere, not just in Pataliputra and other towns but also in the households of Ashoka's siblings and relatives.
10. Lahiri, *Ashoka in Ancient India*, pp. 126–127. No royal messages/orders of any kind prior to Ashoka have survived. Palm leaf, birch bark, cotton cloth and wooden boards were the usual surfaces for writing but all are perishable and there are no extant specimens except for a birch bark of the first millennium BCE from a settlement at Sringaverapura near the Ganga's banks. Some of Ashoka's missives, too, might have used these materials but after Kalinga, it was all stone. See pp.120–121. For a discussion on the different surfaces used for the Ashokan edicts, see pp.121–123.
11. Ibid., p.127; K.R. Norman, 'The Languages of the Composition and Transmission of the Ashokan Inscriptions', in P. Olivelle, J. Leoshko, and H.P. Ray, eds. *Reimagining Asoka—Memory and History*, Oxford University Press, p.49.
12. Lahiri, *Ashoka in Ancient India*, p.128. See also D.C. Sircar, *Asokan Studies*, Indian Museum Calcutta, 1979, rpt 2000, p.4. P.K. Anderson, 'Notes on the Engraving Procedures for the Erragudi Version of Asoka's Minor Rock Edict', *Indo Iranian Journal*, 34, 1991, p.268.
13. His complete royal title was Devanampiya Piyadassi Raja Ashoka. Romila Thapar feels that Ashoka was his personal name, Piyadassi his official one and Devanampiya a generally known royal title of the time. Devanampiya was used in Ceylonese literature not for Ashoka but his contemporary, Tissa. It was adopted as a title by his grandson, Dasharatha and several Ceylonese kings after

Tissa, so it was a well-used royal one. See Thapar, *Asoka and the Decline of the Mauryas*, pp.348–349.

14. See Singh, *A History of Ancient and Early Medieval India*, p.348 where this is cited.
15. Ibid., p.345.
16. Where earlier 'hundred thousands of living beings' were slaughtered in his kitchen 'for the sake of curry', the number had come down to three (two birds and one animal) and even these 'shall not be killed in future'. See, for instance, Lahiri, *Ashoka in Ancient India*, p.193 where this is cited.
17. Incidentally, the word dharma is used by Hindus, Buddhists, Jainas and Sikhs to describe the proper practice of religion and the ultimate reality. In Hindu usage, it spans an even wider application—from the correct performance of religious rules to ethical conduct and the application of law. The normative Dharmashastras or lawbooks cover all this. See Allen, *Ashoka—The Search for India's Lost Emperor*, pp.xviii–xix.
18. Actually, they were ascetic renunciants that included more categories than Buddhist monks.
19. See Robert Hayden et.al., eds. *Antagonistic Tolerance—Competitive Sharing of Religious Sites and Spaces*, Routledge, 2016 for an explanation of the term and examples of it from around the world in different time periods.
20. Upinder Singh, *Ancient India: Culture of Contradictions*, Aleph, 2021, pp. 172–176. For another comparison or 'parallelism' between the Ashokan edicts and the *Arthashastra*, see R.K. Mookerji, *Chandragupta Maurya and His Times*, Motilal Banarsidass, 1966, rpt.1988, pp.236–245. See also Thapar, *Asoka and the Decline of the Mauryas*, p.347. She feels that Vishnugupta (usually regarded as one of Kautilya's names) was, in fact, someone else who worked over the entire text, including any interpolations, in the third or fourth century CE. The form in which we read it today is his.
21. See Rangarajan, *Kautilya—The Arthashastr*a, pp.75–77.

13

THE WOMEN IN ASHOKA'S LIFE

If your hair stood on end when you read about Ashoka burning the denizens of his harem during his early days as ruler, you must have already formed the impression that he was (at least, initially) cold and ruthless, a complete stranger to the gentler passions of romance, and probably entirely incapable of making a woman happy with protestations and attestations of love. The sources beg to differ, though. It appears that Ashoka was entirely capable of being smitten—and that, too, more than once. Let us begin with the oft-told tale of Devi, a brief but alluring one. The daughter of a prominent merchant in the city of Vidisha (modern Besnagar) in central India, Ashoka met her—and the complicated ramifications of love for the first time in his young life—when he was sent as Bindusara's viceroy to Avanti in the Malwa region.[1]

A reminder here—this is the same area that was ruled by Pradyota who had those strange skirmishes with Bimbisara, the Magadhan ruler, and his formidable son, Ajatashatru. In fact, Ajatashatru was inclined to be a bit nervous about Pradyota's designs, which is why he apparently strengthened Rajagriha's fortifications, in the first place. That anyone could get under the Machiavellian Ajatashatru's skin to such an extent seems slightly farfetched, though!

Very little is known about Devi except that she caught Ashoka's eye, presumably on account of her beauty, whereupon they married and moved on to Ujjayini, his base while administering Avanti. Unmoved by the exciting and clearly whirlwind nature of their courtship, however, the Buddhist literary sources stodgily mention her son, Mahinda (Mahendra) and daughter, Samghamita (Sanghamitra), that resulted from this union. Then they move on to the next item of interest in their narrative without any of the whys and wherefores thereof.

And so, we are left with disappointingly meagre information about this affair of the heart except that it probably happened around 282 BCE, a decade or so before Bindusara's death. That the children were born two years apart in Ujjayini indicates that Ashoka stayed there for quite a while. Whether this was due to his fascination with Devi or with Avanti in general remains unclear. What we do know, though, is that both Mahendra and Sanghamitra subsequently played a pivotal role as Ashoka's emissaries in spreading Buddhism to Sri Lanka—and so, Devi's sole purpose, as far as the Buddhist tradition is concerned, is in providing him with offspring.[2]

There is a bit of controversy regarding their marriage and Devi's legal status, however.[3] Some historians feel that as a specific marriage ceremony is not spoken of in the *Dipavamsa* and the fact that Devi did not become Ashoka's chief queen makes one conclude they were living in sin and Devi's tainted status thereby barred her from the exalted post. It is most unlikely, though, that the wilful Ashoka would have cowered behind some prescribed rule and so, he probably *did* marry Devi and give her children a measure of prominence but eventually preferred someone else by his side. After all, rulers are notoriously fickle with lamentably short attention spans. It could, equally, be that Devi tired of Ashoka's weird, mercurial mood swings in time and preferred to stay as far away from him as she could. Such is, as poets will assure us, the path of most wild infatuations and passions—they eventually fizzle out.

Another question that arises here is whether Devi was a practising Buddhist and, by extension, whether she inspired Ashoka, in some intangible way, to adopt her religion at a point of personal crisis. Incidentally, most secondary historical narratives are acutely hysterical about women's piety—or the lack of it—while describing royal personages down the ages. Let us take the case of Didda (mentioned earlier) who ruled Kashmir from CE 980/1–1003 and had been in charge behind the scenes, in any case, for a couple of decades before her formal ascension to the throne.[4] She was a formidable ruler by any standards and administered Kashmir with an iron hand. This involved a fair amount of blood and gore, her viewing her own family members with a jaundiced eye when it came to their ability to rule, and finally sweeping them aside to mount the throne herself as being the best bet for the land. Thereafter, she is supposed to have given Kashmir a long period of stability and prosperity, and to have brooked no nonsense or dissension from any (male) quarter.

'Yes, but did she visit temples?' 'Did she *pray*?' 'Was she a *good* person?' Was she everything a woman ought to be?'—thus, unbelievingly, shriek the purveyors of Kashmir's history from the earliest times to the present, desperately clinging to the hope that Didda was not really that despicable thing: a contravention of a feminine stereotype. When the evidence stares them in the face, though, they withdraw in a unanimous and coldly disapproving huddle. 'She was not really a woman!' they say, heaping her with other wonderful epithets: 'notorious' and 'dissolute' being prominent among them. Didda did not particularly help her case by building a series of religious and secular structures all over Kashmir, and then blithely naming them after herself so as to perpetuate her power and presence more firmly on the physical landscape. And this is just one of the numerous cases from our collective past.

Here is another. Kanauj, in the seventh century CE, was associated with the golden Harsha/Harshavardhana (CE 606–648) who apparently made it the most powerful kingdom in north India and, simultaneously, his contemporaries jealous and miserable. Much is made of his religious choices, of his supposed conversion from Shaivism to Buddhism, at some point, and there is a great deal of frenzied speculation on his motives thereof. Hardly any attention is paid to his younger sister, Rajyashri, who, incidentally, enabled him to get the throne of Kanauj, probably ruled it jointly with him for a period of time, was otherwise very vocal in court debates, accompanied Harsha on military campaigns—and who might very well have influenced her brother's religious proclivities, in the first place, for she was a Buddhist herself and actively encouraged discussions on religion, notably with Xuanzang, the visiting Chinese pilgrim, who has recorded her interest in this regard. But, of course, such a vibrant woman figure must immediately be conventionalised and so, there is a rush to portray her as a weak, weeping creature who needed her magnificent older brother to prop her up and take decisions on her behalf, while all other evidence of her influence and presence, in the political and religious sphere, is routinely ignored.

So here we have two examples—of a queen who was not

particularly moral or religious and of another who was vocal about her religious choices—but both have been invisibilised or trivialised. The writing on the wall is clear for women in history: be pious and/or dependent in your religious choices and we will include you in the narrative; challenge this stereotype and we will condemn you to the shadows. Back to Devi and the facts concerning her religion. The places associated with her bear strong Buddhist connections. Vidisha, for instance, has an intrinsic link to the Buddhist monuments of Sanchi. Furthermore, local traditions link the largest stupa at Ujjayini, the Kanipura, with Devi as having been built for her; it has been dubbed the Vaishya Tekri (Vaishya caste's mound) in local parlance: Devi's father was a merchant, a typically Vaishya occupation. In addition, the Buddhist Pali texts imply that she was following the doctrine of Buddhism much before her royal husband converted to it. The *Mahavamsa* talks of her taking her son Mahinda, by then a monk, uphill to the Vedisagiri vihara (Sanchi, in all probability), suggesting that she was a Buddhist and associated with it.

Devi might even have been a Buddhist when she first met Ashoka in Vidisha and Cupid struck. And, quite possibly therefore, she could have been the factor behind his turning to Buddhism, his spiritual metamorphosis, after the Kalinga massacre. And so, Devi's sole purpose remains procreation and Ashoka is left to achieve enlightenment all on his own with, perhaps, some helpful nudges provided by men. Heaven forbid that we should actually show a woman influencing a man in a very decisive way! In any case, Devi's little paradise was rudely interrupted ten years into Ashoka's sojourn in Ujjayini when his father, Bindusara, fell ill and he promptly raced back to Pataliputra and the throne like a bloodhound on the trail.

Ashoka was not immune to the temptation of graffiti, though, while in the throes of love, according to Charles Allen.[5] Panguraria, near Devi's town of Vidisha, was apparently witness to the rambles of this besotted couple early in their courtship—and Ashoka clearly felt an irresistible urge to record this fact on his return to this place many years later, now in the throes of nostalgia. High up on the face of a rock shelter, carved casually—and, therefore, clumsily—with a chisel and stick in bold letters is the following legend: 'The king, who (now, after consecration) is called Piyadassi, (once) came to this place on a pleasure tour while he was still a (ruling) prince, living together with his unwedded consort.' And thus was an unguarded royal moment, when the cares of administration took a backseat to romantic remembrances and simpler days, captured for posterity!

And then, of course, there is Karuvaki, that powerful woman figure in his life, so earnestly depicted in celluloid by the green-eyed actress, Kareena Kapoor, and, therefore, an aspect of this period that the public at large is aware of, not least because Shahrukh Khan, the permanent Bollywood idol, essayed the role of the emperor. As noted earlier, movie versions of historical figures (and *Asoka* is no exception!) are apt to contain a whole lot of fiction and infinitesimal fact but the manner in which they are lapped up by eager viewers is, undoubtedly, heartening.

It also apparently makes some of them resident experts in the field, such that they will profess to know anything and everything about Ashoka's life—and, by extension, the Mauryan period—on the strength of this three-hour tale alone, where, among other things, the emperor's heart is shown to belong only to the feisty Karuvaki. (They might even extend their newly-acquired expertise to embrace all aspects of the ancient period in Indian history—and from there, it is a mere step to covering the entire past, which is why you have legions of people claiming to know this and that about history and ferociously challenging anyone, even academics, who would deem otherwise. But this is neither here nor there!)

So what does historical evidence say about Karuvaki? For a start, she was definitely powerful and had no qualms in stating so—this comes through very clearly in the inscription known as the Queen's Edict on the Allahabad pillar (alluded to earlier), where she declares that whatever gifts have been made by her, 'the second queen', such as mango groves, gardens, alms-houses and the like, were to be registered in her name. It ends with a deceptively mild statement: 'This (is) (the request) of the second queen, the mother of Tivala, the Karuvaki', yet it is evident that she wants to be known—for the present and, presumably, posterity—as the donor of the gifts. This is definitely not the statement of a shy, shrinking personage who wants to avoid the limelight while donating for noble, pious reasons. No, this is someone who has a will of her own and wants a specific act of philanthropy to be regarded and recorded as hers alone.[6]

And so, we come to the other powerful woman figure in Ashoka's life, Tissarakkha or Tishyarakshita (depending on whether you go by Pali or Sanskrit accounts, respectively). This character possessed shades of the wily Ajatashatru but went several steps further in terms of vengefulness and scheming and general unpleasantness to justifiably earn the epithet of Lady Macbeth that Nayanjot Lahiri, for one, bestows on her.[7] To understand her story, though, one has to first move off at a tangent and examine the tale of the Bodhi tree under which the Buddha is recorded as having achieved enlightenment and, consequently, of great significance to Ashoka.

The *Mahavamsa* talks of a sapling of this sacred tree having been brought to Sri Lanka in the eighteenth year of Ashoka's reign by his daughter, Sanghamitra, who had carefully carried it all the way from the eastern Indian port of Tamralipti, vanquishing certain snakes or *nagas* enroute who wanted to lay their hands on it, so to speak. It was planted in the Maha-megha-vanarama and thrived, thereafter, for a long time. But what of the original, the one dear to Ashoka's heart, and why and how is it connected with Tishyarakshita? Ah, there lies a twisted tale, indeed!

The sorry saga of Ashoka's Bodhi tree seems to have started with the death of Asamdhimitta/Asandhimitra, his 'dear consort' and ardent devotee of the Buddha, in 241 BCE, a year after Ashoka issued his Seventh Pillar Edict, and the twenty-ninth year of his reign. We know very little about this chief queen, clearly a more suitable choice for the post than Devi and probably hailing, as Charles Allen speculates, from a small kingdom north of Delhi—Assandh boasts of the biggest Ashokan stupa in India.[8] Ashoka seems to have been devastated by Asandhimitra's passing away and his state of mourning lasted a fairly long while.

After around eight years, however, he began to revive a bit and take an interest in his surroundings, which is when his eye fell on the beautiful but vengeful Tishyarakshita who soon took the place of his beloved Asamdhimitta in his affections and at court. Thrilled at her newfound power and status, Tishyarakshita was enjoying life until she discovered that Ashoka always sent the most precious jewels to some Bodhi, not her. This appallingly ignorant woman promptly assumed that Bodhi was a rival and decided to tackle her accordingly.

The *Ashokavadana* reveals, in dark detail, Tishyarakshita's dastardly scheme of paying a sorceress to destroy Bodhi. The latter, clearly not as clueless as her royal employer, tied a thread around the Bodhi tree and chanted a spell to hurry things along. And so, the tree began to droop and wither. This dismal turn of events had an equally dismal effect on Ashoka whereby he fainted and had to be strenuously revived only for him to announce that he would die if Bodhi perished. Tishyarakshita, still inexplicably clueless—and this really does not speak well for her general level of awareness!—consoled Ashoka with an enchanting prospect: Bodhi may die but she, on the other hand, would always remain with him and give him pleasure. An irresistible prospect, no doubt, but Tishyarakshita's delusion hit Ashoka like a ton of bricks. One can picture him painstakingly explaining the truth to her ('Bodhi is not a *woman*; it is a *tree*!') and the light of knowledge finally dawning in her eye.

And so, Tishyarakshita instructed the sorceress to revive the tree and all was well. Or was it? While the *Mahavamsa* implies gloom and doom not just for the emperor but also for Buddhism in India (the story in question being highly metaphorical in content and intent), the *Ashokavadana* suggests that everything continued as before (in both spheres) after this unfortunate glitch. However, the writing on the wall was now clear: if Ashoka could not even protect his precious Bodhi tree, he was no longer in control of anything. Thus, Tishyarakshita becomes synonymous with his end—as in the time-honoured literary tradition of associating women with the downfall and destruction of men.

This, incidentally, is a trope that is faithfully echoed by an alarming number of historians, past and present. Is the end of a king and/or a dynasty near? Quick, look for a woman. It's bound to be her fault! (It could also be the other way around. Is a woman anywhere on the scene? Oh, dear, the king and/or the dynasty is bound to fall!). There is another ludicrous speculation that Karuvaki's edict indicates a weakening of Ashoka's control as it was not engraved on his orders but seemingly issued by the queen herself.[9] No speculation, for instance, that the queen in question had an independent and palpable presence in court, and could very well issue her own donative inscription, but much moaning, instead, about Ashoka's implied decline!

There are two more related and hair-raising incidents involving Tishyarakshita that would make anyone's blood run cold. The first of these pertained to Kunala, Ashoka's son by a Queen Padmavati (another entity that we do not know much about). Born as Dharma-vivardhana, his eyes were apparently beautiful like that of the Himalayan bird *kunala*, which is why Ashoka promptly gave him the same name. Kunala, by all accounts, was a pleasant, sensible personality, inclined towards spirituality and, in fact, entirely suited to follow his father to the throne. Tishyarakshita, though, suddenly fell madly in love—or, rather, lust—with this hapless prince (actually, with his eyes, the *Ashokavadana* claims) and had no qualms in telling him so.

Aghast, Kunala explained that he regarded her as a mother and that this was not an appropriate move on her part. The spurned Tishyarakshita was neither embarrassed nor chastened; instead, she told the miserable Kunala that he was not destined to last much longer and began plotting his end with diabolic glee. However, much to her chagrin, no readymade opportunity presented itself, so she sat about biding her time. Kunala departed soon after to quell a rebellion in Taxila and that was that.

At this point, Ashoka was suddenly felled by a violent

and gruesome sickness in that 'excrement' apparently started issuing from his mouth, while, at the same time, something undefinable began to ooze out of all his pores. The royal physicians were baffled and the emperor, inclined to gloomy thoughts in his old age, promptly decided that he was going to die, and asked for Kunala to be recalled from Taxila and ascend the throne as his successor. This turn of events would have dismayed anyone in Tishyarakshita's place but she was made of sterner stuff. Coldly aware of what would happen to her if Kunala returned and told the truth, she set about tackling the problem with methodical ruthlessness. She first banned all Ashoka's doctors from treating him (which probably made them relieved!) and then asked for anyone suffering from a similar problem to be brought to her.

Tishyarakshita's orders were obeyed with alacrity and soon after, she was face-to-face with a man whose ailment mirrored Ashoka's. Now any normal person would have quailed at the task that she set herself but, as we have observed, Tishyarakshita, although somewhat lacking in awareness and discernment, was neither squeamish nor cowardly. So she had the poor man killed and then split open his stomach, examining his entrails with frank (or should that be ghoulish?) interest. Looking at it dispassionately, the Mauryan period was rife with post-mortems of different kinds, if you strictly believe the written word, that is. We have Kautilya trying to extricate the unborn Bindusara from his mother's womb and now we have Tishyarakshita crouching over her victim's belly. Clearly, men and women of iron stomachs, these Mauryans!

What Tishyarakshita found in the man's stomach was disgusting but revelatory: a massive worm that was causing all the flows and oozing with its movements. What she did next was a triumph of science and clinical experimentation:

when peppers and ginger yielded no result, she gave onion to the worm, which promptly died and passed out of the body through the intestinal tract. And so, she presented Ashoka with an onion and told him to eat it, which he promptly did, its raw pungency being a clearly more savoury alternative to having an alien creature in his innards!

His miraculous recovery, thereafter, was lauded by all (incidentally, further cementing the onion's reputation for being a wonder food, although it took a long, long while for certain categories of people to approach it without recoiling in distaste). The grateful emperor decided—in yet another time-honoured literary tradition (recall the *Ramayana*!)—to grant his wifely saviour a boon and we already know, therefore, that disaster hovered in the air. Tishyarakshita, determined to wring every last drop from this opportunity, asked to be made the ruler for a week, and a besotted and physically weak Ashoka agreed without pausing to reflect on the strangeness of her request.

Accordingly, an order was sent soon after to the people of Taxila in her name, instructing them to put out Kunala's eyes. Initially baffled but later presuming that some obscure wisdom underlay it, the citizens obeyed the royal missive and blinded Kunala, whereupon he returned to Pataliputra to expose her villainy. Years of calming Buddhist thought had clearly not extinguished Ashoka's natural inclination to rage, which now rose within him like a roused monster to turn its full power on the villainous Tishyarakshita. The texts tell us that he vowed to tear her eyes out, rip open her body with rakes, impale her on a spit, cut off her nose with a saw and her tongue with a razor, and kill her with poison—a distinct echo of the young Ashoka who had allegedly devised outrageous ways to torture his victims.

But this was a different time and a different place and Kunala, horrified at his father's bloodthirsty designs that so militated against his spiritual coil, urged him to forgive Tishyarakshita. This generosity of spirit apparently—and miraculously—resulted in Kunala's sight being restored but he was unable to protect his assaulter from his father's wrath. She was burned to death and, to top it all, the confused citizens of Taxila were executed for their part in the deed.

All ends well—or, actually, not, in some ways. Kunala seems not to have recovered from this incident (whether physically or mentally is unclear) because he is now no longer Ashoka's successor; his son, Sampadin, is declared the heir. Ashoka, now rid of murderous wives and their machinations, throws himself even more wholeheartedly into donations, sending gold all over the place to different monasteries, until Sampadin and the ministers step in to save the state treasury from this indiscriminate depletion. He manages to thwart them, though, by discovering another, clever way of donation: giving away his gold, silver and copper plates, in turn, until there is nothing left to serve his food on. Bitterly aware of the disapproval that surrounds him, in this regard, he likens his reduced state to a river that is repulsed when it strikes a mountain cliff.

Finally—and dramatically, he is left with nothing but half an *amalaka*/myrobalan—a cherry plum, in other words. One can picture him brooding over it (one presumes he was not in fact, eating it!) until the realisation of its being his very last possession strikes him, whereupon he orders that it be given to the monks at the Kukkutarama monastery.[10] There is a rider, though—as this is his last offering to the Buddhist community, it should be savoured by everyone. And so, the half-fruit is put into a soup that the entire community consumes and enjoys.

It is even used as an instructive metaphor by the leader of the monastery to his monks thus: 'A great donor, the lord of men, the eminent Maurya Asoka, has gone from being lord of Jambudvipa to being lord of half a myrobalan…' This, in fact, forms a striking parallel with Harsha of Kanauj who, in true Ashoka-fashion and witnessed by Xuanzang many centuries later, gave away everything he possessed to his people and eventually had to borrow a cloth from his sister, Rajyashri, to cover himself!

There is one more grand donative gesture made by Ashoka just before he passes away. Conscious of his quickly-ebbing life, the emperor proceeds to donate the entire earth to the Buddhist sangha, excluding the treasury, and inscribes this record with his teeth. No, this was not the final act of a witless person; it was a very deliberate move to confer royal authority on the donation in a most definitive way. Incidentally, this act was mimicked—unknowingly or otherwise—many centuries later in an altogether different locale. Lahiri points out that William the Conqueror of England once donated lands and bit the wax on the document to seal his order in the most emphatic manner possible.[11]

It might be pertinent to note that not all royal records through the ages received this treatment—presumably, wax was not a pleasant substance to sink one's teeth into and there were, after all, other ways of ensuring that orders were enacted. Additionally, this final act was not made so that Ashoka could leave traces of his DNA behind but to obtain 'sovereignty of the mind'. So a man who once sought kingship and visceral glory and power—and had no compunction in killing to achieve these—realises his true priorities, after all. Such are usually the nature of deathbed assertions and in Ashoka's case, it becomes all the more poignant: the man who was hysterical about obtaining an empire gave it all away with his last breath.

Ashoka's death soon after his donative act precipitated a bit of a crisis in that the ministers of the Mauryan court had to buy back the dominions that he had so magnanimously donated to the Buddhist sangha in order that a new king could take over the reins. This they did by ingeniously giving four *kotis* of gold pieces to the sangha to complete the shortfall—a gesture enabled by the sensible exclusion of the state treasury from the overall donation. Incidentally, the Tibetan lama, Taranatha, provides a postscript to Ashoka's tale that is, in fact, quite in keeping with his capricious personality.[12] A woman attendant who was fanning him during his dying moments fell asleep in the noon heat and dropped her yak-tail whisk on him, greatly annoying Ashoka thereby who mused that where he was once served so carefully even by great kings, he was now being insulted by the lowest of his minions. And so, as he died with anger in his mind, he had to be 'reborn as a Naga (snake king) in a big lake of Pataliputra'.

The question of what really happened after this extraordinary emperor's death is an unresolved one. His successors are not mentioned in the Pali chronicles of Sri Lanka, presumably because the emissaries he had sent there had already established firm roots for Buddhism and so, there was no real interest in the aftermath of his rule. To complicate matters, there are glaring discrepancies in the list of his successors in the texts of the northern Buddhist tradition and the Brahmanical Puranas.[13] Together, they list between two and seven names who followed Ashoka on the Mauryan throne.

When you consider that the first three rulers of this powerful line accounted for some eighty-five years between themselves, then Ashoka's successors must have ruled for only fifty-two years altogether because the dynasty itself was extinguished in around 180 BCE. Furthermore, we have very little information on them. For instance, there is no evidence as to whether they continued Ashoka's policy of benevolent governance or dispensed with it entirely.

And then, of course, there is the usual intense squabbling between the Buddhist and Jaina literary traditions. Sample this: the *Ashokavadana*'s version of events is that Sampadin, who succeeded Ashoka on the throne (the Jaina texts insist that Sampadin or Samprati converted to the Jaina faith and did for it what Ashoka did for Buddhism), had a son named Brihaspati who was followed by Vrishasena, who was followed, in turn, by Pushyadharman who was followed by Pushyamitra, which, incidentally, is also the name of the person who killed the last Mauryan ruler and started the Shunga line. So were there two Pushyamitras, one who was the last Mauryan ruler and the other, his namesake who killed him? This sounds impossibly complicated and makes you wonder whether the one who was compiling details for the *Ashokavadana* actually bothered to check their facts!

According to the Puranas and Banabhatta's *Harshacharita*—and this is yet another instance of the muddying of historical waters—the latter Pushyamitra was, in fact, a general in the army of the last Mauryan ruler, Brihadratha, from whom he usurped the throne in a parade-ground coup and founded the Shunga dynasty. The *Ashokavadana* regards him, though, as an anti-Buddhist Mauryan and, therefore, with grave suspicion, ascribing his dubious choices to a nasty brahman priest who urged him to destroy the religion by erasing its monks and monasteries. But—and here we need to furrow our brows in disbelief yet again—a *yaksha* (basically, a nature-spirit that could be nice or nasty) obligingly came along, at this juncture, and ensured Pushyamitra's death (he flattened him under a mountain).

And this is, the text claims, how the Mauryan line ended. The account, as noted earlier, tests the limits of our credulity and it is well-nigh impossible to assess its historical veracity. However—and this is curious given that the dynasty is supposed to have ended in around 180 BCE—there are some references to later rulers who are related to the Mauryas. For instance, Xuanzang, the Chinese pilgrim, refers to Purnavarman, apparently the last of Ashoka's race, who restored the Bodhi tree destroyed by Shashanka of Bengal and who ruled some time before his visit, which, being in the seventh century CE, renders one truly baffled, unless, of course, he was a minor king who was trying to legitimise his rule by claiming a connection with Ashoka.

Shashanka, incidentally (and here we go off on another historical tangent), was caught in an imbroglio with Harshavardhana of Kanauj: not only did he abet the kidnapping of Rajyashri, Harsha's sister, but he was also implicated in the deaths of Rajyashri's husband, Grihavarman, and brother, Rajyavardhana. This had Harsha screaming imprecations and baying for Shashanka's blood, or so the *Harshacharita* claims, and setting out on a grand campaign of retribution, which must have ended in a sort of whimper, though—there is no clear evidence that Harsha ever defeated Shashanka but this uncomfortable fact is usually whipped out of sight in the largely eulogistic narratives of Harsha that exist.

Back to the knotty tale of the Mauryan succession and the significant fact here is that Ashoka *did* have an emulator among his descendants. Dasharatha, one of his grandsons who is mentioned in both the Puranic and Buddhist traditions, and can be pinpointed as someone who actually ruled because he features in a contemporary source, proclaimed his presence through engravings on rock in various structures commissioned by him. He clearly thought that he needed to be worthy of the giant shadow he had stepped into. Not only did he call himself *devanampriya*, a clear duplication of his grandfather's title, but he also inscribed dedicatory inscriptions, mentioning himself and his donees, at caves similar to those at Barabar in the adjacent Nagarjuni hill, and which are associated with Ashoka.

The recipients of Dasharatha's largesse were the Ajivikas (a sect mentioned earlier in connection with Bindusara, if you remember), the caves to be used as rainy season retreats. An interesting fact here: the word *ajivikehi* was later removed or scratched out from the Mauryan inscriptions in the Barabar and Nagarjuni caves, which meant that other religious groups took them over and decided to efface the proof of their earlier occupation. So the Ajivikas were, clearly, turfed out and left to fend for themselves, at some point. There is no other evidence of any ruler in the dynasties that followed the Mauryans having patronised them.

Yet why the Mauryan dynasty collapsed in the manner in which it did is the subject of another chapter altogether.

Notes

1. Central India here pertains to Madhya Pradesh. Vidisha was on the way from Pataliputra to Ujjayini and was an important urban centre of the time. It also has a strong pre-Mauryan core with the first historical phase of occupation in around 500 BCE. See Nayanjot Lahiri, *Ashoka in Ancient India*, Permanent Black, 2015, p.99.
2. Romila Thapar, for one, questions Sanghamitra's role in spreading Buddhism and provides a more plausible story of her life. See

Romila Thapar, *Asoka and the Decline of the Mauryas*, Oxford University Press, 3rd edn, 2021, p.30. However, see Lahiri, *Ashoka in Ancient India*, pp.282–283 where she discusses Sanghamitra's role in bringing the Bodhi-tree to Sri Lanka (as per the *Mahavamsa*), encountering dreadful dangers enroute. Thus, as she is the protector of the plant in this island while Tishyarakshita is its destroyer back home, both symbolise the fate/history of Buddhism in these respective places.

3. See for this and the subsequent discussion on Devi's religion, Lahiri, *Ashoka in Ancient India*, pp.97–101. She is also referred to in the *Mahavamsha* as Vedisa(Vidisha)-Mahadevi-Shakyakumari. It is speculated that she did not follow Ashoka to Pataliputra but remained in Vidisha. See, for instance, R.K. Mookerji, *Chandragupta Maurya and His Times*, Motilal Banarsidass, 1966, rpt.1988, p.82.
4. For this and the discussion that follows, see Devika Rangachari, *Invisible Women, Visible Histories—Gender, Polity and Society in Early Medieval North India (7th to 12th century AD)*, Manohar Books, 2006.
5. Charles Allen, *Ashoka—The Search for India's Lost Emperor*, Abacus, 2012, pp.350–351.
6. This was Minor Pillar Edict 3 on the Allahabad-Kosam pillar. Karuvaki's residence was in the outlying part of Kaushambi. Ashoka also mentions, in one of his edicts, his harems and those of his brothers, as well as the residences of his sisters in Pataliputra and the outlying towns. In another, he talks of his queens and harem at Pataliputra and in the provinces, and refers to his sons—and these could either be those born to his queens or his other consorts. See Rock Edict 5 and Pillar Edict 8 for more information. See also Rock Edict 12 where he creates special officers to oversee the concerns of women. Mookerji, *Chandragupta Maurya and His Times*, p.82. Incidentally, a Prince Samva was apparently put in charge of the monastery at Panguraria, near Vidisha, according to a Minor Rock Edict, but it is unclear whether he was Ashoka's son. The *Rajatarangini* mentions Jalauka, another son, who ruled Kashmir after Ashoka's death. A daughter named Charumati is supposed to have married into Nepal and presided over monasteries with her husband. See, for instance, Allen, *Ashoka—The Search for*

India's Lost Emperor, pp.379, 446. However, as regards Ashoka's other wives, concubines and offspring, everything is a confused muddle of sources and conjecture, with most of them remaining in shadow.

7. Lahiri, *Ashoka in Ancient India*, p.283. Incidentally, Romila Thapar believes that Karuvaki and Tishyarakshita were the same person, the former being her personal name and the latter, her official one after she became chief queen. Both are mentioned as Ashoka's second queens. See Thapar, *Asoka and the Decline of the Mauryas*, p.232.
8. Allen, *Ashoka—The Search for India's Lost Emperor*, pp.376–377.
9. See Thapar, *Asoka and the Decline of the Mauryas*, p.308 where this is cited. She sensibly notes that this should be interpreted as officials recording Ashoka's orders (*devanampiya-vacanena*) rather than his losing control.
10. Incidentally, Xuanzang, the Chinese pilgrim, visits the remains of this 'Cock monastery' as his last royal monument during his travels in Pataliputra. It was situated to the southeast of the old city.
11. Lahiri, *Ashoka in Ancient India*, p.288.
12. Allen, *Ashoka—The Search for India's Lost Emperor*, p.199.
13. In fact, the disdain of the Puranas for Ashoka due to his Buddhist exertions manifests itself in them not giving him the epithet 'great', as also a general disinterest in his successors. Incidentally, the term *devanampiya*, too, becomes pejorative over time. For a detailed discussion on who exactly succeeded Ashoka, see Thapar, *Asoka and the Decline of the Mauryas*, pp.228–246.

14

THE LATER LEGACY OF ASHOKA

Before we begin with surveying Ashoka's influence through time, let us answer a question that usually occurs to those who become acquainted with his story, and the extraordinary twists and turns therein: do we know what he looked like, or, alternatively, is there any physical representation of this highly remarkable character? This is, one must confess, a question that occurs to all of us when we read about *any* person in history who is not impossibly drab and colourless, and whose life was no run-of-the-mill one, by any means. Unfortunately, the further back in time you go, the less is the likelihood of you satisfying your curiosity with corroborative facts and discoveries of this sort.

However, the interesting point here is that Ashoka is not just a faceless voice—there is, for instance, a stone portrait of him that exists at Kanaganahalli near Sannati in the Gulbarga district of Karnataka, which was itself discovered in the most dramatic way. In 1993, some archaeologists were inspecting the area around Sannati to provide the mandatory environmental clearance for a dam to be built across the river Bhima. At Kanaganahalli, on the Bhima's left bank, preliminary excavations revealed part of a large brick stupa, as also several carved limestone slabs, pillars, railings and sculptures, along with coins and other evidence pertaining to the Satavahana dynasty, which enabled the stupa to be dated to between the first and third centuries CE. Of pertinence to our story is the discovery of a broken relief sculpture depicting a king and queen—looking somewhat adoringly at each other—and their female attendants, two of whom are bearing a parasol and fly whisk—accepted symbols of sovereignty, as also a Brahmi inscription that reads *Ranyo Ashoka* (King Ashoka).

Now one may debate for hours on end on whether sculptural representations are accurate or not. And if we are, in addition, dealing with the complicated matter of fragmented evidence, how do we, then, automatically presume that a critical part of the depiction has not broken away and/or quite simply vanished? In this case, though, it is fairly safe to believe that the inscription and depiction pertain to the Ashoka of our tale, reinforced, in no small measure, by subsequent discoveries of Buddhism-related material at the same site in further excavations.[1] Now whether he did, in fact, have thick, protruding lips and huge ears, and shared a disconcerting similarity in the structure of his nose with his queen *and* the other attendants is a matter for conjecture.

Artistic license and fanciful imaginings have ever been the forte of creative people, and there is no reason to assume that this particular sculptor was immune to such quirks just because he belonged to a very ancient context. Whether Ashoka himself commissioned this portrait is not clear; it could, equally, have been made in connection with a royal visit. It might be pertinent to note here that a relief panel at Sanchi had earlier been identified as a representation of Ashoka but there is no convenient inscription to confirm it, which merely adds to the status and lustre of the Kanaganahalli find.

There are other sites that are equally memorable, in this regard. Although Ashoka does not appear in the Buddhist iconography at the site of Bharhut, for instance, historians have correlated some of the sculptural depictions at Sanchi as narrating his visits to Buddhist pilgrimage sites.[2] And there is, in addition, the Ramagrama stupa in Nepal whose southern gateway/*torana* commemorates his visit, along with his royal entourage. He is shown with all his magnificent insignia while on a chariot and leading a procession, and being met by the guardian deities, the Naga kings. This ties in neatly with the *Ashokavadana*'s assertion that Ashoka had gone to Ramagrama to take possession of an original relic deposit of the Buddha. However, it is the western pillar that grabs our attention as it shows him in the throes of grief while visiting his beloved Bodhi tree, which, as we know, had been temporarily felled by Tishyarakshita's machinations. He is supported by two queens (so we know that Tishyarakshita had more to contend with than just an alleged tree-rival, at the time, although this is hardly basis for exoneration!) and exudes misery.

Another panel above it depicts an adorned Bodhi tree, surrounded by a temple, which is probably the one Ashoka built. A similar representation is at Sanchi where one of the carvings again show Ashoka supported by two queens amongst his royal attendants. Interestingly, Tishyarakshita's wickedness as an artistic theme seems to have been quite popular. Abanindranath Tagore, a nephew of the renowned poet, Rabindranath Tagore, and the pioneer of the Bengal school of art, painted her looking at the wilting Bodhi tree with, apparently, a mixture of triumph and regret—although the set of her eyebrows seems to indicate the former emotion more strongly. Other sculptural emblems associated strongly with Ashoka include wheel-bearing pillars, monoliths crowned with capitals of four lions and the *vajrasana* (throne) at Mahabodhi. These were all carved into the gateways of Sanchi, for instance.

Charles Allen also points to two stone sculptures from Langudi in Orissa, sporting Brahmi inscriptions and seeming to refer to Ashoka.[3] One is the upper part of a man with long, piled-up hair and large earrings, apparently the portrait of a donor named 'King Ashoka'. The other is of an enthroned male with a turban, earrings and bangles, and referring to Ashoka as a lay Buddhist. Allen's ruminations on the subject, though, seem somewhat precipitate. He wonders, for instance, whether Ashoka suffered from epilepsy, the key to his fainting episodes captured in stone and perhaps the reason behind him being rejected as a potential heir to the throne, in the first place.[4]

Ashoka and his legacy came within the purview of the Chinese monks and travellers, Faxian and Xuanzang, as well. These two names are a staple of every history textbook (with varying spellings of their names through the ages!), and students are routinely required to trot out the details of their visits to India and the information they left behind—a chore that usually buries their significance in young minds committed to rote. The truth is that both these pilgrims were fascinating, intrepid personalities who undertook the arduous trek from China to India in search of Buddhist texts but, in the process, penned their observations and comments on almost everything they saw and all the interactions they underwent, resulting in a corpus of evidence that is, at once, memorable and immensely significant—and, we might add, considerably more accurate than that of Megasthenes, for one.

Here is a case in point: it is Xuanzang who provides the

critical evidence for the role of Rajyashri, the sister of Harsha of Kanauj, whom we had alluded to earlier. While Harsha's inscriptions maintain a complete silence on her, Xuanzang, while documenting his visit to the court of Kanauj in the seventh century, talks about this young, vibrant woman volubly participating in court debates on religion and accompanying Harsha on military campaigns. And thus, we can resurrect her from general oblivion and put her back at the centrestage of polity and society where she rightfully belongs. And this is just one of the many pointers to our past that Xuanzang—and, of course, Faxian—helpfully provide us with.[5]

Let us tackle them in chronological order. Faxian, in the fifth century CE, was one of the earliest Buddhist Chinese monks to travel to India. He came from Shensi, crossed central Asia, travelled extensively in India and then moved to Sri Lanka—all in pursuit of the correct rules and regulations of the *Vinaya Pitaka* texts of Buddhism, an entirely admirable bibliographic commitment. Among the numerous aspects of the landscape of colour and people and stories and festivals and languages and buildings that he plunged through was the fact that Ashoka lived on in collective memory across a wide geographical span from the hills of northwest India to the Gangetic plains in the east.

What he records of the long-dead emperor is a quaint mix of legends, local retellings and bits from the *Ashokavadana* that he would have already been conversant with. He mentions, for instance, Sankisa as the place where Ashoka planted a stone pillar thirty cubits high with the figure of a lion on top and Pataliputra as the city where he reigned (wherein the palace, 'with its various halls, all built by spirits who piled up stones', and with its elaborate designs 'after no human fashion', was apparently still in existence!).[6] Interestingly, the knowledge of the Brahmi script seems to have faded away by this time and people interpreted the Ashokan stone missives in every which way to suit their fancies, another delightful proof of the human tendency to familiarise the essentially unfamiliar. 'So what if we can't *read* it,' you can hear them say. 'We *understand* what it says.'

Xuanzang, some two centuries later and cast in his illustrious predecessor's mould as far as his travel diaries went, seemed to keep bumping into Ashokan pillars—at Shravasti, Varanasi and Lumbini, to name a few places. He provides solemn yet enchanting appraisals of some of them: the Lumbini pillar was broken in the middle because a dragon had caused it to fall whereas the one near Varanasi shone like a mirror, its surface smooth as ice. In addition, Xuanzang's narrative bristles with stories concerning stupas built by 'Ashoka Raja', again in a wide sweep from Gandhara to the Gangetic plains.

While most of these stupas appear to mark events in the life of the Buddha, there are some that have a deep resonance with Ashoka's personal history. The one outside Taxila, in Xuanzang's view, marked the place where the unfortunate Kunala was blinded on Tishyarakshita's orders, which apparently now possessed the power to restore sight to the devout sightless. It is unclear whether Ashoka commissioned the building of all these stupas that Xuanzang painstakingly recorded because some of them were made of stone whereas Ashokan stupas were usually of brick. However, they were all lumped together as being of Mauryan vintage, by this time.

Another way in which Ashoka has been frozen in time, as it were, is through an interesting inscription issued by a woman many centuries later—Kumaradevi, the queen of Govindachandra, the Gahadavala ruler of Kanauj (*c.*1109/1114–1154), who uses it to proclaim, among other things, the fact that she is a proud Buddhist in contrast to her husband who follows the Brahmanical religion. She also stresses the importance of her natal family, which takes precedence in the inscription over the family she is married into. But what is its relevance to Ashoka, you may ask. This Sarnath inscription, as it is called, records the construction of a vihara with the image of the Buddhist goddess, Arya-Vasudhara, by Kumaradevi. She is also stated to have restored the *shri-dharma-chakra-jina* image of the Buddha and placed it in this vihara or had another one constructed for the purpose. The epigraph contains the following important lines—'This Lord of the turning of the Wheel was restored by her in accordance with the way in which he existed in the days of Dharmashoka…and even more wonderfully, and this vihara for that *sthavira* was elaborately erected by her.'[7]

The message is not as incomprehensible as it first appears for, after all, elaborate language is the basis of most royal inscriptions in the past. What it establishes beyond a doubt, though, is that the memory of Ashoka and the things he did to promote Buddhism was alive and well in the early twelfth century and an allusion to this was considered prestigious enough for an intelligent and confident queen to make use of in her own record. Ashoka's life was dramatic enough but the manner in which he keeps jumping in and out of the shadows of memory and known history is equally striking, verging on the theatrical, at times. Going from a context where he was just about everywhere to one where his missives could not be read at all to being mentioned in this record is an eventful trajectory. It is a veritable 'now you see me, now you don't' situation. You can't help wonder whether the young, untamed Ashoka would have enjoyed startling people thus. He probably would!

A word about Kumaradevi—and Govindachandra. The largely ubiquitous presumption is that queens followed the faiths of their husbands, particularly in a royal scenario. Yet here is Kumaradevi not only openly announcing that she is a Buddhist but probably also influencing a very generous donation that Govindachandra later makes in a Buddhist cause. Shades of Rajyashri and Harsha here but as with the former, Kumaradevi and her role evokes very little interest among historians! Incidentally, Govindachandra himself made various donations along with his other queens—and so did his mother, Ralhadevi/Ralhanadevi. Ralhadevi seems to have been a forceful personality because her inscriptions indicate that she virtually ran the administration during the reign of her husband (and Govindachandra's father), Madanapala, a highly ineffective character, along with another of his wives, Prithvi-Shrika—more instances of powerful, remarkable women who have been virtually removed from the historical narrative.

There is yet another wonderful story concealed here that is worth recalling even if it means we are moving off at a tangent once again. For this, we have to visit contemporary Bengal or Gauda, as it was known then (although it was also called Vanga and, just to complicate matters, both Gauda and Vanga were used interchangeably for Bengal, even though the specific Gauda territory could be distinguished from Pundra in the north and Vanga and Samatata in the south/south-east. Yes, this is exactly the sort of confusion that historians routinely deal with and hopefully, your respect for them would have risen exponentially by now).

Our tale is rooted in the Pala dynasty that ruled for around four hundred years from the eighth century CE, and controlled significant areas of Bengal and Bihar. There is a lot of epigraphic evidence available for the Palas, as well as a text named the *Ramacharita*, written by Sandhyakara Nandi, which provides their history from CE 1070 to 1121. All in all, a well-documented period but one that again reveals much gender bias in the handling. This tale begins with the three sons of the Pala ruler, Vigrahapala III (*c.* 1043–1070)—Mahipala II, Shurapala and Ramapala—and the rivalry between them. Mahipala, as the eldest son, succeeded Vigrahapala to the throne but turned out to be completely obnoxious. He not only imprisoned his other brothers in the belief that they were plotting for the throne but also had a great time oppressing his subjects, and generally being intolerant and unreasonable.

And so, in the time-honoured tradition of all tyrants, he was set aside by the Kaivarta Divya, whose family took over the Pala throne. Shurapala and Ramapala managed to get free in the ensuing confusion whereupon the former conveniently vanished into the shadows while Ramapala speedily became the hero of the Pala saga. So where does he go, all alone and friendless? He runs straight into the open arms of his maternal uncle, Mathana of Anga, who promptly and efficiently sets a damage control mechanism in operation.

But here we pause and ask—who was Mathana of Anga, to begin with? He is, of course, the brother of Ramapala's mother but who this woman was and where she came from is a question that has been avoided by almost all historians except for a vague speculation that she was a Rashtrakuta princess, discerned from the fact that Vigrahapala's other wife, Yauvanashri, is mentioned in the records as a Kalachuri. Other than this, there is lamentably little interest in her identity whereas the identities of several royal males in the Pala line, for instance, have been the focus of ferocious debate.

Back to the tale and we see Mathana, at this juncture,

assuming centrestage by proferring mental, material and financial aid to his nephew. Ramapala is able to win over his feudatories through a bribe-and-coercion mixture, laced with extravagant promises of land and wealth, all backed by Mathana's resources. Mathana later sends his sons to scout the usurped Pala land and then enables Ramapala to make a triumphant return from exile via a 'bridge of boats'. The Kaivarta Bhima, now on the throne, is killed and Ramapala becomes the rightful Pala ruler, acknowledging that the throne has been regained and revitalised on the strength of this crucial maternal bond. The relationship between uncle and son endures: Mathana seemingly devotes his life to Ramapala's prosperity and when he eventually dies, his 'overwhelmed' grief-stricken nephew drowns himself in the Ganga at Monghyr.

But what does any of this have to do with Kumaradevi and Govindachandra, you may ask. The answer is quite unexpected and also goes to show that the world is not only a very small place but is also full of surprising connections. During Ramapala's painstaking feudatory-resumption period, Mathana managed to neutralise one of his nephew's foremost foes, Devarakshita of Pithi, by a simple yet startlingly effective diplomatic manoeuvre: he married his daughter, Shankaradevi, to Devarakshita, thereby enlisting the latter in Ramapala's camp. Mathana went one step further some years later—he kept the Gahadavala kingdom of Kanauj from turning covetous eyes on the Pala region by marrying his granddaughter, Kumaradevi (the daughter of Shankaradevi and Devarakshita), to Govindachandra, its ruler.

So our story has come full circle, ending where it began—as is the wont of most satisfying tales. A large part of Kumaradevi's Sarnath inscription talks about Mathana and the marriage connections he engineered in Ramapala's favour while delineating her natal ancestry. Unfortunately, though, historians haven't actually spotted and acknowledged the import of these maternal links. This isn't altogether surprising—women, their role and their probable influences (as repeatedly noted in this work), aren't exactly the focus of mainstream historical narratives! Yet that the study of any historical personage (in this case, Ashoka) involves sourcing material from a wide range of time and evidence is underscored—and often this *will* involve women.

Ashoka was, indeed, memorialised in stone many times over, but his memorialisation in other ways and other times is, at the same time, an enigmatic yet vital point of research. The fact is that when you reflect on how strongly and fondly Ashoka is remembered today, and the liberal use of his name to resurrect anything from relative obscurity to instant greatness (awards, naval vessels and political jargon spring to mind), you are bound to wonder anew at his having been in the shadows of known history for so long. One of those quintessential hidden-in-plain-sight affairs! So what are the myriad ways in which we recall him and why is he so pivotal to our collective consciousness?

Perhaps we should begin by surveying the legacy of his material remains and then move on to the more profound realms of situating him vis-à-vis the national psyche. Let us start with his spokespeople, as it were—his pillars and rocks, and turn right away to the *Tarikh-i-Firuz Shahi*, written by Shams Siraj Afif in the fourteenth century, and intended to eulogise Firuz Shah Tughlaq, the ruler of the Delhi Sultanate who built the sixth of the many cities of Delhi, and whose insatiable curiosity and penchant for restoration made him otherwise quite remarkable.[8]

Incidentally, Firuz Shah was the successor to the unfortunate Muhammad bin Tughlaq, who had allegedly obtained the throne by upending a pavilion onto his father, Ghiyasuddin Tughlaq's head, and then promptly turned contrary and weird, forcing his subjects to trail miserably up and down the country while he whimsically changed capitals, inaugurated currency reforms that confounded the economy, and swung from one policy to another like a seesaw gone rogue. And so, Firuz Shah's accession was like a breath of fresh air—literally so with his other penchant for creating green spaces.

But we are veering off at a tangent here. The pertinent point in all this is that the *Tarikh-i-Firuz Shahi* provides a very interesting account of two Ashokan pillars, the Delhi-Topra and the Delhi-Meerut, pertaining to areas in modern Haryana and Uttar Pradesh, respectively. It seems that Firuz Shah Tughlaq came upon them in the course of his military campaigns at Topra and Meerut, and was impressed enough to decide that they be immediately sent to Delhi. Such are the often-wild, impulsive urges of rulers and one can only feel for the hapless ministers who had to execute them.

As the tale goes, this was an enterprise of monumental proportions, involving the people in and around Topra being made to assemble at the pillar with reams of silk cotton, the pillar being carefully extricated from the soil and made to fall on its carefully-prepared silk cotton bed whereupon it was covered in reeds and hides and moved onto a special carriage of forty-two wheels, the carriage being dragged to the Yamuna where the Sultan arrived to cheerfully direct the proceedings, the pillar being transferred to a raft of boats and floated to Delhi, and it being hoisted to a position in the palace complex at Firuzabad (modern Firuz/Firoz Shah Kotla, the city named after its founder).

At this point, some brahmanas appeared on the scene to decipher the inscription, confidently—and conveniently—claiming that it contained a prophecy to the effect that no one would be able to remove the pillar from its original location until the time of a great king called Firuz Shah Tughlaq. Now Ashoka was a man of many talents but it is fairly safe to say that he was not a visionary or seer who peeped into the future and exclaimed, 'Oh, look, *there* is Firuz Shah Tughlaq and I want only *him* to transport my pillar all over the place!' Ashokan Brahmi had become a linguistic mystery all over again by this time but there was no one to challenge the brahmanas to an on-the-spot script-decipherment test. And so, the pillar proudly remained in its new home and came to be known as the Minar-i-Zarin or the Golden Column.

Incidentally, painted illustrations of the Topra pillar's adventures are also available to prop up the tale. So is a poem attributed to Firuz Shah Tughlaq that celebrates his 'column of gold' wherein he also ponders over its meaning: 'Is it the *Tuba* (the Lote-tree of Paradise) which the angels have planted on the earth, or is it the *Sidya* (the Plum-tree of Paradise) which men have taken to be a mountain?'[9] Meanwhile, the Meerut pillar was installed in the Sultan's hunting palace/lodge, so he had both his finds safely within sight and could gloat over them whenever he chose.

There is an ironic postscript to this tale, though: chronicles about Firuz Shah Tughlaq do not mention the original creator of these itinerant pillars. Ashoka, therefore, had presumably passed from public memory by this time. Even more ironically, the pillar in Firuz Shah's hunting lodge was blown into fragments sometime in the early 1700s due to the explosion of a powder magazine. It was later carefully reassembled a few centuries on and lodged in the British Museum in London, with, however, one piece still missing.[10]

Interestingly, several Ashokan pillars contain inscriptions pertaining to later periods. Apart from the names of people scratched into them at regular intervals, proving that the practice of graffiti in monuments is an ancient one that remained healthy and thriving down the ages (not that this is any kind of license to emulate our scribbling ancestors!), there are records of later rulers that thriftily made use of the same durable material to document important matters. Not that there was a paucity of similar substances but sharing space with an ancient record would automatically confer respectability and gravitas by association—an opinion presumably shared by later royal engravers who might not have understood the content of Ashoka's missives but appreciated their intended import.

We have already alluded to the Girnar rock that bore inscriptions pertaining to Rudradaman, Chandragupta Maurya and Ashoka. If we consider the Delhi-Topra pillar, its fame after Ashoka does not necessarily begin and end with Firuz Shah Tughlaq: it also bears three twelfth century inscriptions of Vigraharaja IV, the Chauhan king, that reiterate his victories and greatness. In a similar vein, the Delhi-Meerut pillar has three early medieval Sanskrit inscriptions. And the Lauriya-Nandangarh pillar inscription of Ashoka abuts a Persian inscription of the Mughal emperor, Aurangzeb's time, as also that of an English surveyor, Reuben Burrow (this epigraph is terse: 'Reuben Burrow, 1792').

However, if we are talking about famous inscriptions jostling for space, we must consider the Allahabad-Kosam pillar, which, like the Delhi-Topra—was an itinerant one as it refers to the mahamatas of Kaushambi, implying that it moved from Allahabad to Kaushambi, at some point. Apart from Ashoka's renowned schism edict, it also bears the much-cited Allahabad *prashasti* (eulogy) of the Gupta emperor, Samudragupta, composed by his clearly-adoring court poet, Harishena, for whom he was the last word in rulership and military prowess and talent and culture. In addition, the pillar has an epigraph that provides the genealogy of Jahangir, the Mughal emperor, bringing the grand total of its emperor-usage to three—no mean feat this! And it does not end here—it also has names of random people scratched into it over different periods.

Other Ashokan pillars have been repurposed and reused over this huge span of time—a fate not uncommon to historical artefacts in general. Two fragments have been identified at Hissar and Fatehabad, both in Haryana—the former, a part of a composite pillar before a mosque built by Firuz Shah Tughlaq; the latter, also a part of a composite pillar, bearing information on the same ruler. However, there are some other, outrightly peculiar usages of Ashokan pillars. For instance, there are records of some of them and/or their fragments being worshipped as Shiva *lingas*. A similarly inexplicable use is of them being associated in local tradition with the Pandava brothers of the *Mahabharata*, especially the much-muscled Bhima, and are dubbed *Bhim-ki-lat* or *Bhim-ka-danda* (Bhima's pillar or stick). The whys and wherefores of this particular trajectory are unclear but such is the history of the human race and its persistent desire to adopt the unfamiliar and give it a cosy status. One wonders whether Ashoka would have approved of this!

His deeds spawned several powerful admirers, though.[11] In China, for instance, Emperor Lu of the Liang dynasty (CE 502–549) tried to imitate Ashoka by building stupas, and curtailing the consumption of meat and alcohol. We also have the Empress Wu Zetian (*c.* CE 623–705) who liked to portray herself as a *chakravartin*, an image of kingship synonymous with Ashoka. And, of course, as repeatedly noted, he has been immortalised in the Sanskrit *Ashokavadana*, and in the Sri Lankan Pali chronicles, the *Dipavamsa* and the *Mahavamsa*, that have, together, wrung every detail out of his remarkable life and captured them for posterity. You never know the ways in which influence works and the forms it can take. In fact, Romila Thapar speculates that Yudhisthira's views against violence and the evils of war in that amazing tome, the *Mahabharata*, might reflect a debate among post-Ashokan polities that arose from the whole dhamma question and Ashoka's lived experience of it, which, if you think about it, makes a lot of sense.[12]

Ashoka was—and continues to be—the focus of narrative non-fiction and fiction, often used as an entry point to analyse Buddhism, and issues of religious tolerance and peace, among other things; alternatively, more often than not, as a riveting biographical subject.[13] There was a frenzy of monograph-writing on Ashoka in the early twentieth century. Writing on him, says Thapar, was like 'a rite of passage' for ancient Indian historians.[14] Accordingly, he swung from being an autocrat, monk, missionary and dreamer to someone who was respected for his 'extraordinary vision'. Much has been said about Ashoka inspiring veteran political leaders, such as Mahatma Gandhi and Jawaharlal Nehru.[15]

More recently, he is routinely invoked (for political or other reasons) in triumphant attestations of India's non-violent heritage; in the context of unification, nation and democracy; and in assertions that India's past also sports magnificent historical figures to run alongside similar characters in the world arena—or as H.G. Wells very generously puts it (albeit in the context of the 1920s) that more men 'cherish his memory today than ever heard the names of Constantine or Charlemagne'.[16] Ashoka would have definitely approved of this sentiment!

He is still in the public eye at the time of writing this. 2022 being the 2,327th birth anniversary of the emperor by the Bharatiya Janata Party's (BJP) reckoning seemed to be a fortuitous time to investigate his caste.[17] With the caste cauldron of Uttar Pradesh roiling ahead of the Assembly polls, a battle for appropriation sprang up between rival parties in neighbouring Bihar, the state which has long claimed the king as its own. The BJP, according to an article, has always looked out for 'icons covered in the cobwebs of history' and was, therefore, one of the first entities to acknowledge his political value—and to gain mileage from this: in 2015, the BJP in Bihar commemorated his 2,320th birth anniversary with the party government at the centre issuing a postal stamp on him. However, others were equally quick to jump on to the bandwagon and claim Ashoka for themselves, especially the OBC (Other Reserved Caste) Kushwaha community and backward class leaders across parties, such as the BJP, JD(U) and the RJD. The emperor was even dubbed 'a grand OBC face and voice of the subaltern' by one among them. The operative part here, of course, is that the present-day Maurya community are Kushwahas; the latter forms eight percent of Bihar's population and are an important part of the JD(U)'s OBC base with a fair sprinkling among the BJP and RJD, too.

The current appropriation embroilment began when Daya Prakash Sinha, a former government officer and BJP worker, as well as a Sahitya Akademi Award winner for his play, *Samrat Ashoka*, declared that his research led him to similarities between Ashoka and the Mughal emperor, Aurangzeb, in terms of their youthful excesses and subsequent 'over-religiosity' so as to divert the people's attention from their sins. He also reiterated that several Buddhist works describe Ashoka as 'very ugly'. This set the cat among the pigeons with three Kushwaha leaders from three different parties jumping to Ashoka's defence, managing to rally other politicos behind them, in the process.

The BJP, in particular, hit back hard: they filed an FIR against Sinha 'for hurting people's sentiments' and distanced themselves from him despite Sinha's claim that he was the national convener of the BJP's cultural cell. Meanwhile, demands from different political quarters that Sinha's literary award be recalled grew shriller. One of the reasons attributed to this brouhaha was that the BJP, having lost some OBC leaders to the Samajwadi Party (SP), was loath to be party to any issue that might antagonise the OBCs further. The important point, for our purposes, is that Ashoka remains eminently relevant in the politico-social context even now.

He continues to cast a giant shadow today.

Notes

1. It has also been speculated that his children, Mahendra and Sanghamitra, are captured in the frieze.
2. While Prasenajit of Kosala and Ajatashatru figure in the Bharhut iconography as the Buddha's contemporaries, it took a couple of centuries for Ashoka to be similarly depicted—on the columns and gateways of Sanchi. Unlike Bharhut, though, there are no identifying epigraphs or labels accompanying the Sanchi figures and his presence in them is based on the conjunction of sculpture and story. See Nayanjot Lahiri, *Ashoka in Ancient India*, Permanent Black, 2015, p.295.
3. Charles Allen, *Ashoka—The Search for India's Lost Emperor*, Abacus, 2012, p.361.
4. He also points to Ashoka's ugliness showing through in panels that depict him as corpulent and/or with a/balloon-like face. See

ibid., pp.343, 346, 375. Incidentally, he also wonders why there are no sculptures of Ashoka despite his probable awareness of the royal personality cults of the Persians and Greeks. He thinks that images of Ashoka were made in his lifetime but that they have not survived. See p.336.

5. Incidentally, as Charles Allen points out, Faxian's *A Record of Buddhistic Kingdoms* and Xuanzang's *Great Tang Records of the Western Regions* remained unknown outside China until well into the nineteenth century. See ibid., p.220.
6. See R.K. Mookerji, *Chandragupta Maurya and His Times*, Motilal Banarsidass, 1966, rpt.1988, pp.71–72.
7. See Devika Rangachari, *Invisible Women, Visible Histories—Gender, Society and Polity in North India (Seventh to Twelfth Century AD)*, Manohar, 2009, p.349. The verse in question is vv.22, 23.
8. See, for instance, Allen, *Ashoka—The Search for India's Lost Emperor*, pp.9–11.
9. Ibid., p.14.
10. Ibid., p.20.
11. Lahiri, *Ashoka in Ancient India*, p.5; M. Deeg, 'Asoka: Model Ruler without a Name?' in P. Olivelle, J. Leoshko and H.P. Ray, eds. *Reimagining Asoka: Memory and History*, Oxford University Press, 2012, pp.362–379.
12. See Romila Thapar, *Asoka and the Decline of the Mauryas*, Oxford University Press, 3rd edn, 2021, pp.xxvi–xxviii.
13. Some of these biographies were totally arbitrary in their choice of source material, though. V.A. Smith, for instance, rejected the two prime Buddhist sources as 'the silly fictions of mendacious monks' in his book on Ashoka, cited in the bibliography (although his was the first modern rendition of Ashoka's life based on his words). See Allen, *Ashoka—The Search for India's Lost Emperor*, p.346. R.K. Mookerji, on the other hand, while seeking to situate Ashoka in a wider historical context, notes that he has been likened to David, Solomon, Constantine, Marcus Aurelius, Charlemagne, Oliver Cromwell, Khalif Omar and Emperor Akbar—basically, the gamut of world leaders who ever wrote or said or did anything noteworthy through the ages. See p.347 where this is cited.
14. Thapar, *Asoka and the Decline of the Mauryas*, pp.xxxiv–xxxvii. Other biographies of Ashoka followed V.A. Smith's, such as those

by D.R. Bhandarkar (which focused on his engagement with Buddhism), R.K. Mookerji (cited earlier), B.M. Barua (who used sources like the *Arthashastra* as well for a more comprehensive analysis) and, of course, Romila Thapar's iconic work (cited above in this very note), which placed Ashoka in the context of his times. Apart from these, there are several works on the Ashokan artefacts alone. See Lahiri, *Ashoka in Ancient India*, pp.17–20.

15. To put it simply, Gandhi's belief in non-violence was partly derived from Ashoka's worldview and his political value system; Nehru concretised the link between modern Indian democracy and Ashoka with the adoption of the Sarnath pillar capital as the national emblem and the wheel (Ashoka chakra) on the Indian flag. See Lahiri, *Ashoka in Ancient India*, p.14.
16. Ibid., p.5. Note Nayanjot Lahiri's poetic summation of Ashoka's 'afterlife', which, 'like his real life, remains poised between legend and the truth'. See p.307.
17. Santosh Singh, 'OBC upheaval fallout: What caste was King Ashoka?', *The Indian Express*, January 15, 2022, Patna, p.7.

15

THE MAURYAN ADMINISTRATION

There are some issues in history that elicit a sort of Pavlovian response among historians: the reaction is immediate and familiar. The structure of the Mauryan empire is one such, with the battlelines clearly drawn, and the respective arguments of the opposing sides already known to all and sundry. However, if one were to set down each and every point thereof, this work would take on the unwelcome dimensions of a standard textbook. Therefore, we will confine ourselves to the basics and, in this case, it is whether the empire was centralised or not.

The first stumbling block is that of the sources and the maddening uncertainty that cloaks them as regards their dating and content, and, consequently, their pertinence to the Mauryan empire—although all of them were intrinsically connected to the Mauryan court. The *Arthashastra*, as discussed earlier, is, technically, a theoretical work, of how a state *should be* in an ideal world. Therefore, how much of it actually reflects the functioning Mauryan state is unclear. And then, of course, we have the *Indica*, whose numerous exaggerations and errors have already been noted, so one can hardly hold it up as a source par excellence! Ashoka's inscriptions are, indisputably, brilliant historical sources as their dating is beyond question and they contain his authentic voice. There is one problem, though: they talk extensively about Ashoka's dhamma but rather cursorily about his administration, so we return to the realm of conjecture again. And then there is the small matter of the numismatic and archaeological finds not having been hitherto analysed from the point of view of their political implications.

The initial view was that the Mauryan empire was a very highly centralised entity and was largely derived from a surface reading of the *Arthashastra*, which presents a state that has a stranglehold over its people and resources. Then, as is usually the case, some people went over to the opposite side altogether. Gerard Fussman's view is regarded with much reverence, in this regard.[1] He argues that the Mauryan empire could not have been so centralised given the expansive nature of the realm and the communication networks at the time. The picture is this, instead: several existing political units who already govern themselves but who have Mauryan rule superimposed on them anyway. That the local officials and administration had a generous measure of agency is clear from the fact that the script, language and content of Ashoka's inscriptions, for instance, change according to the exigencies of the province in question. And let us not forget that the choice of location of these missives was left to the local officials—Ashoka was definitely not scrambling over hilly terrain and scouting suitable surfaces himself!

Romila Thapar, the renowned Indian historian who has done stellar work vis-à-vis the Mauryas, first adhered to the centralised control theory and then revised her views to posit an image of the Mauryan empire as a behemoth of sorts, encompassing varied economies, polities and ways of living.[2] So she believes that the empire itself consisted of metropolitan, core and peripheral areas. The core included existing states, the periphery included pre-state societies and Magadha was the metropolitan state.[3] While the empire definitely had some central control, there must have also been delegation of authority at all other levels—provincial, district and village, given its massive size, covering practically all of the subcontinent and extending into the northwest, so it is not entirely necessary to dub it centralised or decentralised. It was an exceedingly sophisticated and cultured empire, too, with its monumental sculpture and architecture, and its relations with other courts—Hellenistic for diplomatic purposes and Ceylonese, among others, for religious ones, the latter underscored by Ashoka's boast of having attained dhamma-vijaya (victory through dhamma) in the realms of other rulers.

So how do we approach this tangled mess of sources, and figure out which ones to use more with regard to the question at hand and which to approach with caution? The problems with the *Indica* and Ashoka's inscriptions have already been pointed out but let us first accord the *Arthashastra* a closer look. We know that we cannot use it as a straightforward rendition of the Mauryan state and its ramifications in prose but we *do* know that at least a part of it, most probably the core, was written in this period. It is safe to presume that Kautilya had an astounding brain but to further assume that he concocted an image of such a powerful and immaculately-run state with such an advanced knowledge of politics without encountering it anywhere else than in his mind is bending the bounds of credulity somewhat. Therefore, he must have based his work on something that he saw around him, on political institutions and political thought that was contemporary, something—in all likelihood—that he had helped set up.

Here is the bottomline, the crux, as it were: the *Arthashastra* is the first Indian text to define a state (as noted earlier) and, moreover, adds seven components to its definition as being essential for the latter's existence[4]—in other words, the *saptanga rajya* or seven-limbed state. We will come to the seven parts in due course but it should be noted that this picture of the state was adopted with minor changes by several other texts, such as the Dharmashastras (or law books), the Puranas and the *Mahabharata*. And this is precisely why we need to know what these seven aspects are—they underpin every idea of the state as we know it in our prescriptive and epic/narrative literature.

So we start off with the *swami*, the lord/king—or, in more fanciful imagery, the spider at the heart of the political web. The instructions in the *Arthashastra* are, in fact, addressed to this very personage, ranging from the acquisition and maintenance of political power by the *vijigishu* or aspiring conqueror to the general obligations of a king. Incidentally, Kautilya's ruler is always a male; there is no room for a woman ruler in his scheme of things unless matters go horribly wrong. And in this, he mirrors the sentiments of other lawgivers and prescriptive texts who shudder at the prospect of a woman at the helm. The *Mahabharata*, for instance, darkly observes that any polity ruled by a woman, a child or a gambler 'sinks helplessly as a stone raft in a river'.[5]

So the ideal Mauryan state envisaged was a monarchy with a powerful king at the centre of the polity. Also, as we know—and just to shore things up a little, Ashoka makes an attempt to link his mortal self with divinity by dint of his titles. Kautilya's king is impossibly exposed and vulnerable, however, and needs to be guarded at all times from attacks launched, particularly, by women and other close relatives.

Meanwhile, he is to maintain and increase his power while also indulging in a sort of paternalistic rule whereby he looks after his subjects like a father would his children, protecting them from calamities, for one, and ensuring their spiritual salvation, on the other. Being a father also involved wagging one's finger in reproof at rebellious entities who sought to break rules and generally act tough, as Ashoka so splendidly did in Rock Edict 2.

The second limb in Kautilya's grand state plan was the *amatya*, which is usually—and loosely—translated as the minister but could also be a senior official, counsellor or departmental head. There is a plethora of information, in this regard, from Ashoka's inscriptions alone. There seem to have been two consultative bodies of these officials (again, all male) that met regularly to deliberate on important matters and this, coupled with Ashoka's assertion of being available night and day for any matter, conveys an image of a well-oiled system where portfolios were clearly allocated and everyone knew what they had to do with the ruler hovering above them all. And we even have textual corroboration, in this case, which is a cause for rejoicing whenever it occurs in history. Patanjali's *Mahabhashya*, that invaluable compendium of Sanskrit grammar of the second century BCE, refers to Chandragupta's *sabha*, and Megasthenes to a similar body via the words *sumbouloi* and *sunedroi* (the latter meaning 'those who sit together').

Luminaries existed, too: the *samahartri* (chief revenue collector), the *samnidhatri* (treasurer and royal storekeeper), the *antaravamshika* (chief of the palace guard—and the potential preventer of treacherous assassination bids) and the *purohita* (royal priest who—talking of unfair job expectations—was meant to prevent *both* divine and human calamities!). If we needed clues as to the influence some of these men wielded, we have only to look at Radhagupta, Bindusara's minister, who purportedly—and singlehandedly—swung the entire succession battle in Ashoka's favour. And then, of course, we have the elite group of mahamatas/mahamatras in Ashoka's time who had various assigned tasks, a particularly significant one being the itthijhakka-mahamatas or mahamatas in charge of women's welfare, and the most exalted of them all—the dhamma-mahamatas, a core group specially created by Ashoka thirteen years into his reign to spread dhamma all over the Mauryan realm.

Incidentally, being an officer in the Mauryan court was not exactly a cakewalk. Apart from the stringent intellectual and other requirements, there was a code of conduct to be observed at all times in which seriousness and gravity were paramount, and no room at all for levity.[6] In fact, laughing loudly 'when there is nothing to laugh about' or, conversely, laughing too loudly 'when there is cause' were unacceptable. So, too, were indulging in unseemly gestures like 'winking, biting the lips and frowning'. Imagine, if you will, an official with a carefully-schooled deadpan expression, thinking carefully over anything that emerges from his mouth and endeavouring to provide nothing but the strictest satisfaction to his royal employer—and you have the Mauryan court minion, who was clearly made of very stern stuff, in a nutshell!

Kautilya's third required limb is *janapada*, a term that indicates the territory and the people. The Mauryan realm was so huge as to be positively unwieldy but there is nothing like a bit of order to infuse sense into things. Accordingly, it was divided up into four basic provinces, each with its administrative base and governor—the north under Taxila, the south under Suvarnagiri, the west under Ujjayini and the east under Toshali. If you remember, Ashoka cut his teeth in two of them—Taxila, which, being a somewhat rebellious province, could not have been an easy sojourn for him; and Ujjayini, where he met the love of his life (or, at least, one of them). These were administered by governors, usually the royal princes—and we know this from Ashoka's inscriptions where they are addressed as kumara or aryaputra. (Incidentally, there is not much evidence of the provinces under Chandragupta but if we use a method of inference, Ashoka does not claim any of the provinces in his inscriptions to be his own creation. And where he does meddle and/or change the machinery handed down to him, he specifically mentions it in his records. Hence, it is safe to assume that he continued the same provincial divisions as his worthy grandfather and father.)

And there were more official minions to back up the governors—the *pradeshika*, *rajuka* and *yukta* of Ashoka's edicts, for instance. Of these, the *rajukas* seemed to have shouldered a fair share of the administrative burden: under Ashoka, they were senior officials who had to deal with public welfare measures, judicial duties and the propagation of dhamma. The *Arthashastra* only mentions the *yukta* and not them but Kautilya had a great deal to say about the structure of administration, which being a complicated mathematical formula can be a little hard to comprehend.

Sample this: he advises the king to establish a base called the *sthaniya* to administer each unit of eight hundred villages, a *dronamukha* in a unit of four hundred villages, a *karvatika* in a unit of two hundred villages and a *samgrahana* in a unit of ten villages. The *sthanika* administered units similar to districts and the *gopas*, who commanded units of five to ten villages, were under them, and then the village headmen or *gramikas*. And the list goes on but we will stop here before your heart quails at the thought of tackling more intricate categories. Before we turn away, though, we should note that Megasthenes talks about city administration but his account is probably pertinent to Pataliputra, the capital. There were six committees of five members each, in this regard, and these grandees monitored the following things: arts, the comings and goings of foreigners, births and deaths, trade and commerce, and the sale of goods and collection of taxes thereof.

The fourth ideal Kautilyan limb was the *durga* or fortified capital, which can be interpreted in manifold ways. In fact, Kautilya's intense preoccupation with looming danger and betrayal and imminent treachery makes one wonder why this was not heralded as the foremost requirement of a state. Much has been said about his elaborate plans to circumvent these (to him) ghastly eventualities. A well-run intelligence system was pivotal to Kautilya's conception of the state, and the amount that is said about espionage and counter-espionage and the machinations thereof in the text would have made the greatest spy novelists retire, abashed. He would have heartily disapproved of James Bond, the legendary one-man spy machine, for instance—the onus should never be on one man alone, in Kautilya's view, but there ought to be spies stationed in one place (*sanstha*) *and* those who roamed around (*sanchara*), as well as a mechanism to track their efficacy.

You could not just take on this job because you fancied yourself in a beard and wanted to satisfy your wanderlust. No, you had to prove yourself, and your credentials and progress were monitored closely. Ashoka goes a step further and talks of the *pativedakas*, who seem to have been spies or reporters, and the *pulisani* (incidentally mentioned by Megasthenes as the episcopoi), who were of higher rank and had more wide-ranging duties. Together, they kept the ruler informed of everything that was happening around him.

Kautilya takes an unexpected plunge into architecture, at this juncture. He draws up plans for the construction of the main fort in the capital, recommending a mud rampart with brick or stone parapets, and three moats filled with lotuses and crocodiles (exceedingly odd combination, this!) surrounding the fort walls. The fort, which ought to have secret escape routes, was to be stocked with supplies to tide over sieges. Having demonstrated his designing skills, Kautilya now immerses himself in military strategising. He advises the construction of a series of frontier posts, the recruitment of a fort garrison, the placing of troops along the approaches to the fort, and a standing army maintained by the state.

Infantry, cavalry, chariots and elephants were to be the four divisions of the army to be placed under particular officials (with the rather pompous-sounding titles of *ashvadhyaksha*, *rathadhyaksha* and so on). Megasthenes adds his somewhat dubious two-bit here. He seems to have had a fascination for the six-committees-and-five-members trope because he uses it again with regard to the Mauryan defence: the departments, in this case, were of the navy (not even hinted at by Kautilya!), transport, infantry, cavalry, chariots and elephants. On the other hand, the army administration remains cloaked in silence in Ashoka's inscriptions, although there is no evidence that he actually disbanded his army in his pursuit of pacifism.

The fifth limb was the *kosha* or treasury, a category to be treated with much reverence in Kautilya's eyes. After all, the title of his text and much of his advice is inextricably linked with wealth, and its acquisition and enhancement, even if the path to it seems intimately connected with power. The more there is in a treasury, the greater is your capacity to expend it in power-and-wealth-related ventures—such was his timeless logic. Land, as always, was paramount—the most critical state and revenue resource.[7] There is much frenzied speculation among the Greek writers on the specific taxes levied and the relevant fractions and the state's share and so on, which, if recounted here, would not add much to a general comprehension of the Mauryan empire.

Suffice it to say that Kautilya mentions a whole lot of taxes (*kara*, *bali* and *bhaga*, among others). The king's share was one-sixth of the produce and additional levies that could be imposed if the treasury were ever to be depleted. And here is an interestingly radical method employed by the Mauryans, as noted by the venerable grammarian, Patanjali, to raise revenue. Apparently, when the need arose, they took to manufacturing images of deities and trading them for profit. The images used in these transactions (and so, tainted, in a sense) were named differently from those that were worshipped.[8]

Kautilya also has some extremely sensible, revenue-related ideas to share, such as the recommendation that the king grant land unsuitable for cultivation in the wilderness to ascetics for their use and the maintenance of a grain buffer stock for lean times. The overall state control of and participation in every aspect of the economy—markets, trade, sale of goods, price fixation, guilds, weights and measures and so on (basically, all agriculture, industry and trade)—that he envisages is startling, even remarkable, but as Upinder Singh, for one, cautions, it is highly unlikely that the Mauryan state actually functioned in this exact manner.[9] On the one hand, to visualise such overweening control over the society and economy in an ancient context is far-fetched but on the other, some of what Kautilya says must have been partially based on the existence of a powerful state in this period that had the potential to do so. He seems to have extrapolated his utopian ideal onto the Mauryan state but the very fact that such an entity existed, at least in part, is a significant fact to consider.

The sixth Kautilyan limb was *danda*, interpreted as force or justice, not necessarily punishment, which is, quite literally, what the word otherwise means. Justice seems to have been one of Kautilya's pet subjects because he pontificates on its administration, particularly with reference to crime, redressals for which could range from fines to bodily mutilation to outright death. And here is the sensitive part—the nature of punishments did not just depend on its type and the circumstances thereof but also on the varna or caste of the wrongdoer and the aggrieved. Predictably, the higher varnas got off lightly. Let us presume for the sake of argument that a kshatriya has committed a crime in Kautilya's world. He could, quite conceivably, escape with a hefty fine but the very same offence could result in a vaishya being divested of his property and a shudra being burnt to death. However, as Kautilya's strictures always veered towards the strict and severe, it does not necessarily imply that this was what, in fact, happened on a daily basis.

As far as judicial officers were concerned, Ashoka narrowed (or expanded, depending on which way you look at it) the job credentials somewhat. Rock Edict 1 notes that every five years, the king would send a gentle officer, who was neither fierce nor harsh, on a tour of inspection to ensure that the mahamatas of the city were being impartial and sympathetic, and that no one was being unfairly or unjustifiably harassed or imprisoned. One wonders how the entire recruitment process in the Mauryan realm would have panned out. On the one hand, Kautilya was looking for those who were naturally suspicious, cautious, and adept at spying and disguising themselves, to shore up the state's security. And then there was Ashoka, looking for mild, tender-hearted individuals to keep a benign eye over the populace. Also, one can't help wonder whether the ascription of these qualities was on the basis of outward appearances or probing interviews.

Either way, the system clearly worked; there is no evidence, for instance, of a judicial officer claiming to be gentle and then unleashing his hidden malevolence on the hapless subjects! However, Ashoka had other checks and balances in place. The same edict notes that the prince/governor of Ujjayini should despatch an inspection team every three years, and that mahamatas from Taxila should add this to their other duties. And here is a classic example of a sugar-coated pill: Pillar Edict 4 talks of a three-day respite for those on death row so that they could appeal against their verdict, meet their relatives and generally prepare themselves but this clearly indicates that even though Ashoka had raised his own gentleness quotient by several notches, he did not do away with the death penalty. Take this in conjunction with his warnings to his subjects to toe the line and we know that this ruler meant business and his mildness, if any, could be cast aside when needed.

So now we come to Kautilya's seventh and final state prerequisite—*mitra* or ally; literally, friend. Here again, he lapses into convoluted, near-mathematical permutations and combinations that can be hard to comprehend right away, requiring several reads and re-reads for his logic (which is, nevertheless, of the best kind!) to sink in. It is not possible to skim over this because it is one of the most remarkable parts of Kautilya's political philosophy and gives you more insights into his genius, maverick mind. A chessboard world of would-be conquerors and kings, whose mutual—and intrinsically slippery—equations should, in his view, be assessed and revised all the time, according to the political exigencies of the moment.

Kautilya starts off with a basis circle of kings (*raja-mandala*) of whom the main players are the *vijigishu* (aspiring conqueror), *ari* (enemy), *madhyama* (middle king) and *udasina* (the indifferent, neutral king). 'This is a Game of Thrones scenario!' you cry. 'We know who each one is.' Once you have nobly resisted the temptation to compare worlds, you can understand the sheer brilliance of Kautilya's plotting and appreciate what a pioneer he was, in this regard. After laying out the players, he comes up with six policies or guidelines (*shad-gunya*), as it were, that a king (any king, just not a woman) should follow depending on the circumstances.[10] If one is weaker than the enemy, the policy of *sandhi* (devising a peace treaty) should be adopted. If, on the other hand, one is stronger than the enemy, the policy of *vigraha* (hostility) should be followed. However, if one's power is equal to that of the enemy, then one should follow the policy of *asana* (keeping quiet).

And if one is considerably stronger than the enemy, then *yana* (embarking on a military expedition) is the policy to be followed. If one is extremely weak, though, then one should follow the policy of *samshraya* (seeking shelter with another king or in a fort). Finally, if it is possible to fight the enemy with the help of an ally, then one should adopt the dual policy of *dvaidhibhava* (*sandhi*/peace with one king and *vigraha*/ hostility with another). So, if you follow his logic, your enemy's enemy is, in fact, your friend with whom you can team up and defeat your original foe. But the friend of your enemy's enemy can turn out to be your enemy, too, if they combine forces and turn against *you*, in turn.

If your head is (justifiably) reeling by this time, it might help to reiterate that the *Arthashastra* projected a theoretical reality and we do not know how much of its intense pragmatism was translated into action, although—and this cannot be discounted—it could very well have been based on real tussles between contemporary rulers that Kautilya might have observed or even helped resolve. We know, for instance, that Chandragupta Maurya led most of the Mauryan military triumphs but we have no idea whether this was the policy (or policies!) he followed.

And while on the subject of this very king, we must add that despite him having apparently left Pataliputra for Karnataka in the wake of a prolonged famine, the *Arthashastra*, in fact, stipulates a very rigorous famine code, which, therefore, raises the whole reality versus theory spectre, as regards the text, again. Kautilya envisages all sorts of famine-related contingencies and offers a range of remedies that range from the standard (providing food and/or employment to the people) to the truly innovative (moving the famine-stricken to another country).[11] This begs the question of whether these measures were actually employed during Magadha's famine (probably not if it lasted for twelve long years!) or merely remained within the pages of the text.

Questions and more questions but the answers aren't exactly pouring in!

Notes

1. Fussman, Gerard, 'Central and Provincial Administration in Ancient India: The Problem of the Mauryan Empire', *Indian Historical Review*, 14 (1–2), pp.43–72; Upinder Singh, *A History of Ancient and Early Medieval India—From the Stone Age to the 12th Century*, Pearson/Dorling Kindersley, 2008, pp.340–341.
2. Ibid., p.341. See also Romila Thapar, *Asoka and the Decline of the Mauryas*, Oxford University Press, 3rd edn, 2021, pp.119–121.
3. Magadha, the metropolitan state, had centralised bureaucratic control much before the Mauryas; the core areas were already states before they were conquered by the Mauryas, such as Gandhara and Avanti; and the peripheral regions were areas of relative isolation with no history of state formation but with natural resources valued by the Mauryans. See Nayanjot Lahiri, *Ashoka in Ancient India*, Permanent Black, 2015, p.172.
4. Singh, *A History of Ancient and Early Medieval India*, pp.341–342. For a detailed discussion of the limbs, see pp.340–349.
5. See Devika Rangachari, *Invisible Women, Visible Histories—Gender, Society and Polity in North India (Seventh to Twelfth Century AD)*, Manohar, 2009, p.85. It contains illuminating examples of women ruling capably, and not having their kingdoms crash and burn.
6. L.N. Rangarajan, ed. and trans. *Kautilya—The Arthashastra*, Penguin, 1992, pp. 175–176, 5.4.8–10, 14. Much is stern and purposeful in Kautilya's world. Take, for instance, his recommendation that villages were not to be provided with pleasure-gardens or halls for dramatic, dance or musical performances, 'disturbing the work of helpless agriculturists'. Towns were spared from this injunction, though, and had bands of actors, dancers, musicians, storytellers and magicians with, presumably, institutions to showcase their talents, so they were definitely spoilt for choice there! See R.K. Mookerji, *Chandragupta Maurya and His Times*, Motilal Banarsidass, 1966, rpt.1988, pp.126, 140.
7. The economy of the Ganga plain was largely based on agriculture with increasing areas brought under cultivation with state-organised peasant settlements. See, for instance, Thapar, *Asoka and the Decline of the Mauryas*, p.xix.
8. See Mookerji, *Chandragupta Maurya and His Times*, p.76.

9. Singh, *A History of Ancient and Early Medieval India*, p.346; R.P. Kangle, *The Kautilya Arthasastra—English Translation with Critical and Explanatory Notes*, Part III, University of Bombay, 1965, pp.166–194.
10. Singh, *A History of Ancient and Early Medieval India*, pp.348–349.
11. See, for instance, Mookerji, *Chandragupta Maurya and His Times*, p.76. The Sohgaura copperplate inscription in Uttar Pradesh and the Mahasthangarh inscription in Bangladesh deal with famine relief measures. These were probably issued during Chandragupta's reign. See, for instance, Thapar, *Asoka and the Decline of the Mauryas*, p.10.

16

WHAT THE MAURYAS BUILT

So much of what we know of a culture is based on its art and architecture—the buildings and sculptures that are meant to remain its permanent markers on the physical landscape and, often, when its other pertinent sources fade or disappear, stay on as its lone reference points, assuming greater and greater historical significance the further back in time they relate to. This particular aspect takes on an added meaning during Ashoka's reign when he sought to unite the entire Mauryan realm through his mammoth creative endeavour.

But let us begin at the beginning and reiterate a crucial fact: the Mauryan period was remarkable for its monumental stone sculpture and architecture—a direct reflection of its imperial power and seen for the first time since the Harappan civilisation—as well as pivotal beginnings in rock-cut and stupa architecture. If you think this need not necessarily concern you as you engage with the larger Mauryan tale, consider the sheer volume of tourist traffic to Sanchi and Sarnath in today's context, for instance, and, by extension, to Ajanta and Ellora.

The Mauryans who built, in the urban context, obviously had wealth in abundance but most of the structural remains of this empire can be directly linked to royal patronage, particularly of Ashoka. Artistic links are not very evident in the case of Chandragupta, who was obviously preoccupied with setting his newfound dynasty on an even keel, or Bindusara, who was busy trying to maintain the power he had inherited, on the one hand, and cold-shouldering his son, on the other. But it was not just the royals and the privileged court circles who built; there is evidence of what is termed 'popular art' in the form of terracotta figurines, sculptures, ring stones and the like, indicating that artistic activity was also within the purview of the non-royal strata of society. You may recall, in this regard, Chapada, the enterprising artist who left his signature on the rocks at Brahmagiri and Rameshvara.

When we talk of artistic activity in the Mauryan times, our attention springs foremost to Ashoka and his inscribed pillars.[1] These, it has been discovered, are more or less similar to each other in form and size, indicating that a standard template for them was conceived and followed all through the realm. Here again, we run into an unresolved debate—some say the pillars are monoliths or carved out of single pieces of stone but Vidula Jayaswal, for instance, claims that some of them, such as the Lauriya-Nandangarh and Vaishali pillars, were made of several pieces of stone. The details of this impasse, though, are nowhere as important as her actual discovery: the Ashokan pillars were hewn out of stone that was quarried at Chunar in eastern Uttar Pradesh.

It seems Jayaswal was examining megalithic structures in nearby Baragaon when she and her team stumbled upon signs of ancient stone quarries, including large, cylindrical stone blocks, in the Chunar hills.[2] The more they investigated, the more concrete was the evidence that the sandstone from here was used for sculptures and buildings from the third century BCE to the medieval period. She also discovered an interesting continuity of sorts: the modern inhabitants of Baragaon are mostly stone-cutters, although they do not extract stone from the old quarries any longer, which they refer to as *mara patthar* (dead stone) to distinguish it from the more recent, not-as-weathered ones, which they call *zinda patthar* (living stone).

This brings to mind a completely unrelated but equally fortuitous—and spectacular—discovery: the Indian archaeologist, V.S. Wakankar, stumbling upon the Bhimbetka rock shelters in Madhya Pradesh (following up on an oddity of terrain glimpsed from a train window, of all things!), thereby uncovering the oldest-known rock art—and the earliest traces of human life—in India; also, the oldest petroglyphs (a fancy word for prehistoric rock carvings) in the world. As oft-repeated, such thrilling, totally unexpected finds go on to patch up the historical narrative, and as more and more gaps are filled in, the more vibrant the field becomes. Historians exist for these intermittent bursts of joy—it makes the tedium of their research work worthwhile.[3]

Back to the Ashokan pillars, all of them being smooth, highly-polished creations, except, of course, for the Delhi-Meerut pillar, which was dragged around from place to place, and others with a similarly turbulent history. But what really concerns us—even the non-art-afficionados—are the motifs associated with the Ashokan pillars and their capitals (or the stones atop their shafts), which are carved in different shapes. Most of the former are derived from Indian religious mores, so apart from pretty run-of-the-mill designs of the floral sort, you also have the wheel, seen as representing the *dharmachakra* (the wheel of dharma) or the Buddha's first sermon, or even more conveniently, sovereignty (which, eventually, makes its way into the Indian flag).[4]

And then we have the lotus, strongly associated with both Brahmanical and Buddhist traditions—the former with purity, the latter with adorning the baby Buddha's first steps, among other things. The lion motif could be appropriated as a Brahmanical solar symbol but, then, the Buddha is also the *Sakya-simha* (lion of the Sakyas) in Buddhist lore. And, of course, the elephant is claimed by everyone—the Brahmanas, who associate it with Goddess Lakshmi; the Buddhists, for whom the white elephant is one of the Buddha's forms; and the Jainas, for whom the white elephant (again!) heralded Mahavira's birth in his mother, Trishala's dreams.

There are several more animal motifs on the Ashokan pillars that straddle traditions but the most easily identifiable one is of the quadruple lions that appears on the Sanchi and Sarnath capitals. As the Sarnath capital has been adapted and adopted as the emblem of the Indian nation, it faithfully appears on Indian currency, passports, all government letterheads and visiting cards, and the President's seal, among other things, and literally represents the ultimate stamp of official approval. The original was more elaborate: four lions standing back-to-back on an abacus with a frieze of a horse, elephant, bull and lion—all separated by wheels, with the *dharma-chakra* over it all as the crowning glory, as it were. The choice of motifs could hardly have been an arbitrary one, left to the artistic whimsies of the empire's craftsmen. Given that Ashoka virtually poured his soul into his messages, he must have devoted as much attention to the motifs that would accompany them. Sagacious choices these—with a distinct Buddhist significance but equally resonant with the culture at large.

Here is another pillar-related debate. It has been suggested that Ashoka was influenced by the Persians (and even the

Greeks), in this regard: the Achaemenids inscribed pillars, and there is some similarity between the wording of their epigraphs and the look of the end product. Admittedly, there were close links between the ancient Indians and Iranians but there are some distinct differences between the Mauryan and Persian pillars in terms of the shape and ornamentation.[5] And, of course, there is simply no comparison between sporadic attempts at engraving proclamations and Ashoka's astonishing feat of marking his presence through them virtually *everywhere* and imbuing them with a significance that went far beyond the mundane.

And again, artistic influence is as intangible and unquantifiable and non-specific now as it was then. Art *does* travel and there must have been a common pool of motifs and symbols for its practitioners to draw upon in the ancient world but that doesn't mean that similar ideas couldn't strike two artists situated in two different areas at the same time, so that one is tempted to draw an arrow between the two and label it as a direct influence of one upon the other (which a lot of scholars are wont to do). Today, this might even be seen as plunging into the murky waters of plagiarism and copyright! Suffice it to say that the Ashokan pillars might or might not be directly attributable to Persian influence but as everything comes from something, to begin with, there must have been an incipient carving-and-sculpting tradition that we are currently unaware of but which later blossomed into this high art.

Also, it is not as if Ashoka's period was the sole repository of Mauryan art and architecture. He definitely had some precedents to work on, at least as far as Chandragupta went—and perhaps even further back than that. Take the archaeological excavations in and around the Mauryan capital of Pataliputra, for instance, that have revealed it to be a city of magnificent proportions. The Chinese pilgrim, Xuanzang, using a confused mix of observation and legend, claims that the city was created by Ashoka. Here is what he says: '... there was a king called Ashoka (O-shu-kia), who was the great-grandson of Bimbisara-raja. He changed his capital from Rajagriha to Patali(pura), and built an outside rampart to surround the old city.' Xuanzang, though, could only see the old foundation walls that remained.[6]

Now Ashoka was clearly a revered name even in the seventh century, which was why he was invoked in hearsay and legend. However, he had absolutely nothing to do with making Pataliputra the Magadhan capital; the credit for that, if you remember, goes to Ajatashatru, the son of Bimbisara, in the sixth century BCE, neither of them having any connection whatsoever with Ashoka. So whether Bindusara's name and memory were mangled by Xuanzang or his informants is unclear but here is additional proof of his being pushed into the shadows yet again—a tacit endeavour by all and sundry through the ages, it seems! One can't really blame the pilgrim, though. To the untrained ear, and even to students today who wrestle with this part of history, Bindusara sounds *exactly* like Bimbisara, and only a history enthusiast would want to split hairs about the chronological differences thereof!

Ajatashatru, that wily fox of yore, wanted Pataliputra, situated in the Ganga plains on the right bank of the river, to be his new headquarters during his ambitious Lichchhavi campaign (which, as we know, he won hands down). He had it aggressively fortified so as to safeguard Magadha's exposed riverside flank. Rajagriha was, otherwise, an ideal capital with natural hilly defences and fortresses whereas Pataliputra, more than a hundred kilometres away, was more like a swampy morass, so this might have seemed like a very odd choice unless you consider the fact that the states at the time were at each other's throats and Magadha, which hoped to win, could not be governed in splendid isolation from a place that was in the interior, leaving a long swathe of territory unguarded along the river. And so, the pragmatic, far-seeing Ajatashatru switched base to Pataliputra, which, around fifty years later, during the reign of his successor, Udayin, was declared the Magadhan capital. And so it remained through to the Mauryan times and later.

Incidentally, this switch had already been anticipated by divine foresight without crediting its real executor. The Buddha apparently looked back at Magadha after a visit and told his disciple, Ananda, that 'a hundred years hence there shall be a King Asoka; he shall build here his capital and establish his court…'[7] The stone upon which he impressed his feet while making this prophecy was observed by Xuanzang who was suddenly seized by the desire to be very precise and factual. Accordingly, he notes the dimensions of the Buddha's footprints on the stone (18 inches long, 6 inches broad), and the signs of divinity marking his feet and toes. He goes a step further: near the stone, he notes, there was a huge stone pillar bearing a damaged inscription to the effect that 'Ashoka-raja with a firm principle of faith' had bestowed the country as a religious offering to the Buddha and the faith no less than three times and had also redeemed it with his wealth (also thrice). No known Ashokan pillar says anything of the sort, so this was either a figment of Xuanzang's imagination or the local interpretation of the inscription.

In fact, there are more divine prophecies surrounding Pataliputra and its future paramountcy in the Magadhan scheme of things. When it was little more than a village, the

Buddha apparently saw magical creatures frolicking around it, which, to him, was a sign that a fortress was to be built there. He also predicted to Ananda (who was clearly more of a companion than a disciple and privy to all sorts of confidences!) that while Pataliputra (or Patali-puta, as he called it) would become an important commercial hub, three dangers, pretty much like Damocles's sword, would hover over it—that of fire, water and dissension among friends.[8] A word of caution here: the Buddhist literary tradition tends to invoke the Buddha's name to sanction or legitimise most important occurrences, so whether he actually said this is a moot point. Nevertheless, the part about Pataliputra becoming a vital trade centre is true. It was also the heart and soul of the Magadhan empire, crisscrossed by vital political and economic bonds that extended over the entire realm.

Megasthenes's Palimbothra (Pataliputra) was, to him, the greatest city in India. His description of its impressive fortifications and other striking features has been noted elsewhere but if we adhere to his calculations, it would have been a city of some 4,500 hectares.[9] This does not exactly correspond to the archaeological excavations but the ruins indicate that it was, in fact, a very large city. According to F.R. Allchin, for instance, it would have been 'far larger than any other South Asian city of its day'. Nayanjot Lahiri claims that even if Ashoka's princely sojourns brought him to cities 'with massive ramparts and overlooked rivers', they would have appeared 'Lilliputian' to him as compared to the 'enormous sprawl' of Pataliputra.[10]

Weirdly enough, Megasthenes does not see fit to describe the palace, which must have been an impressive building in itself. Frustratingly, archaeological evidence for this royal residence is also minimal except for sundry, disconnected remains of structures that pop up during construction works. There are remains of the wooden palisade on the boundaries, though, and as Megasthenes is quite verbose about them, he clearly (at least in this instance!) set down exactly what he saw. There were two parallel rows of walls made of wood, paved and covered with it, creating a sort of tunnel-like passage, the kind that would have gladdened Kautilya's heart.

The city's drains were made of wood, too—and we know all this from excavations at Bulandibagh in Patna, conducted painstakingly by D.B. Spooner (this was from 1915–17; others took over later). Why wood, you may ask. Remember that Pataliputra was a swamp, more or less, and, therefore, prone to waterlogging, which was why wood was used for defences and drains—and this wasn't just any old wood from trees that grew in the vicinity but the carefully-procured *sal*, hard and ideal for these conditions but, to complicate matters, not native to the area. So it was clearly carted here from some unknown place by someone with great engineering insight; Pataliputra became the first city in the Magadhan region to use this wood to build an entire urban metropolis. And it has survived to this day, over two thousand years later! Other things have come to light apart from the palisade and a large wooden drain; among them, a big spoked chariot wheel with an iron rim and the probable foundation of a wooden jetty.

Spooner, though, had made another spectacular discovery some years earlier: seventy-two pillars arranged in a chessboard pattern at Kumrahar in Patna. Eight more were later discovered by A.S. Altekar and V.K. Misra, so here were the remains of a massive pillared hall, which must have been used for some grand ceremonial and/or congregational purpose but we have no supporting evidence for this. All we can say is that these (Chunar) sandstone pillars were thinner and shorter than the

Ashokan ones, and were originally fixed on square wooden bases.[11] The hall seems to have been open on all sides—there are no traces of walls—but it (or, specifically, the floor and roof) seems to have been burnt, at some point: a large amount of ash and burnt wood discovered indicate this.

Incidentally, seven wooden platforms of the inimitable *sal* wood were excavated near the hall and perhaps these supported a (wooden) staircase leading to it. Some scholars have gone further and suggested that a canal might have connected this spot to the Son river. Spooner has drawn an exciting parallel between this splendid pillared hall at Kumrahar and the Hall of Public Audience of the Persian king, Darius, at Persepolis in Iran but the former is a more elaborate structure. We still do not know what it was used for.

This chapter is not a treatise on art and architecture, so we will cite just a few more examples in the Mauryan context that would interest even the aesthetically-challenged. We have, for instance, a hoard of Mauryan soapstone discs to consider that are beautifully-moulded and decorated with the usual suspects: lotuses, nude women, and several birds and animals. Workmanship under the Mauryas was clearly exemplary but what these delicately exquisite pieces were used for is not clear. Also, Megasthenes might have walked among display stalls in the market or even seen them used at court but he does not mention them at all. One suspects he did not particularly have an eye for art or subtleties thereof but, rather, for the visually obvious and/or the glaringly unfamiliar.

Then there is the Dhauli rock sculpture in Odisha of the front part of an elephant, which is so realistically carved with the right leg tilted and the left one bent that it seems as if it is walking out of the stone, a sight that is both spellbinding and slightly eerie, in turn. We also have a torso of a nude male—of Chunar sandstone, polished and rather graphically carved—recovered from Lohanipur in Patna, with the potential to offend the prudish. On the subject of nude art in the ancient context (whether in stone or terracotta), there is a ubiquitous tendency to label those of women as varying depictions of the mother goddess, the fertility goddess and/or goddesses in general. Nude male figures are not accorded this level of retrospective reverence—they are just seen as ordinary men, sometimes of society's higher echelons (if richly-adorned). So women can't be treated normally in art as well. The wheels of gender bias in perennial motion.

Rock-cut architecture also seems to have been a pioneering Mauryan offering to posterity. There are several caves in the Barabar and Nagarjuni hills near Bodhgaya, outwardly plain but with highly-polished interiors, that contain inscriptions of Ashoka and Dasharatha (noted earlier), and with some fancy sculptural ornamentation in the Lomasha Rishi cave, in particular. Ashoka also forged ahead—in a somewhat dramatic and frenzied manner—with building stupas, emblematic of the Buddha. It seems that he distributed the Buddha's relics among pivotal towns and ordered the construction of stupas over them.[12] There are remains of hundreds of Buddhist monastic settlements built around stupas all over India and extending into Afghanistan. Some were built from scratch, some merely enlarged but the place of honour goes to the stupa site at Sanchi in the Raisen district of Madhya Pradesh—a place on the outskirts of ancient Vidisha, which, as you may remember, had a personal importance for Ashoka, being Devi's hometown.

Incidentally, Vidisha also contains a marvellous relic of religious import—the pillar of Heliodorus, the envoy of the Indo-Greek ruler, Antialcidas of Taxila, to King Bhagabhadra (his identity is hotly disputed), who inscribed on it—in the Prakrit language and Brahmi script—his devotion to Vasudeva, 'the god of gods' (another name for Krishna) in the second century BCE. Excavations have, in fact, revealed his pillar to have formed part of an ancient Vasudeva temple site. At the time of its discovery in 1877, it was covered with vermillion and dutifully worshipped by the locals who had given it the somewhat prosaic name of Khamba Baba.

The core of the largest stupa in Sanchi, rather unimaginatively dubbed the Great Stupa or Stupa no.1, was definitely built in Ashoka's time as it shares the same level as his schism pillar edict. The site itself sports several stupas, shrines and monasteries—and sees an enormous amount of tourist traffic every year. (It helps that the Bhimbetka caves and the Heliodorus pillar are a stone's throw away, so a 'Sanchi trip' covers a satisfying number of historical places.) There are other well-known stupa sites, too, that have Mauryan associations: the stupa-monastery complex at Amaravati, the Dharmarajika and Dhamekh stupas at Sarnath, and one at Rajgir, among them.[13]

Some of them were hidden in plain sight, apparently. Upinder Singh, for instance, recounts the story behind P.K. Mishra's discovery of an Ashokan stupa at Deorkothar in the Rewa district of Madhya Pradesh.[14] A brick mound there was explained away as the unfulfilled wish of an ancient king (again, unknown!) who wanted to build a palace but died, all of a sudden, before doing anything about his amassed brick piles. Further archaeological probing revealed all sorts of remains, including a stupa, which, for several sound reasons, has been connected to the Mauryan period and, specifically, Ashoka.

If you walk into the Mathura Museum today, among

the staggering range of ancient antiquities on display is a grey sandstone figure, datable to the Mauryan period, that is likely to take your breath away. This is of the Parkham yaksha, whose sheer size (2.59 m high) and somewhat brooding presence (note the set of the mouth, for instance) borders on the intimidating, although his broken right arm was probably raised in the time-honoured protection-granting gesture (*abhaya-mudra*).[15] Yakshas (and yakshis, their female counterparts), a vibrant part of popular religion, were otherwise generally friendly deities connected with water, fertility, trees and forests. The third century BCE inscription in Brahmi on this particular sculpture's base indicates that it was an image of the yaksha Manibhadra, the deity of merchants and travellers, and a highly important figure in the commercial world, therefore.

And here is another interesting story of continuity. When the image of the yaksha Manibhadra was removed from Parkham village (where it was found, hence the name) to the Mathura Museum several years ago, he was replaced by a substitute to officiate, so to speak, in the annual Jakhaiya mela (yaksha fair) at Parkham. The latter is a complete parody of the original, though! He is small with an exaggerated grin (or grimace, depending on what you see) and his right arm is raised in a sort of cheerful wave—a far cry from the original colossal image that exudes sheer power and strength and dignity.

There is, as well, the Didarganj yakshi, magnificent in her adornments—but reassuringly real with two rolls of flesh on her stomach, crafted of the same sandstone as the Ashokan pillars and with the same lustrous polish, who was discovered, in 1917, sticking out of the mud beside the Ganga at Didarganj village in Patna. She has been dubbed the Venus de Milo of Indian art, a sobriquet which, Charles Allen, for one, complains, is inadequate as she has 'far more allure'.[16] In fact, Allen goes a step further and speculates that she was crafted 'by the same genius' who produced the spectacular Sarnath lion capital, the 'Mauryan Michelangelo', as it were.

And here is a very recent salute to what the Mauryans built and its enduring legacy: a motorcycle journey undertaken by a bike-and-history enthusiast who went visiting the edicts of Ashoka in Karnataka and discovered that this route formed a 'perfect bike circuit'.[17] Kiran Balakrishnan embarked on this 'historical trip' after much forethought and research; it took him four days to cover the 1,200 kms along the locations of the Ashokan edicts. And this was a strategic plan in more ways than one: pandemic times meant lesser crowds and a more enjoyable experience, by extension! Besides, most of the edict locations involved hiking uphill, apart from the motoring, which added to the fun of the whole thing.

Accordingly, setting forth from Bengaluru on his steed of choice, the Avenger, Balakrishnan first visited Brahmagiri, Ashoka Siddapura and Jatinga Rameshwara—all within a three-km radius—and then went on to Yadugiri, Nittur and Udegolam in the Bellary district; Maski in the Raichur district (which, incidentally, he was thrilled to see because it is supposed to be the first edict that mentions Ashoka by name); Sannati in Kalaburagi; and finally, Palkigundu and Gavimath in the Koppal district.

Balakrishnan joins the ranks of others who have pondered deeply over the choice of locations of these edicts (and sitting atop a hill beside an ancient relic in grand isolation, as it were, must have been conducive to profound thinking). He adds his two-bit: the nine edicts in Karnataka were in a better state of preservation than the two in Andhra Pradesh but the presence of active mining zones in close proximity to these epigraphs could, quite possibly, destroy them and the boulders they are inscribed on. Time, indeed, for historians and heritage conservationists to put their heads together while Balakrishnan plans his next journey of bike-discovery. Incidentally, this is not the first time that he has sallied forth in search of new frontiers—a few months prior to the Ashokan route, he had gone on a road trip to Assam and Nagaland, managing to cover Guwahati, Dimapur, Kohima, Imphal, Loktak and Moreh, in the process. Hats off to his indomitable spirit—and to his obviously sturdy back!

And, of course, to Ashoka who continues to reinvent himself, albeit unknowingly, in contemporary times.

Notes

1. Incidentally, he might have carved some of his edicts on pre-existing pillars. There are pillars without inscriptions, too. Upinder Singh, *A History of Ancient and Early Medieval India—From the Stone Age to the 12th Century*, Pearson/ Dorling Kindersley, 2008, p.358.
2. Ibid., p.358; Vidula Jayaswal, *From Stone Quarry to Sculpturing Workshop: A Report on the Archaeological Investigations around Chunar, Varanasi and Sarnath*, Agam Kala Prakashan, 1998.
3. Some Mauryan relics have been unearthed in totally unexpected ways. Nayanjot Lahiri points to Mauryan terracottas, ring wells and pottery having been found in modern localities in Patna when sewage lines were being laid, and during the construction and demolition of buildings and other structures. See Nayanjot Lahiri, *Ashoka in Ancient India*, Permanent Black, 2015, p.56.
4. For details of the symbols, see Singh, *A History of Ancient and Early Medieval India*, p.359.
5. For further details, ibid., pp. 359, 361. Ananda Coomaraswamy's interesting contention is that India was once part of an ancient east, extending from the Mediterranean Sea to the Ganga valley, with a similar cultural heritage. See also Niharranjan Ray, *Maurya*

and Post-Maurya Art: A Study in Social and Formal Contacts, Indian Council of Historical Research (ICHR), 1975, pp.24–26.

6. Lahiri, *Ashoka in Ancient India*, pp.42–43; Samuel Beal, *Buddhist Records of the Western Countries, Volumes Two and Three*, Bharatiya Publishing House, 1884 (rpt.1980), pp.332–333.
7. Lahiri, *Ashoka in Ancient India*, p.45.
8. Ibid., pp.46–47; T.W. Rhys Davids, trans. *Dialogues of the Buddha—Translated from the Pali of the Digha Nikaya*, Low Price Publications, 1910 (rpt.2001), vol. 2, p.92.
9. Lahiri, *Ashoka in Ancient India*, p.53; F.R. Allchin, 'Early Cities and States beyond the Ganges Valley', in F.R. Allchin, *The Archaeology of Early Historic South Asia—The Emergence of Cities and States*, 1995, p.202.
10. Lahiri, *Ashoka in Ancient India*, p.54. Also, she points out that Ashoka's presence in Pataliputra is not much in evidence, perhaps because much of the ancient city is buried under modern Patna and most excavations have focused on the outskirts. He might, however, be connected to the pillared hall at Kumrahar. See pp.250–251. For an excellent survey of the town planning and other details of Pataliputra, and the other cities of the Mauryan empire, see Singh, *A History of Ancient and Early Medieval India*, pp.335–339.
11. Singh, *A History of Ancient and Early Medieval India*, p.357.
12. Charles Allen dubs it his 'Sakya relic redistribution programme', described in the *Ashokavadana*, Xuanzang and other sources. Piprahwa in the Magadhan heartland occupies centrestage here. See Charles Allen, *Ashoka—The Search for India's Lost Emperor*, Abacus, 2012, pp.328–330.
13. Another example is the Mahabodhi temple at Bodhgaya and its Ashokan remains. For an interesting account, see ibid., pp.300–302. Apart from sections of the original Ashokan railings and pillars, a most rewarding discovery was that of a slab of the Diamond Throne placed by Ashoka at the base of the Bodhi tree. These correspond with the first depictions of Bodhgaya at Bharhut's bas-reliefs. Apparently the Diamond Throne is barely visible today—its top half is draped with coverings and the lower half is buried underground due to the Bodhi tree's growth.
14. Singh, *A History of Ancient and Early Medieval India*, p.364; P.K.

Mishra, 'Deorkothar Stupa: New Light on Early Buddhism', *Marg*, 52(1), 2001, pp.64–74.

15. Ibid., p.365; Upinder Singh, 'Cults and Shrines in Early Historical Mathura (c.200 BC-AD 200)', *World Archaeology*, 36(3), pp.378–398.
16. Allen, *Ashoka—The Search for India's Lost Emperor*, pp.322–324, 335. There is some controversy about her date, though. See Singh, *A History of Ancient and Early Medieval India*, p.364.
17. Melvin Mathew, 'Tripping on Ashoka the Great', *Bangalore Mirror Bureau*, January 3, 2022.

17

WHAT HAPPENED TO THE MAURYAS

There has always been much excitement surrounding the Mauryan empire ever since its details were painstakingly put together by historians. After all, this was the first known ruling line to have commanded such an extensive realm—a feat that only the Mughals were able to parallel much later—and, to all appearances, with such admirable control. Beginning with Chandragupta, almost all of India was united under one yoke with one central administration. Communications, trade, urbanism and the economy grew in leaps and bounds. This was an astonishing achievement for the times—and the baton passed smoothly (in this regard, at least!) to Bindusara and Ashoka, worthy inheritors of the Maurya mantle. So why did the dynasty more or less fold up after Ashoka's passing away? This question, it must be cautioned, remains as much of a puzzle as it was when first mooted.

Ironically, the principal factor behind the Mauryan glory is also blamed for its eclipse. Many fingers point to Ashoka as having pushed the empire towards oblivion through his policies. It has been suggested by Haraprasad Sastri, for instance, that the Shunga rise was, in fact, the manifestation of a rebellion by brahmanas who were sorely tried by the maverick emperor's ostensibly anti-brahmana policies and his support of heterodox sects (the latter, incidentally, being something that he shared in common with his father and grandfather). Ashoka's ban on animal sacrifices and his widescale appointment of dhamma-mahamatas are seen as the main offending factors: they chipped away at the brahmanas' livelihood and their longstanding status as society's moral conscience keepers, respectively.[1]

Viewing Pushyamitra Shunga as the restorer of Brahmanical authority ties in with this. He has been labelled a 'violent anti-Buddhist' for destroying several important Ashokan Buddhist sites, such as the Kukkutarama monastery (of the *amalaka* soup fame), Deorkothar, Bharhut and Sanchi.[2] However, smashed sculptures and pillars could, equally, have been the handiwork of natural disasters and/or human interference. Also, ironically, the Sanchi stupa underwent a reconstruction in the second century BCE, following the end of the Mauryan dynasty and *during* the Shunga period: it was enlarged and encased in its present stone covering, and saw a virtual explosion in donations by a whole range of (mostly non-royal) people from near and far. The whole thing might have had something to do with the seesaw nature of patronage—either Pushyamitra or his successor, Agnimitra, reversed their policy to support Buddhism all over again. Several later Shunga rulers followed suit.

Yet here we can cite a piece of evidence that directly counters Sastri's contention, which proves, for the hundredth time, how important it is to read a source carefully before you set about interpreting it and asserting your conclusions. To Sastri, Rock Edict 1 contains Ashoka's boastful claim that he had revealed the brahmanas to be false gods. This promptly set the cat among the pigeons and it was a short step from here to branding Ashoka the culprit behind the empire's downfall. If you mess with the religious equilibrium, then you only have yourself to blame, agreed fellow-adherents of this view. Not that this exonerated Pushyamitra Shunga's murder of the last Mauryan king but there were clearly extenuating circumstances behind the act. As it turns out, though, Sastri's reading of the pertinent sentence was wrong: it actually states that gods and men had come to the point of mingling, so to speak, and all due to Ashoka's efforts. This, juxtaposed with his oft-repeated pleas to his subjects to respect brahmanas and shramanas, turns Sastri's theory on its head. Quite clearly, therefore, the Mauryan dynasty did not end due to angry brahmanas revolting and/or taking revenge.[3]

Fingers point to Ashoka again but this time around for his pacifist policy. Enveloped in a glow of spiritual awakening and perpetually exhorting your subjects to refrain from violence sends out the best sort of message to rival powers: you eschew bloodshed of all kinds and are, by extension, weak—the perfect time, therefore, for them to launch an attack. Nevertheless, there is a single contrary fact—Ashoka did not disband his army, even in the immediate aftermath of his Kalinga trauma when his aversion to war was at its peak. He might have undergone a radical internal transformation but his core identity as the ruler of the mighty Mauryan empire remained the same—and he was very well aware of this. Practical considerations dictated that his army remain intact and so it did.[4]

Put this together with his veiled warnings in his edicts to recalcitrant tribal elements and the fact that he did not abolish capital punishment at any point in his reign, and you start to question the culpability of his policy of peace in the downfall of the empire. However, to be completely fair, Ashoka's army was only involved in one major military campaign, that of Kalinga, and probably skulked around, thereafter, in a state of semi-preparedness while their ruler strove to direct his realm in another direction altogether. This was probably the reason behind the successful invasion of the Bactrian Greeks, at a later stage, which further weakened the empire.

Or could it be the partition theory proposed by Romila Thapar with the empire's eastern part coming under Dasharatha and the western under Kunala due to which the Greeks could not be held off?[5] The administration was generally crippled, too, as per this theory—the eastern part with Pataliputra continued much as before but the western part, which included the volatile province of Taxila and the northwest, had to hastily emulate the former, so its hands were full and its priorities were different. It is also likely that we need to look somewhere else altogether.

Perhaps the dhamma-mahamatas were the real culprits, probably assuming overweening powers in the waning years of Ashoka's reign, and generally demanding favours from and harassing the public on account of their exalted status. A resentful public would, therefore, have welcomed a change, a respite. This applies to the officials at large, too. If they owed their loyalty to the king in question due to them being personally selected, any change at the helm would result in fresh recruitments—and resultant chaos.[6] The first three rulers might have handpicked their assistants with care; the others might not have been as bothered.

A lot depends on how you choose to view the Mauryan empire. If it was a deeply centralised political system, then a weak ruler or one with suddenly altered priorities could, perhaps, be singled out as the reason for its decline. After all, when the pivot crumbles, it takes the system with it. However, as pointed out earlier, a lot of evidence has been cobbled together to show that the Mauryan empire was probably not as centralised as once believed and so, this theory does not really hold. There are other decline theories that have been proposed, such as the Mauryan empire having faced some sort of financial crisis or a generalised economic crisis, (centred on spiralling taxes, for one; extracting revenue from existing resources instead of creating new ones, for another) but the evidence, if any, is unsatisfactory, so these might not be credible.

Much of the problem is caused by our trying to solve the riddles of the past with the solutions of the present, as if one situation can be so easily extrapolated onto the other. Each period of history remains rooted in its own specific context with its own particular priorities and compulsions—and we are all very well aware of this—but still the tendency remains: an instinctive attempt to read elements of the present as also being relevant to the past. This might, of course, hold true but only to a limited extent. So, for instance, some of the other theories that have been put forward for the Mauryan decline, such as the absence of nationalism and the lack of popular representative institutions in the empire, do not really pertain to the ancient world. Moreover, to accuse the Mauryans of not being able to restructure the economies of the core and peripheral areas, and hold this responsible for their decline, is tantamount to accusing them of not having the planning and strategies of the modern-day world.[7]

The basic point is that the Mauryan empire was a colossal entity. Incorporating a huge territorial span, it also held, within it, diverse people and resources. Control over the realm was always going to be a daunting task but the first three rulers were able to hold it all together by dint of military mechanisms, the administrative structure and, later, a unifying ideology. However, all things have their limit and the Mauryan behemoth eventually began to crack under the strain—in the manner of all massive empires in the ancient landscape. Charisma and confidence are unquantifiable factors, so even if later rulers possessed them to the same degree as their three great predecessors (and the meagre evidence seems *not* to indicate this), it is unclear whether they could have just papered over the cracks and soldiered on.

And a collapsing centre meant the rise of distant provinces who broke away in search of autonomy. All this is mere conjecture, though—there is not much concrete evidence either way. But it *is* true that even before the rise of the Shungas, other local kingdoms had broken away after Ashoka's death and the ensuing confusion; notably, the Satavahanas (south and west of Kalinga), who eventually became a power to reckon with across central and south India—*and* they were Buddhists or liked them anyway. Interestingly, though, Magadha continued as the focal point of large kingdoms in the Ganga plain even though the succeeding dynasties were unrelated to the Mauryas. Eventually, however, a series of invasions from the northwest led to a westward shift in the focus of political power away from the Magadha region.[8]

And so, the Mauryan empire went the way of all great empires—morphing into new ruling lines, new identities and new tales; living on in evidence, legend and hearsay; and holding its own special place in the narrative reconstruction of the Indian past. Also, importantly, its resonances are quite tangible in the present. The streets of Delhi, the national capital, for instance, are rife with Mauryan references. To begin with, we have Chanakyapuri (literally, the 'city of Chanakya'), which houses embassies and diplomatic missions—no simple coincidence, this, but a deliberate choice of name! Admittedly, Chanakya/Kautilya might not have been the most diplomatic or tactful personage around given his levels of paranoic suspicion and general distrust of humans but his mastery of statecraft and political relations cannot be overstated. Therefore, the name Chanakyapuri for this ever-strategising community, otherwise called the Diplomatic Enclave, is very apposite indeed.

We also have Chandragupta Marg (or 'road') within this area that houses more overseas missions, a prominent school and a hospital, among other things. Not too far from it is Kautilya Marg that sports some high commissions and state buildings. And not much further than a stone's throw away is Ashoka Road that leads into Connaught Place, one of the city's commercial hubs. There is, too, the government-run Hotel Ashoka in Chanakyapuri and a street marked Ashoka Drive within the Indian Foreign Service (IFS) Villas' complex in Greater Noida. Bindusara has not been earmarked for similar glory but now you probably understand this oversight a little better. Nor, predictably, have any of the Mauryan royal women: the gender bias also extends into the naming of streets and thoroughfares in urban landscapes, as you likely know.

Another, rather unexpected Mauryan bequest seems to have taken on literary contours. In recent years, there has been a rush of books in the Indian market that claim to provide ways of transacting business and living lives by using Kautilya's dictums.[9] We also have colourful and intensely dramatic reconstructions of his story, one of them, for instance, involving him being cursed and reborn with a generous dollop of hair-raising excitement in every line.[10] The internet also bristles with Youtube videos on Chanakya Niti (loosely 'Chanakya's policy'), and sites and books offering to guide aspiring entrepreneurs using the principles of the *Arthashastra*. (*Chanakya Speaks: The Seven Pillars of Business Success* is the modest title of one of these offerings.)

Kautilya *did* speak profusely, albeit in prose, and *did* have an opinion on most things—and this rediscovery and resurrection of his ideas would have probably flattered the venerable fox. However, he might, equally, have been miffed at this repackaging of his ideas—these were not for everyone's eyes, after all, but for the king alone to absorb and implement. He has also been immortalised on screen, notably by Chandraprakash Dwivedi, whose television series, of several decades vintage now, still has the capacity to enthrall viewers, chiefly due to his excellent rendition of the man himself. The confrontation scene with the Nandas, for instance, is perfectly enacted with a goosebump-raising quality of its own, particularly when the camera focuses on Kautilya's hair hanging loose and his face suffused with fury.

The several ruling lines who came after the Mauryas have been acknowledged and analysed for their respective contributions but none so far have captured our imagination in the manner in which they have. There is something in their story that sets them apart—some intangible element of mystery and passion and adventure that makes you want to know more and to dive deeper into the layers that cloak them. We have a long way to go before their story is laid bare in its entirety but we can still look back on this part of our past with admiration—a bit of concrete proof that dreams and seemingly impractical notions can, if pursued hard enough, suddenly acquire shape and form and substance.

Thus is an empire born; thus is a genius—or many.

Notes

1. Upinder Singh, *A History of Ancient and Early Medieval India—From the Stone Age to the 12th Century*, Pearson/Dorling Kindersley, p.366. Tony Joseph, for instance, wonders whether the defeat of the Mauryas presages the eventual disappearance of Buddhism from the subcontinent and Jainism's decline. Was it, therefore, the orthodox traditions of Aryavarta (and Brahmanism) triumphing over the 'more open, freewheeling, progressive and anti-ritualistic ideologies' of Magadha? See Tony Joseph, *Early Indians—The Story of Our Ancestors and Where We Came From*, Juggernaut, 2018, p.213.
2. Charles Allen, *Ashoka—The Search for India's Lost Emperor*, Abacus, 2012, pp.397, 359.
3. Romila Thapar notes that there was very little in the way of Brahmanical revival as a result of Shunga rule and that, in fact, the post-Mauryan period saw an expansion of Buddhist patronage in the Indian subcontinent and beyond. See Romila Thapar, *Asoka and the Decline of the Mauryas*, Oxford University Press, 3rd edn, 2021, p.xxvi.
4. There are some works of fiction that assume he *did* disband his army after Kalinga. See, for instance, Subhadra Sen Gupta, *Kartik's War*, Rupa, 2002 where the eponymous hero, once an exalted military spy, has to resort to lowly police work after this event.
5. Thapar, *Asoka and the Decline of the Mauryas*, pp.242, 244, 247–248, 250. She cites a text called the *Kunalasutra* whereby Kunala was so successful in governing Taxila that Ashoka decided to divide the empire, placing the area from the Indus to the Chinese frontier under him. It included Gandhara and Kashmir.
6. See ibid., p.260. This system would have created group loyalties and other unpleasant, potentially dangerous situations. Thapar notes (p.335) that the empire coming apart in so short a time suggests either 'oppressive features or inefficiency or both'.
7. Singh, *A History of Ancient and Early Medieval India*, p.366; Thapar, *Asoka and the Decline of the Mauryas*, p.259. Thapar claims that the causes for the Mauryan decline were far more fundamental and included a much wider perspective of Mauryan life than any of the other reasons proposed. The organisation of (the top-heavy) administration and the concept of the state were key factors.

She also argues there that was no national consciousness at the time in the way in which we understand it now. Resistance to outsiders (like the Greeks) was localised, not a concerted effort, and there were huge economic, cultural and linguistic disparities within the Mauryan realm itself. For a nation to exist, common customs, language and historical tradition were required, which did not exist through the area of this empire. See pp.263–266.

8. New areas of the subcontinent transited to city life; the Deccan and the far south to state polity and society. The northwest retained its identity as a major cultural crossroads, though. For details, see Singh, *A History of Ancient and Early Medieval India*, p.369.
9. Shrikant Prasoon's *Rule the World the Way I Did*, published by Pustak Mahal in 2008 and Sunilchandra Dal's *Win In Life With Chanakya's Strategies*, published by White Falcon in 2022 are some of the suggestions that a net search promptly provides.
10. The book in question is Ashwin Sanghi's *Chanakya's Chant*, published by Westland in 2010.

BIBLIOGRAPHY

Agarwal, Deepa, *Chanakya—The Master of Statecraft*, Puffin/Penguin, 2013.

Allchin, F.R., 'Early Cities and States beyond the Ganges Valley', in F.R. Allchin, *The Archaeology of Early Historic South Asia—The Emergence of Cities and States*, 1995, pp.123–151.

Allchin, F.R., *The Archaeology of Early Historic South Asia—The Emergence of Cities and States*, 1995.

Allchin, F.R. and K.R. Norman, 'Guide to the Asokan Inscriptions', *South Asian Studies* 1, 1985, pp.43–50.

Allen, Charles, *Ashoka—The Search for India's Lost Emperor*, Abacus, 2012.

Altekar, A.S. and V.K. Mishra, *Report on Kumrahar Excavations (1951-53)*, 1959, K.P. Jayaswal Research Instotute, 1959.

Anderson, P.K., 'Notes on the Engraving Procedures for the Erragudi Version of Asoka's Minor Rock Edict', *Indo Iranian Journal*, 34, 1991, pp.267–291.

Barua, B.M., *Asoka and His Inscriptions*, New Age Publishers, 1946, rpt 1968.

Basham, A.L., *History and Doctrine of the Ajivikas—A Vanished Indian Religion*, Motilal Banarsidass, 1951, rpt 2009.

Beal, Samuel, 'The Tooth-seal of Asoka', *The Indian Antiquary*, IX, 1880, p.86.

Beal, Samuel, *Buddhist Records of the Western Countries, Volume One*, Susil Gupta (India) Pvt. Ltd, 1884, rpt.1963.

Beal, Samuel, *Buddhist Records of the Western Countries, Volumes Two and Three*, Bharatiya Publishing House, 1884, rpt.1980.

Bhandarkar, D.R., *Asoka*, University of Calcutta, 1925.

Bhandarkar, D.R., 'Asoka and his Successors', in K.A. Nilakanta Sastri, ed. *A Comprehensive History of India—Volume Two: The Mauryas & Satavahanas 325 BC-AD 300*, People's Publishing House, 1957, rpt 1987, pp.20–49.

Bongard-Levin, G.M., 'Megasthenes' "Indica" and the inscriptions of Asoka', in *Studies in Ancient India and Central Asia*, Indian Studies Past and Present, 1971, pp.109–122.

Bose, M.M., 'Ashoka's Rock Edicts I, VIII, IX and XI', *Indian Historical Quarterly* (IV), pp.110-123.

Chakrabarti, D.K., *The Early Use of Iron in India*, Oxford University Press, 1992.

Chakrabarti, D.K., *The Archaeology of Ancient Indian Cities*, Oxford University Press, 1995.

Chakrabarti, D.K., *The Geopolitical Orbits of Ancient India—The Geographical Frames of the Ancient Indian Dynasties*, Oxford University Press, 2010.

Chakrabarti, D.K., *Royal Messages by the Wayside—Historical Geography of the Asokan Edicts*, Aryan Books, 2011.

Chakrabarti, D.K. and M. Lal, eds. *History of Ancient India, Volume III: The Texts, Political History and Administration till c. 200 BC*, Vivekananda International and Aryan Books, 2014.

Chakravarti, Uma, *The Social Dimensions of Early Buddhism*, Oxford University Press, 1987.

Coomaraswamy, Ananda, *History of Indian and Indonesian Art*, Munshiram Manoharlal, 1927, rpt 1972.

Cunningham, Alexander, *Inscriptions of Asoka—Corpus Inscriptionum Indicarum Volume 1*, Indological Book House, 1877, rpt 1961.

Deeg, M., 'Asoka: Model Ruler without a Name?' in P. Olivelle, J. Leoshko and H.P. Ray, eds. *Reimagining Asoka: Memory and History*, Oxford University Press, 2012, pp.362–379.

Deeg, M., 'From the Iron-Wheel to Bodhisattvahood: Asoka in Buddhist Culture and Memory', in P. Olivelle, ed. *Asoka in History and Historical Memory*, Motilal Banarsidass, 2009, pp.109–144.

Falk, H., 'The Fate of Asoka's Donations at Lumbini', in P. Olivelle, J. Leoshko and H.P. Ray, eds. *Reimagining Asoka—Memory and History*, Oxford University Press, 2012.

Filliozat, J., 'Graeco-Aramaic Inscription of Asoka near Kandahar', *Epigraphia Indica*, Vol. XXXIV, 1961-2, pp.1–8.

Fussman, Gerard, 'Central and Provincial Administration in Ancient India: The Problem of the Mauryan Empire', *Indian Historical Review*, 14 (1-2), pp.43–72.

Ghosh, A., 'The Pillars of Asoka: Their Purpose', *East and West*, New Series 17 (3-4), pp.273–275.

Gokhale, B.G., 'Early Buddhist Kingship', *Journal of Asian Studies*, 26 (1), 1966, pp.15–22.

Goyal, S.R., *The Coinage of Ancient India*, Kusumanjali Prakashan, 1995.

Gupta, P.L., *Coins*, National Book Trust, 4th edn 1996.

Gupta, S.P., *The Roots of Indian Art (A Detailed Study of the Formative Period of Indian Art and Architecture: Third and Second Centuries BC—Mauryan and Late Mauryan)*, B.R. Publishing, 1980.

Gupta, Subhadra Sen, *Ashoka—The Great and Compassionate King*, Puffin/Penguin, 2009.

Gupta, Subhadra Sen, *Kartik's War*, Rupa, 2002.

Guruge, A.W.P., *Asoka, the Righteous: A Definitive Biography*, The Central Cultural Fund, 1993.

Hazra, K.L., *Asoka as Depicted in His Edicts*, Munshiram Manoharlal, 2007.

Hayden, Robert M., Tugba Tanyeri-Erdemir, Timothy D. Walker, Aykan Erdemir, Devika Rangachari, Manuel Aguilar-Moreno, Enrique Lopez-Hurtado and Milica Bakic-Hayden, eds. *Antagonistic Tolerance—Competitive Sharing of Religious Sites and Spaces*, Routledge, 2016.

Hultszch, E., *Corpus Inscriptionum Indicarum Vol. 1—Inscriptions of Asoka*, Archaeological Survey of India, 1925, rpt 1991.

Jaini, Padmanabh S., *Gender and Salvation: Jaina Debates on the Spiritual Salvation of Women*, Munshiram Manoharlal, 1992.

Jayaswal, Vidula, *From Stone Quarry to Sculpturing Workshop: A Report on the Archaeological Investigations around Chunar, Varanasi and Sarnath*, Agam Kala Prakashan, 1998.

Joseph, Tony, *Early Indians—The Story of Our Ancestors and Where We Came From*, Juggernaut, 2018.

Kangle, R.P., *The Kautilya Arthasastra (Part 1)*, University of Bombay, 1960.

Kangle, R.P., *The Kautilya Arthasastra (Part II)*, Motilal Banarsidass, 1972 (rpt 2000).

Kangle, R.P., *The Kautilya Arthasastra—English Translation with Critical and Explanatory Notes*, Part III, Motilal Banarsidass, 1965 (rpt 2000).

Kejariwal, O.P., *The Asiatic Society of Bengal and the Discovery of India's Past*, Oxford University Press, 1988.

Kielhorn, F., 'Junagadh Rock Inscription of Rudradaman, The Year 72', *Epigraphia Indica*, Vol. VIII, 1905-6, pp.36–49.

Konow, S., 'Sarnath Inscription of Kumaradevi', *Epigraphia Indica*, Vol. 9, 1907-8, pp.319–328.

Kumar, Anu, ed. *Chanakya: The Kingmaker And The Philosopher—What Chanakya Did, What Chanakya Said*, Hachette, 2013.

Lahiri, Nayanjot, 'Rulers And Their Emblems', *The Indian Express*, 14.7.2022, p.10.

Lahiri, Nayanjot, *Ashoka in Ancient India*, Permanent Black, 2015

Lahiri, Nayanjot, *Finding Forgotten Cities—How the Indus Civilization was Discovered*, Hachette/Permanent Black, 2005, rpt 2011.

Lahiri, Nayanjot, 'Revisiting the Cultural Landscape of Junagadh in the Time of the Mauryas', *Puratattva* 41, 2011, pp.114–130.

Lal, Makkhan, *Settlement History and Rise of Civilization in Ganga-Yamuna Doab (from 1500 BC to 300 AD)*, B.R. Publishing Corporation, 1984.

Lal, Makkhan., 'Iron Tools, Forest Clearance and Urbanisation in the Gangetic Plains', *Man and Environment*, X, 1986, pp.83–90.

Majumdar, R.C., *The Classical Accounts of India*, Firma K.L. Mukhopadhyay, 1960.

McCrindle, J.W., *Ancient India as Described by Megasthenes and Arrian*, Trubner & Co., 1877.

Mathew, Melvin, 'Tripping on Ashoka the Great', *Bangalore Mirror Bureau*, January 3, 2022.

Mishra, P.K., 'Deorkothar Stupa: New Light on Early Buddhism', *Marg*, 52(1), 2001, pp.64–74.

Mookerji, R.K., *Chandragupta Maurya and His Times*, Motilal Banarsidass, 1966, rpt.1988.

Mookerji, R.K., *Asoka*, Motilal Banarsidass, 1928, rpt 2007.

Mookerji, R.K., 'The Foundation of the Mauryan Empire', in K.A. Nilakanta Sastri, ed. *A Comprehensive History of India Volume 2: The Mauryas & Satavahanas 325 BC-AD 300*, People's Publishing House, 1957, pp.1–19.

Mukherjee, B.N., *Studies in the Aramaic Edicts of Asoka*, Indian Museum Calcutta, 1984.

Mukherjee, S.N., ed. *India: History and Thought*, Subarnarekha, 1982.

K.R. Norman, 'The Languages of the Composition and Transmission of the Ashokan Inscriptions', in P. Olivelle, J. Leoshko, and H.P. Ray, eds. *Reimagining Asoka—Memory and History*, Oxford University Press, 2012, pp.38–62.

Oldenberg, H., *The Dipavamsa: An Ancient Buddhist Historical Record*, Asian Educational Services, 1879, rpt 1982.

Olivelle, P., 'Asoka's Inscriptions as Text and Ideology', in P. J. Leoshko and H.P. Ray, eds. *Reimagining Asoka: Memory and History*, Oxford University Press, 2012, pp.157–183.

Olivelle, P., *King, Governance, and Law in Ancient India—Kautilya's Arthashastra*, Oxford University Press, 2013, rpt 2014.

Olivelle, P., ed. *Asoka in History and Historical Memory*, Motilal Banarsidass, 2009.

Olivelle, P., J. Leoshko and H.P. Ray, eds. *Reimagining Asoka—Memory and History*, Oxford University Press, 2012.

Parasher-Sen, Aloka, 'Of Tribes, Hunters and Barbarians: Forest Dwellers in the Mauryan Period', *Studies in History*, n.s., 14 (2), pp.173-191.

Pargiter, F.E., *The Purana Text on the Dynasties of the Kali Age*, Chowkhamba Sanskrit Series, 1913, rpt 1962.

Patra, B., 'Dhauli: An Early Historic Urban Centre of Orissa', *Orissa Review*, 2006, pp.49–53.

Rangarajan, L.N., ed. and trans. *Kautilya—The Arthashastra*, Penguin, 1992.

Rangachari, Devika, *Invisible Women, Visible Histories—Gender, Society and Polity in North India (Seventh to Twelfth Century AD)*, Manohar, 2009.

Rangachari, Devika, *From Obscurity to Light—Women in Early Medieval Orissa (Seventh to Twelfth Centuries AD)*, Manohar, 2020.

Rangachari, Devika, *Queen of Ice*, Duckbill/ Penguin, 2014.

Ray, H.P. and Carla Sinopoli, eds. *Archaeology as History in Early South Asia*, ICHR and Aryan Books, 2004.

Ray, Niharranjan, *Maurya and Post-Maurya Art: A Study in Social and Formal Contacts*, Indian Council of Historical Research (ICHR), 1975.

Raychaudhuri, H.C., *Political History of Ancient India—From the Accession of Parikshit to the Extinction of the Gupta Dynasty*, University of Calcutta, 1953.

Rhys-Davids, T.W., trans. *Dialogues of the Buddha—Translated from the Pali of the Digha Nikaya*, Low Price Publications, 1910, rpt. 2001.

Rhys-Davids, T.W., *Buddhist India*, Motilal Banarsidass, 1903, rpt 1971.

Roy, Kumkum, ed. *Women in Early Indian Societies*, Manohar, 1999.

Sahni, D.R., 'The Yerragudi Rock Edicts of Asoka', *Annual Report of the Archaeological Survey of India 1928-29*, Swati Publications, 1928-9, rpt 1990.

Sahu, B.P., ed. *Iron and Social Change in Early India*, Oxford University Press, 2006.

Salomon, R., 'Asoka and the "Epigraphic Habit" in India', in P. Olivelle, ed. *Asoka in History and Historical Memory*, Motilal Banarsidass, 2009, pp.45–52.

Sarao, K.T.S., 'Janapadas, Mahajanapadas, Kingdoms, and Republics', in D.K. Chakrabarti and M. Lal, eds. *History of Ancient India, Volume III: The Texts, Political History and Administration till c. 200 BC*, Vivekananda International and Aryan Books, 2014, pp.183–204.

Sastri, K.A. Nilakanta, ed. *A Comprehensive History of India Volume 2: The Mauryas & Satavahanas 325 BC-AD 300*, People's Publishing House, 1957, rpt 1987.

Sastri, K.A. Nilakanta, *Age of the Nandas and Mauryas*, Motilal Banarsidass, 1967.

Sealy, I. Allan, *Asoca: A Sutra*, Penguin, 2021.

Sharma, J.P., *Republics in Ancient India c. 1500 B.C.-500 B.C.*, E.J. Brill, 1968.

Sharma, R.S., *Material Culture and Social Formations in Ancient India*, Macmillan, 1983.

Sharma, R.S., *Aspects of Political Ideas and Institutions in Ancient India*, Motilal Banarsidass, 1996.

Singh, Santosh, 'OBC upheaval fallout: What caste was King Ashoka?', *The Indian Express*, January 15, Patna,

Singh, Upinder, 'Sanchi: The History of the Patronage of an Ancient Buddhist Establishment', *The Indian Economic and Social History Review*, 33, 1996, pp.1–35.

Singh, Upinder, 'Texts on Stone: Understanding Asoka's Epigraph-Monuments and their Changing Contexts', *Indian Historical Review*, 24 (1-2), 1997-1998, pp.1–19.

Singh, Upinder, 'Cults and Shrines in Early Historical Mathura (c.200 BC-AD 200)', *World Archaeology*, 36(3), 2004, pp.378–398.

Singh, Upinder, *The Discovery of Ancient India—Early Archaeologists and the Beginnings of Archaeology*, Permanent Black, 2004.

Singh, Upinder, *A History of Ancient and Early Medieval India—From the Stone Age to the 12th Century*, Pearson/ Dorling Kindersley, 2008.

Singh, Upinder, 'Governing the State and the Self: Political Philosophy and Practice in the Edicts of Asoka', *South Asian Studies*, 28 (2), 2012, pp.131–145.

Singh, Upinder, *Political Violence in Ancient India*, Harvard University Press, 2017.

Singh, Upinder, *Ancient India: Culture of Contradictions*, Aleph, 2021.

Sircar, D.C., *Asokan Studies*, Indian Museum Calcutta, 1979, rpt 2000, p.4.

Sircar, D.C., *Select Inscriptions Bearing on Indian History and Civilization*, Vol. 1, V.K. Publishing House, 1942, rpt 1993.

Smith, V.A., *Asoka The Buddhist Emperor of India*, S. Chand, 1909, rpt 1957.

Smith, V.A., 'Graeco-Roman Influence on the Civilization of India', *Journal of the Asiatic Society of Bengal* 58, 1889, pp.107–198.

Spooner, D.B., 'Mr Ratan Tata's Excavations at Pataliputra', *Archaeological Survey of India Annual Report 1912-13*, Swati Publications, 1912-13, rpt 1990, pp.53–86.

Stein, M.A., tr. *Kalhana's Rajatarangini*, Motilal Banarsidass, 3rd rpt 1989, vols. I, II.

Stein, M.A., ed. *Kalhana's Rajatarangini*, Motilal Banarsidass, rpt 1988, vol. III.

Strong, J.S., *The Legend of King Ashoka: A Study and Translation of the Ashokavadana,* Motilal Banarsidass, 1989, rpt 2008.

Thapar, Romila, *Asoka and the Decline of the Mauryas*, Oxford University Press, 3rd edn, 2021.

Thapar, Romila, *Ancient Indian Social History: Some Interpretations,* Orient Longman, 1979.

Thapar, Romila, *The Mauryans Revisited*, K.P. Bagchi & Co., 1984.

Thapar, Romila, *The Past Before Us—Historical Traditions of Early North India*, Permanent Black, 2013.

Thaplyal, K.K., *Asoka—The King and the Man*, Aryan Books, 2012.

Tieken, H., 'The Composition of Asoka's Pillar Edict Series', in P. Olivelle, J. Leoshko and H.P. Ray, eds. *Reimagining Asoka: Memory and History*, Oxford University Press, 2012, pp.184–194.

Trautmann, T.R., 'Elephants and the Mauryas', in S.N. Mukherjee, ed. *India: History and Thought*, Subarnarekha, 1982, pp.254–281.

Waddell, L.A., *Report on the Excavations at Pataliputra (Patna), The Palibothra of the Greeks*, Sanskaran Prakashak, 1903, rpt 1975.

Wagle, Narendra, *Society at the Time of the Buddha*, Popular Prakashan, 1963.

Watters, Thomas, *On Yuan Chwang's Travels in India AD 529-645*, Munshiram Manoharlal, 1904-5, rpt 2012.

Winternitz, Maurice, *A History of Indian Literature Volume II—Buddhist Literature and Jaina Literature*, Oriental Books Reprint Corporation, 1933, rpt 1972.

ACKNOWLEDGEMENTS

This book owes its existence to a chance conversation between Himanjali and me when she asked if I could write it and I promptly said no. I am very grateful to her for her gentle persistence and cheerful support that saw me through all the doubts, angst and panic involved in writing it—and for generally being a good friend, fellow-traveller and fellow-cake-slasher. My gratitude to Sayantan, too, for the tea and laughter at Elma's, and Megha for ploughing through this tome but liking it anyway. And special thanks to Sayoni Basu for responding to our distress call with alacrity, speedreading the manuscript and calming me down.

I owe a debt of gratitude to Prof. Nayanjot Lahiri and Prof. Upinder Singh, outstanding historians and my personal mentors, whose works on the subject I have drawn on considerably for this one, and for always supporting my writing, academic or otherwise. And to Prof. B.P. Sahu who would have been so happy to see this book but, sadly, passed on much before his time.

My family who cloaks me with love and concern, and shores up my morale with excellent advice and suggestions, and whose pride in my work reduces me to tears every single time is the reason I write and the reason for everything I am. As for Gautam who sweetly keeps me supplied with books and laughter and yoghurt—special thanks for being the best agent ever, and for expanding my brain with animal analogies and words and edge-of-the-seat travels.

To all of you: this book is as much yours as mine.

ABOUT THE AUTHOR

Dr Devika Rangachari is an award-winning writer whose book, *Queen of Ice*, was on the White Raven list, won the Neev Young Adult Book Award, and was shortlisted for the Sahitya Akademi's Bal Sahitya Puraskar. Her other books include *The Train to Tanjore, Queen of Fire* (Parag Honour List 2022), *Queen of Earth*(Parag Honour List 2021; shortlisted for the Neev YA and the JK Women AutHer awards), *10 Indian Monarchs Whose Amazing Stories You May Not Know, Tales of Love and Adventure, Swami Vivekananda—A Man with a Vision, Harsha Vardhana, The Merry Mischief of Gopal Bhand, The Wit of Tenali Raman* and *Growing Up* (IBBY Honour List 2002). She also received a prestigious national fellowship of the ministry of culture in India to research aspects of gender and historical fiction in Indian children's literature.

Devika has completed her post-doctoral research on gender in Indian history. Her academic works include *From Obscurity to Light: Women in Early Medieval Orissa (Seventh to Twelfth Centuries AD)* and *Invisible Women, Visible Histories: Gender, Society and Polity in North India (Seventh to Twelfth Century AD)*. She has also published widely in academic journals and been the recipient of several distinguished academic fellowships from the University Grants Commission, as well as the Charles Wallace India Trust.

ABOUT THE AUTHOR